Without Apology

STEPHEN M. JONES, JR.

Without Apology

Copyright © 2005 by Stephen M. Jones, Jr.

All rights reserved. No part of this book may be reproduced or transmitted in any form or by any means without written permission of the author.

ISBN 978-0-615-62406-8

ACKNOWLEDGMENTS

I would like to thank my loving wife, Lisa, for her support throughout the many times my attitude from working on the book affected our relationship. She has stuck with me through thick and thin. Mostly thin. Also I'd like to thank our close friend, Laurie Dunne, who saw quite a few editing issues with a tissue on my 1st submission and graciously came to my rescue to donated her time for a rebel without a cause. And last but not least, Terry Lee Hester, my Cuz, for editing a last moment update at the end of my book called, "*Authors Apocalypse.*"

FORETHOUGHTS

This book is designed for the average, everyday person to read. People like me. There's no ghostwriter here, nope nada. No orthodox spit and shine delivery. You're just not going to get it here.

Nor mind you, was this book written by the slanted views of some reporter, or forensic law professor. If my views are jaded, it's because they were purely motivated by personal emotions from real events. I believe that is obviously evident in this book.

I tried to be objective, even about myself. I don't think I come out smelling like a rose by any means. I made mistakes. I think we all did. This book informs, stripped of varnish, as if you were a fly on the wall in the hotel room with Clinton and Paula as he does the unthinkable.

It is a story of humanistic value that has all the elements of hopes, desires and tragedies. The book has fiery dialogue, commentary and of course, more than its fair share of ridiculous analogies. Being Southern born, you wouldn't expect anything less.

The Republicans may not like it, because I name a few names. The liberals may not like it, because I poke the Clintons square in the eye on more than a few occasions, but it doesn't matter what they think. It's here, ready for you to read and draw your own conclusions.

FOREWORD

I guess some people, and certainly the Washington hypocrisy, can't understand why the Jones Lawsuit won't go away. It affected many people's lives whether they liked it, or not. It forced them to look at their own morality. Maybe people saw a little of Clinton in themselves. There's always a scandal of some type in every work environment; if not, some backbiter will create one. And so it seems that most Americans were willing to give Clinton a free pass. I mean, why not?

We see morality issues in the movies, on the Internet, and in most publications we read. Hell, who says you have to read? Just looking at the pictures will give your five year-old a prerequisite on sex education. Are we less moral as a nation, say as we were twenty years ago? Could you ever imagine watching the NASCAR Winston cup championship with Richard Petty barreling past the checkered flag driving a Viagra sponsored car? Or could it be that the perception of our own morality has changed? Let's come to bear on these sermonic questions.

Most of us want to visualize the White House as a bride-to-be in a white dress; as pure and virgin as a mountain stream. But in reality, we know there are lots of white dresses, and damn few virgin streams. It's the illusion of dignity, respectability, and honor compounded by our economic values. And what do I mean by economic values? I'll answer that by giving you an all too familiar phrase, "Are you better off now than you were five years ago?" You didn't buy into that garbage back then did ya'?

So, with the media frenzy building like a never-ending epic of *Payton Place* uncensored, we Americans, hooked on tabloid news, rush home like going to a drive-up fast-food joint to gorge ourselves on the latest blue plate special. If you think about it, this tabloid all-you-can eat renovation to the White House ensued when the Clintons took possession. Historically, it's not to say that a sore loser hasn't contributed to public scandal to make political hay. That's always plagued a fair share of administrations occupying space in the White

House. That's just the nature of the beast, but the Clinton scandals epitomized our own growing lack of moral judgment.

So here's this guy, with issues, elected to the highest office. The same touchy, feely, fuzzy, friendly persona that got Clinton elected will ultimately be his own legacy.

His successful political career was almost undermined by his unbridled libido. I think the term, *Tricky Dick*, that bannered the Nixon years, was a little premature and better suited to the Clinton administration. Of course, being married to a sexually liberated feminist, with a kinship to alternate, lifestyles didn't help with the rumormongering.

How did all this come about, you ask? Well, a big chip off the old block is the movie industry. When Hollywood shoves a sheep-herding, academy award-winning movie down our psyche, we have to acknowledge that we've journeyed into a new era of tolerance. With that said, maybe it's a testament to Hillary's calculating run in 2008.

Now, I know what you're thinking; what the bjesus do Bill Clinton and Hollywood have in common? I'm glad you asked.

Think I'm mixing my apples and oranges? Exactly my point. I guess I'm not completely lobotomized just yet enough to settle down inside a movie theater crunching on some buttery popcorn and slurping a cold drink while watching two guys suck face without getting a little homophobic. However, I've got a few more years to work out the kinks of what used to be peep shows that are now coming to a box office theater near you.

But hey, what do I know about political correctness? I come from a region where they grow big heads and play banjos. All you have to do is just take a look at James Carville and you'll catch my drift. For those of you who don't get the big heads and banjo thing, I'm being cynical by referring to kissing cousin inbreeding.

This illusion of morality in the White house— did we really care? Or have we become a culture of Jerry Springer yuppies? So, what do we do? We sell out like a half-off sale at Macy's around Christmas time. This sellout didn't happen overnight, it took time for the Clinton administration to go out and plant the seed of deception on the blue cocktail dress of public opinion. Excuse the pun, I couldn't help myself.

What method would be used to indoctrinate the masses? He already had the support from organizations such as the *National Organization Of Women* (N.O.W.) and most of the Hollywood elite. You know, it's amazing how he seemed to gel with an industry based partly on fiction, and moral taboos. Bill could break out his saxophone to entertain as easily as he could wag the dog. It gave us a sense that he was one of them, and that sort of thing goes on all the time in tinsel town. So here you go Bill, free pass.

Now, the JFK *wanna-be thing* definitely worked for him in the partying and womanizing department. While Governor, Bill and his little brother, Roger were the ultimate party boys. They could blow more dust in one night than Mick Jagger's entire band could on tour in Costa Rica. Roger was quoted "My brother, Bill, has a nose like a vacuum cleaner." Eureka! In fact, I heard that the idea of the *Got Milk* theme was inspired by a milk advertising executive who was invited to one of Roger Clinton's many poolside parties. He observed that the *then Governor* had passed out with, what he thought was, a milk mustache.

Why do you think he was the only modern President not to release his medical history to the public? Maybe you're willing to accept the answer generated from the White House spin cycle, saying that every American should reserve the right to keep their medical history private.

I say, hell no! Not if you're running for the highest office in the country. And you had a substance abuse problem that caused you to have an operation to remove your lymph nodes, not to mention a curvature in your penis caused by hard sex. I think being a drug addict, not alone sex addict, could raise some questions as to what is becoming a minority opinion of our perception of a qualified candidate. I believe it's a little more serious than Willie Nelson on top of the White House roof in the Carter administration smoking a doobie.

A lot of Clinton surrogates were on TV, and radio talk shows saying that his personal life is private, and is between him, his wife and God. Personally, I would refer to Hillary as a business associate, sleight of hand politician, or cattle future queen, but a stand-by-my-man wife is a bit of a stretch. *You think a women like Hillary would dump Bill to lose all that political clout when she was about to sink her teeth into something bigger? I think not.*

Again, I get it, some of you are scratching the noggin' and asking, "What in the bohemian is a cattle future queen?" Simply put, Hillary admittedly, with no experience in future's trading, invested sixty-three hundred dollars in the good economical future of cattle and she made nearly a hundred-thousand bucks. Wow! It's good to be the queen. However, her broker, Robert "Red" Bones was suspended for three years for insider shenanigans. Martha Stewart couldn't cook this stuff up without going to jail, but Hillary always had a front man to take the hit. Red Bone's was lucky—it cost Vince Foster his life.

So, without further ado's or explanations, this seed of propaganda took root with the public, case in point. I remember a middle-aged woman screaming at me and Paula as we were rushing to make our connection at the Memphis airport. She was saying, "Clinton's personal life has nothing to do with his public life. He's doing a fine job, leave him alone."

I made the dubious mistake of trying to defuse the situation by explaining to her that Clinton had made inappropriate advances to Paula, who was one of his subordinate employees. I was running late, so I touched her on the shoulder to say that I had a flight to catch. She smiled back at me. In my mind, I'm now thinking, *she understands. I've turned her around and she is moving to the light at the end of the tunnel.* To my astonishment she screamed with a raging force of flying spit particles that coated my face like an out-take of the movie, *The Exorcist*, minus the spinning head, saying in a deep hellish voice "Police! He hit me, police—"

From that day on, I saw a new cult beginning to take form where its members took an oath of blind faith and secrecy; a cult that would have made Rev. Moon proud. I refer to these mindless followers as Clintonologists. These disciples worked feverishly on every new network show that sprung up like a gold mining boomtown of the 1800's. Like the boomtowns, the networks lined their pockets with the misfortune of those that were named, or fingered in the unfolding drama.

James Carville was the highest-ranking Guru of the Clintonologists. He was chosen to indoctrinate the masses. I believe James was cloned from dark hearts and big heads in Area 51, because nothing that condescendingly ugly can come from a woman's womb, seriously.

Carville, with corn crop circle deception, sent disciples to the far reaches of universal opinion. These converts would profess, "There's a right wing conspiracy to impeach the President and these people are behind the Jones' lawsuit. The President has the highest rating than any President in history. He's balanced the budget, he's reformed welfare as we know it, he's put women in key positions in his administration, he's raised the minimum wage for our young people, he's tackling our dwindling social security for our senior citizens, he's putting new programs out there for single moms, and he's proposing a tax cut for middle-class families with children. The President has accepted responsibility for his lack of judgment, and he's asked forgiveness from those he has hurt."

Hot damn, makes ya' wanna vote for him all over again.

However, they conveniently forgot to mention that this heartfelt speech came only after Bill's uncontrolled outburst of DNA was a match on Monica's blue cocktail dress. Too bad, huh? The Johnny Cochran metaphor in the O.J. Simpson case would've worked great. Can you imagine Bob Bennett, Clinton's lawyer, saying in a stuffed shirt bravado, "If the DNA stain on that blue cocktail dress doesn't fit —isn't a match, then you'll have to acquit."

But his personal misconduct has nothing to do with his public capacity to run the nation. They say, "It takes a village (of idiots) and a *stand-by-your-man* woman." So build that bridge of deception. If you build it, they will come. Do you remember all that yada, yada, yada? This was the opening script that was drummed into our psyche for as long as four-scores ago, well, maybe not that long ago Abe, but the Clintonologists were on every radio and TV show until nearly a state of comatose set in. Hell, I almost felt his pain. Maybe I was wrong and Clinton was the victim, and Paula dropped her skirt to the ankles.

The right wing Clinton-hater's theory worked pretty well for a while. Combined with the bimbo eruption and James Carville's epithet referring to Paula as white, trailer park trash by dragging a dollar bill through a trailer park, even though she never lived in a trailer park. (Now you know why I'm a little indignant when speaking of Carville.)

I had rented a trailer for three months on a lake for one summer, years earlier, so it peeved me when anyone insinuated that people who lived in a trailer park were trash. Statistically if that were so, I'd say half the trash in Arkansas elected Clinton Governor, because probably half the people who reside in the state of Arkansas live in house trailers.

Most importantly, they were talking about my wife, the mother of my sons. Paula had my name, and when you die, people remember you by the legacy you leave. Being Southern born, reputation and honor mean a lot to me. I wanted to set things right and an apology would do just fine. An apology is about being accountable for your actions. Clinton should have had the backbone to see that an indiscretion had been made on his part, and he had more than one opportunity to set things right.

A simple apology about a misunderstanding that shouldn't have happened in the first place was all that was needed and it would have been over with! We wouldn't have known about the dirty-kneed Intern, Clinton wouldn't have had to lie about it in our deposition, which cultivated the Starr investigation that launched the impeachment proceedings. Boy—woulda, coulda, shoulda.

This was not about money for me, as some disingenuous reporters wrote. It was about having the backbone to do the right thing. But because of hardheadedness, bad legal advice, or a combination of both, all of us as a nation were drawn into a moral issue on what constitutes sexual harassment in the work place.

To the highest branches of Government to the smallest business enterprise, no one should be subjected to lewd behavior on the job. The Jones lawsuit would not go away, simply, because it was *Without Apology*.

This is my true story; the names have not been changed because there's no innocence to protect.

Chapter One

In 1994 there was a grass root movement going on by conservative fundamentalists to take back the country before it turned into a Canadian totalitarian society. Many foundations came together to form this coalition of conservative thought. The Jones vs. Clinton case was just a pawn to a bigger game being played. I believe you saw the effects from the Clinton legacy in the *then* newly elected majority of the house and the senate. This was by design, not fate, or blind luck, as some might suggest. It was a calculated move capitalizing on the weakest link in the chain. Historically speaking, this is nothing new. It's been done many times over. From ancient to modern civilizations, control to push forward an ideology will be replayed again and again long after we're dust to dust.

The infamous Ken Starr, not yet a household name, talked to Paula's attorney Gil, on strategy concerning presidential immunity. He almost submitted a brief in support of Paula, only to bow out due to conflict of interest in his newly appointed role as independent counsel.

Here we were lining up all our ducks in a row. Ready to prove Clinton's pattern of behavior with women, and boom—Starr shows up at the penny arcade with his Red Rider BB gun, and pings one of our ducks. He crosses over from Whitewater to Lewinsky to drive a stake deep into the heartbeat of the case. Damn claim jumper.

Without Apology

Judge Wright set the parameters of which women we could subpoena. If Clinton had any sexual relations that resulted in harassment, job promotion, or appointment of position, then they were fair game. If any of the many women we subpoenaed fell into this category, it was Lewinsky. Starr called Judge Wright to say we were interfering in a possible federal indictment, so the Judge disallowed Lewinsky's deposition, reneging on her own parameters she had set.

Needless to say when Starr intervened, the bigger game was about to sacrifice the pawn.

How on earth did a quest for an apology for sexual harassment evolve into a conservative crusade? Easy, most conservatives believe they hold the moral high ground, and liberals are immoral and corrupt. I capitalized on this train of thought to reach the ends to my means. Problem was, you can't have it both ways. You can't use people without being used yourself. There's always collateral damage. Question is, is it manageable? I thought so, but I was wrong. Clinton thought so, and he was wrong.

Let me ask you a question, "Do you think Bennett, Clinton's lawyer, believed his client?" Remember, I said believed, not believed in.

Bennett let the goose out of the bag when he said he wanted the sealed affidavit containing the description by Paula of Clinton's lower extremities. Bennett's own words were, "I want that affidavit, I think it's horseshit, but I want it".

There's the twitch. Did you see it? I did, when he said, "I think, and I want."

Here's a big roller, high stakes lawyer boy who had just made an elementary mistake. He let his big mouth ego overload his insecurities about his client, and spilled the beans. Hey now, hold on—justa cotton pickin' minute. Don't fall in the pit of troglodytes that would lead you to believe that Bennett simply wanted the affidavit to prove there were no characteristics. Collateral damage is the name of the game. Bennett knew about Clinton's womanizing, that was easy to do battle, and win, when the only witness is a *he says, she says*.

Stephen M. Jones, Jr.

Throw into the mix distinguishing characteristics, and you have a lawyer with a perplexity.

Is he going to ask the President to prove it, or is he going to take his word for it. Looks to me like he took the latter and that has to get under the skin of a big shot like Bennett. If you're going to be in a position to wheel and deal, you better damn well have all the answers to all the questions, especially if you're representing the President of the United States. Law School 101, don't ever ask a question you don't already know the answer to. When opportunity knocks, take it. There is leverage when the other side, right under your nose, uses words like, "I think, and I want."

I mean think about it, why would a fat dog attorney want to negotiate to buy worthless horseshit? I guess there's a fine line between horseshit, and being full of it.

Too bad I didn't learn about Bennett's comments until almost two weeks after the fact inside another Little Rock hotel room the night before going in front of Judge Wright to schedule the case for trial. That bit of knowledge most definitely reinforced my resolve to stick to my guns when secret negotiations were going on behind our backs between Paula's attorneys, and Clinton's.

On the flip side, Paula's attorneys weren't a hundred percent sure of their client's credibility given her historical pedigree. So there you go, pretty much a stalemate with political overtones from both sides. Like Arkansas road kill, all the buzzards surrounded the courthouse posed for a media feast.

I believe sexual harassment transcends all barriers, especially political. Read between the sheets, what do you believe?

In 1989, I was working for an airline as a customer service agent in Memphis. The airline had a reduction in force. Basically, a polite company term for taking it up the wah'zoo. So along with four other agents, I used my seniority to bump into the Little Rock station.

The Little Rock station was small, about three flights a day, so you had to work the ramp loading planes as well as providing passenger service at the ticket counter.

3

Without Apology

I liked the change. Little Rock, like the station, was small with an air of tranquility and serenity. I was just getting over a seesaw relationship, so this was a clean slate of new pasture for me. I leased a house in North Little Rock and started to settle into this country homey feeling.

That feeling didn't last long. I left the airport at the end of my shift and headed home down Roosevelt Blvd. toward the expressway that would take me north. As I was about to turn on the exit ramp to my right, I noticed a woman at a Texaco service station in distress. She was waving her hands above her head frantically trying to get my attention. Being of the southern gentlemen's society, I pulled over to see what, if any, assistance I could be in her moment of need. I came to a stop, and rolled down the window on the passenger's side, and asked her what happened? "Were you in an accident?"

She kept saying something about her head, but I didn't see any cuts, or bruises. As she tried to lean in further, I did notice her breasts, the size of cantaloupes, were damn near fully exposed. Could she have been raped? I couldn't understand a word she was saying. Finally I turned down my car radio and forced my mind to stop racing to conclusions, so as to listen. Her words became clear and direct. She wasn't saying her head was injured, she was asking me if I wanted some head. Hells bells, she was a prostitute working the street corner, not a damsel in distress. I've seen things like this in Las Vegas, but not in Dog Patch USA.

Boy, that popped my perception of Little Rock in a hurry. Embarrassed by my premature interpretation of events, I took off without her fully moving clear of my vehicle.

I did learn one fact however, the elasticity of a woman's breast.

After about six months went by, I was informed by my landlord that his son would be getting out of a half-way house in thirty days and would be moving back home. I said, "That's nice, but how does this exciting news concern me?"

And so he replied, "Well, I was a'renting this here place for my son until he got out of jail for drug running. Oh, I'm sorry, by the look on your face, I mus'ta forgotten ta' mention it. But don't you worry, not one little bit. I've told my son all about ya' and he's happy to have a roommate. Sort of like a big brother and all. You know, to help rehabilitate him back into society. Especially with all them homo's he had to deal with in jail, you'll be a breath of fresh air for him."

I acted like I was thinking about it for a second or two, just to be polite. Then I wished him all the luck in the world with his boy, and that I'd be out as soon as I could find a new place.

It seems that Little Rock was on the cutting edge of redefining my perceptions. So, I moved a little further north to Sherwood into a two-bedroom townhouse, which suited me just fine.

I worked the afternoon shift like the other guys that came over from Memphis. Since we were all new to town and pretty much in the same inoculation situation, we flocked together. After work a tradition was born in the employee parking lot by backing your truck bed back to back, and letting the tailgate down as if it were a pre-game block party. Us guys would pop the top of a few cold ones, and shoot the breeze, or someone would suggest bringing our fishing rods to fish the Arkansas spillway until the wee hours of dawn. It was a simple, but effective psychological rehab from being home alone.

It was on such a night, with pole in hand, on the banks of the Arkansas River that I was told of a country and western honky-tonk dance hall, called BJ's. I didn't feel much like going to any more bars, and clubs. I went through that disco era thing and that pretty much did me in. But eventually, I had to give into my inner needs to cohabitate with the opposite sex. It sure beat the hell out of playing bingo on Friday nights down at the local community center where the air was acrid with *Aqua Net* and *Ben Gay*. BJ's honky-tonk looked like a Home Depot with neon lights. I pulled into its huge lot and stepped out onto the pavement wearing my new pair of Durango boots, which felt like razor blades digging into both pinky toes. It looked like a hundred and fifty yards to that damn front door. So about halfway there, I'm thinking, *this better be good because if not, I'm going to Disneyland where they have shuttles in their parking lots.*

I paid the cover charge, and managed to make my way over to the standing room only edge of the dance floor which, by the way, looked like a hockey rink. At the back end of the floor was the front cab of an 18-wheeler truck with a disk jockey inside cranking out the latest country songs.

Once I got my bearing, I walked like Festus in *Gun Smoke* toward one of the two bars, and ordered a shot of bourbon with a beer chaser hoping that the alcohol might deaden the pain in my pinky toes still being held in captivity by the Durango brothers.

Before long, I noticed a particular girl who was grazing in and out of the acres of cow gals, and cow pals. She seemed to know at least one heifer, or bull in each herd that had grouped together like cattle in a rainstorm. She was a hundred and five pound brunette that had jeans on that were so tight that she must have laid down on her bed for an hour wiggling like a newborn tadpole just to get them on.

I worked my way in close, being careful not to spook the herd. I was close now, very close. She had her back to me swishing her tail back and forth, suddenly she bolted. I was ready. I reached out and lassoed her hoof; I mean *hand* to ask her to dance.

She radiated a raw submissive expression that inspired native drums to go off in my sensory glands. (More likely the boilermaker I had just drunk.) Without a word mentioned, we headed to the dance floor. I was about to go into my jungle mating ritual that I had picked up by watching half-naked natives doing ceremonial dances around campfires on *National Geographic*. I've been told my rendition resembles the mating ritual of the gooney bird having a seizure. But before this romance ritual could be consummated, a woman of giganotosaurus proportions came up and started chatting to her while we were still in the preliminary invocation.

Then as quick as lightning, my cowgirl bolts off into the sunset of flashing neon lights. She left me—right there on the dance floor with the man-eater. Damn that was bold! Better yet, I don't think she thought twice about it. I politely excused myself to go find this blue ribbon bullette that had just bruised my manhood. It didn't take me long to locate her, she was moving

Stephen M. Jones, Jr.

through the crowd of cowboy hats casually stopping to talk like a honey bee in a flower garden. I went up to her, and introduced myself. I asked her three questions in succession. What's your name? Would you have dinner with me? And what's your phone number?"

She replied, "My name is Paula, I already have a boyfriend, and I don't give my number out to strangers. She started to walk away then turned back to me, and said, "If you really want to call me, I'm in the phone book in Cabot, Arkansas.

And with that, she quickly melted into the surrounding crowd of obscurity. I stood there for a moment, going over in my head what had just transpired. I thought to myself, she's good. She worked me like two Mormons on bicycles.

I gave myself a week to wash this chance encounter out of my head. On the second week the urge to call got the better of me. Since I only had her first name, I wondered if she had given me her real name. Did she live in Cabot, and if so, how many Paula's were listed in that phone book? I also had the uncanny feeling that maybe I wasn't the only dumb ass going through the Cabot Directory. I found myself being overcome by the urgency to find this woman like a bad habit out of control.

After about an hour going from A to Z in the phone book, I came up with a handful of Paula's. Thank God I wasn't looking for Elmer Fudds and Farmer Johns.

As luck would have it, on or about the third call, a familiar child-like voice answers the phone. I almost instinctively wanted to say, "Is your mother home little girl?"

Paula has a very distinctive, child-like voice overlaid by a heavy southern twang that was cute, and affective. I asked her if she remembered me from BJ's a few weeks ago. I went on to explain the name game, and the extreme lengths I had gone through to locate her. Thinking to myself, *like she really gives a damn Stephen, but hey if I dramatize it, maybe she'll go out with me at least long enough to wash the effects out of my system.*

7

Paula, "Oh yeah, I remember now. Yer the guy I left on the dance floor. What's yer name again?"

Damn, slap me naked and hide my clothes in the bushes, that hurt. She didn't even remember my name. So I say, "That's alright, I'll make sure you don't forget this time. You know, it's a good thing you weren't looking for my name in the phone book."

"Why's that?" She asked.

"Because my last name is Jones."

"Oh my, yer right, there are a lot of men with yer name running around, that's for sure."

Paula, and I talked on the phone for over an hour about anything, and everything; God, that woman could talk. At the time, I took this as a good sign, later I would find out that this would be an omen from the future of the fortuneteller Ma Bell.

Every day Paula kept in touch with family and friends by phone. Shut off notices were like candy wrappers at Halloween. Oops, that just slipped out. Bad memory—bad memory. I'm getting a little ahead of myself, so let me back up.

Anyhow, I asked her out on a date, and she accepted. We went to a restaurant called *Mexico Chiquita's* near the McCain Mall. The conversation stretched into different topics, one overlapping the other. It was exactly how a first date should go, never having a loss for words, or moments of silence that sometimes permeates from lack of interest.

Paula laughed at all my locker room jokes, and was genuinely interested in what I liked to do. Me, being an avid sportsman, this was great that she enjoyed the outdoors.

Only one problem. She did have a boyfriend named Carl who lived in Dallas, but she seemed disenchanted about the relationship. She said he smoked dope with her brother-in-law, Mark, when he was in town, and made fun of her when she refused to watch X-rated movies at Mark's trailer home.

She indicated that we could still be friends, and go out, but nothing serious. I thought about what she had just said, but her actions told a different story. At that moment, our eyes met as she slowly flicked the salt off her frozen margarita with her tongue. I felt myself consumed in an erotic trance as she worked her way around that glass knowing full well I was hooked in the gills.

Well I said, "Friends can be a good thing. Waiter, more salt."

I asked Paula out again, she wanted me to meet her and some of her friends at a place called *Bobbie Socks*. As the name implies it's a back to the fifties place that was part of the airport *Holiday Inn*. I was to meet her after I got off work. I walked into the place, and like the *BJ's* honky-tonk with the 18-wheeler inside, *Bobby Socks* had a 57 Chevy parked inside the front door. Arkadians must have a fixation about using old autos to decorate their landscape.

I stood at the bar to see if I could spot her. I wanted to sit back unnoticed for a while, and watch her movements. I spotted her at a table with some girls and guys. Then Paula and a girlfriend got up to cruise the bar. I ducked my head as they snaked through the crowd.

It sort of bothered me, and I thought about leaving, but hey, this was not a date, and she only considered me as a guy friend, so I made my way over to her table. She warmly greeted me, and introduced me to her friends. I told her that I had been here for a while, and had watched her cruising the bar scene.

She just laughed, explaining, "We do that all the time just to get the guys to buy us drinks."

I stayed for a little while longer, and then told Paula that it was getting late and I had to get to work early the next morning. She asked if I could take her home.

"Definitely, not a problem," I said.

We started to leave, but Paula headed to the little girls room to powder her nose first. On the way out some guy grabbed her on the ass, I mean not your run of the mill adolescent male quickie to impress your buds pinch. He took the Neanderthal grab between the legs approach that lifted her off the floor.

I figured one good turn deserves another. I came up behind him, and grabbed his testicles, putting my forearm at the back of his neck pinning him to the wall. A little thing I learned from moonlighting as a bouncer in Memphis.

As I started to escort him to the front door, I noticed he was walking on his toes. I guess he thought by walking on his tippy toes that it would take the pressure off his balls. Wrong. A friend of his joined the ballgame, which was unfortunate for the guy's balls I was still clutching. His friend's action caused me to turn off balance, much like a shortstop fielding a grounder, tossing his balls underhanded to second base for a double play.

Just as soon as it started it was over. Two police officers that were standing in the hotel lobby enjoying the fringe benefits of the donuts, and hot Joe the hotel provided stopped the play of game, and ruled it a foul ball. Ass grabber, turned choirboy, will think twice before picking a flower from someone else's rosebush.

In September Paula's birthday rolled around, and I bought her a Gucci purse, and birthstone ring. I wanted to express how much I liked her, and I wanted to be more than just a guy friend. I think she got the hint, because we were seeing each other every week without the barfly scene.

Instead, I chose to go to Petty Jean Mountain for a trial hike where the mountain water runoff cascades down to form narrow raging rapids that race alongside much of the forest-covered trail. With the crisp cool hint of autumn breezes that lapped at your senses, and rustles through the leaves bursting in colors of yellow, and crimson that no artist could ever recreate on canvas. It is a sensuous place of unique beauty and tranquility. One is at peace with the sounds and smells of nature.

This transition from friendship to courtship on an autumn weekend was momentarily interrupted by my four-footed, man's best friend. A 65-pound English Pit-Bull Terrier named Mitzie. She was always ready for play, would lick you like a bear on a honey tree, and had gas like a bunch of crazed jungle monkeys after devouring too many green bananas.

Mitzie hated anything fur bearing, mostly squirrels and cats; at this moment it was squirrels. The woods were full of them. Paula happened to be the unfortunate soul holding the leash when a busy squirrel foraging for nuts scampered by.

Like a runaway locomotive pulling a caboose, Mitzie bolted. Before I could react, Paula was dragged over the hills, and through the dells, way the hell past Grandmothers house! With a puff of dust, they were soon out of sight. When I caught up with them I tried to sugar-coat the situation by saying, "You guys were so close, you really gave that squirrel a run for his nuts."

Paula, finding no humor in my remark, handed me Mitzie's leash and started back down the trail.

We managed to catch the sunset as I slowly picked out the leaves and twigs still lodged in her hair.

One November weekend, I took Paula to Mississippi to go deer hunting with a buddy of mine. I felt that she needed some practice handling a gun. We went to an open field to shoot skeet. For people who don't know, skeet shooting is where one shoots a shotgun at a circular disk made of clay that is tossed into the air by a spring-loaded machine called a trap.

Paula told me that she had dated a guy in high school who lived on a farm and he had taken her duck hunting all the time. This gave me the impression that she was this little Annie Oakley. Paula was the first one up to bat, I told her to say pull when she was ready. She did, the gun went booyah, and water began to pour out of her eyes.

I ran up to see what had happened, and noticed a trickle of blood from her nose.

"Are you all right, honey? What happened?"

Through her sobs, and feeling somewhat embarrassed she said,

"I don't know what happened. I pulled the trigger, and the gun jumped up, and hit me in the nose."

I took a folded tissue from a roll of toilet paper out from under my hat to plug her bleeding nose. A habit I'd learned from my granddaddy, "Stevie don't ever go into the field without something to wipe your butt."

11

I checked the shell, and found out it was buckshot instead of birdshot. Buckshot is a very powerful load that delivers a walloping recoil. By mistake, I had reached into my hunting vest, and loaded the sweet sixteen-pump with a hot shell. I don't believe, until she reads this, that she ever knew.

The next day we loaded up, and headed to deer camp. A few days before, I had bought Paula an insulated camouflaged jumpsuit. I got her a fluorescent orange vest, so not to be mistaken for a deer and shot. Deer are colorblind, they only see in black and white.

However, your chances of security diminish quickly if there is a high rate of Bubbas hunting in your area. We set up base camp, and did a little scouting to find out where the deer were moving.

You know you can do your homework to find the most remote area thinking, it's just you and Mother Nature out here. Wrong. Sure enough, not a half-mile away we spotted Camp Bubba. Oh well, we'll steer clear, and hunt the north end.

We were hunting in a heavily wooded area with hundreds of acres. So it was crucial to get your bearing, even an experienced woodsman can easily get lost. Remember, this is before a city boy could buy a handy dandy pocket global satellite system, referred to as a GPS. Go ahead and ask me if I have one now? You're damn skippy I do. Heck, I don't want to get lost either.

About an hour before daylight, we set out making as little noise as possible. I wanted to get a head start on Camp Bubba. Now depending on the terrain, I either hunted with a model 1911, 12-gauge trench gun loaded in successions of buckshot, then slug to finish the job. This type of weaponry is good for heavy brush, or I use a high caliber rifle with scope for long range. Paula wanted nothing to do with the shotgun because of the nose damage she had suffered, so she used the rifle. We put her on a tree stand, high on a ridge, and told her to stay there until we got back.

After about an hour, I circled around to check on her, and to my astonishment she was gone. Damnit, "I told her to stay put." I bolted back to my buddy to secure his help to find Paula double-quick.

Stephen M. Jones, Jr.

We split up, and formed a search grid about a hundred yards apart, working back toward each other every twenty yards. We agreed to fire two shots in the air if either one of us found her. Now with Camp Bubba not too far away, I'm thinking in the back of my head about that damn movie *Deliverance.* In the movie two hillbillies abduct two city slickers, making one watch while the other is man loved and made to squeal like a pig. (Sorta like *Brokeback Mountain* without the forced entry.)

Just thinking about the possibilities caused my blood to rush faster. My anxiety intensified when I spotted her camouflaged jumpsuit hanging in a fork of a tree with Paula nowhere in sight. Now I started moving through the woods like a madman thinking she's being raped by a pack of toothless Bubba's. Damn, this is all my fault. I should never have brought her out here in the first place. If something happens to her. I'll never, never forgive myself. My mind was spinning when I heard this tiny voice saying; "Shush…You're making too much noise, and spooking all the little deer."

"Oh God, what happened, honey? Are you all right? Did those bastards hurt you?" Paula said in a hushed voice.

"What are you talking about?"

"But, I saw your—your clothes—you left them back there in a fork of a tree. I thought something happened to you."

Well Paula said nonchalantly, "Obviously not. I got hot, so I took them off is all."

My concern turned to anger. "Paula you just don't take your orange vest off, and walk around when the woods are full of hunters. And for the last time, will you please take that damn big ass bow out of your hair before one of those rednecks mistakes it for antlers, and shoots you."

Paula said, "Well, alright then…Don't get yourself all lathered up into a tiffy. There, you satisfied? All I'm saying, Stephen Jones, is I got bored sitting up there all by myself, and…"

I made a gesture by rolling my eyes.

"Don't you give me that look. You jus' look somewhere else mister." I bit my lip, and shot two rounds off in the air halting the senseless no resolve conversation, but scaring the bejesus out of Paula.

"Sometimes you can take the woman out of the city, but you can't take the city out of the woman." Paula's portrayal to me as a country girl tomboy was the first of many misconceptions that would set the prelude of things to come.

On Thanksgiving Day I met Paula's family at her mother's apartment. Paula's father had died when she was in High School, years earlier. As we drove up, Ms. Corbin was sitting on her front porch in an old metal picnic chair with a flyswatter in one hand, and the Good Book in the other. Paula's apartment was just a stone's throw away in the same complex. I learned Ms. Corbin usually ended up paying Paula's rent at the end of the month.

Paula's mother, Delmer Corbin, looked like a robust lady in her mid-sixties, the perfect storybook caricature of a grandmother. Her hair, white with streaks of silver pulled tight into a cumber bun, had never been cut for religious beliefs.

She stood up out of her chair recognizing Paula as we arrived. She was courting a depression era flower print dress that hung the length of her shinbone. Her slip-on house shoes with white tube socks made up the difference of exposed skin.

On the way over Paula had mentioned that her mother is a devote Pentecostal. She said that Pentecostals believed in plain living.

"Hey," I said, "That's what life's all about."

"I don't think you understand," Paula said.

"Sure I do, honey."

"No. you don't Stephen. They don't believe in wearin' make-up and they…"

"Honey" I said, "Looks like ya' mus'ta rebelled somewhere along the way, because I see no signs of Pentecostal influence with you in that department."

"Oh, shut up and let me finish. You never let me finish my thoughts before you burst right in."

Stephen M. Jones, Jr.

"Okay…okay, I catch your drift, gourd ahead. I'm sorry I interrupted ya'."

"Well" she said, "You'll really like this; they don't believe in TV, they think it's an instrument of the devil."

"Hold it right there—justa cotton picking' minute baby. Are you telling me that we're going over to your mama's house on Thanksgiving, and she doesn't have a TV?"

"That's right," Paula said.

"She ain't got no TV."

"No way. It can't be. Oh man, I'm turning this car around."

"Oh no you don't, Steve Jones, you're gonna go to my mama's house for Thanksgiving, and you're gonna like it."

"Well I might go, but I ain't gonna like it. I mean, what's more religious than watching football on Thanksgiving Day. Honey, I sure wish you woulda told me before now."

"Mama's got a radio."

"Radio," I exclaimed, "What am I gonna do with a radio?"

"Well Stephen, maybe you kin find a game on one of the stations."

"Hot damn—shit fire! I don't believe it. That doesn't make any sense to have a radio, and not a TV. They can have bad things on the radio just like they can on TV. If she doesn't like something she sees, she can change the channel just like I'm sure she does with the radio when she hears something she doesn't like. It doesn't make a hill 'o beans difference. I mean, think about it Paula, if that's what your mama thinks, then the radio is an instrument of the devil too. Your mama has a warped since of religion."

"Don't you talk about my mama like that, especially sense you've never met her."

"Well I don't mean to be disrespectful, but I hope she knows they have gospel programs on TV twenty-four hours a day. This isn't the dust bowl of the 1930's with everybody sitting around waiting to listen to *The Shadow*. This is the 1990's. You tell your mama to let go."

Paula laughed at my futile effort to justify my personal rebellion against her mama's plain living that I just moments earlier was praising.

15

"My mama won't let one of them things in her house. She would say, "It's different when it comes to a radio, and a TV."

"Paula, it's no different."

"I know it sounds crazy, but that's what she believes. When we were kids, I remember my daddy had arguments with mama about buying one, but every time we felt daddy was winning the battle, and figured we'd get one, mama would get all hysterical, running around the house shouting that we'd all die and go to hell. Daddy would always back down. Anyhow, we ended up sneaking out over to our friend's house to watch television."

"So, Paula, what does your mama do if she visits somebody that has a TV on?"

"My mama will sit with her back to the TV if she can't get them to turn it off."

"Boy ol' boy, that's just pitiful. You poor thing, you mus'ta' had a heck of a childhood. No wonder you overdo everything. Your mama deprived you from what most other kids take for granted. I guess this means no football at mama's house. The sacrifices men go through for the sake of courtship. But I'll tell you one thing, you can bet next Thanksgiving your mama will be sitting with her back to the TV."

Paula, with an expression of recollection exclaimed, "That's my mama."

Ms. Corbin made a large baking dish of chicken and dumplings. I thought to myself, *where's the turkey?* But boy howdy, how the aroma from the chicken and dumplings filled the little two-bedroom apartment and reminded me of my own grandparent's house. I soon forgot all about the turkey, and almost the football.

Inside Ms. Corbin's apartment were her hand crocheted blankets that she displayed across the back of a Herculean couch, and a rocking chair. She fashioned small doilies with biblical figurines on top. These figurines, along with family pictures, were all around the living room. I got the feeling that this was her way of keeping her family beliefs, past and present, close to her heart.

Paula's family tree grew in the front yard of an old, large two-story house. Paula said her daddy, Bobby Gene Corbin, was a preacher, but dabbled in business opportunities outside the church to bring in extra income. Ms. Corbin was the penny-pincher of the household. She could literally spend hours in a grocery store price comparing. I can tell you this was a gene trait that Paula never received from her mama.

I remember years later, after Paula and I were married, we invited her family to a Christmas dinner. We had gifts for all the kids and adults. I went a little overboard, but hey, twas the season. Not expecting anything in return, Paula's mother gave me a box of Arm & Hammer baking soda. I was, as expected, taken back a little when I unwrapped it, but quickly regained my composure. I smiled at Ms. Corbin, and remarked facetiously, "I hope you didn't spend too much on me."

"Oh lordy, no, Mr. Steve. I had a buy one, get one free coupon."

Paula said it was a gag gift, but I had my doubts.

Mrs. Corbin (Delmer) held the key to Mr. Corbin's (Bobby Gene) wallet, and would never fully allow him to make family financial decisions that she felt might jeopardize the Corbin nest egg. Paula said that her daddy blamed her mama for holding him back from success. Their animosities toward each other drove a wedge between the marriage. By the early 1980's dissention started to take its toll on the Corbin family.

Bobby Gene now rarely preached, except for an occasional revival. Delmer had a nervous breakdown that impaired her from driving. It's not that she is physically unable to operate a car, she's just too nervous to get behind the wheel. She has to be shuttled around by family and friends.

Although the Corbin marriage stayed intact, they lived separate lives. Bobby Gene was spending much of his time away from the house either fishing, playing the piano or visiting his own circle of friends some of whom were female. Paula said it was a dirty rumor that floated around town that her daddy was not only a spiritual, but a physical inspiration.

It was of such a day when he had a massive heart attack and died while tickling the ivory keys in the home of a lady friend.

I believe Bobby Gene's untimely fate affected Paula in two ways. First, before she met me, she dated, and seemed to be drawn to older men as a father figure. Second, her daddy's rumors of transgressions made her so insecure that she would constantly accuse those close to her of infidelities, to the point of hysteria. Sound familiar?

Paula loved her daddy dearly. She often reminisced about him, saying how big his sweet tooth was.

"My daddy would get so mad at us girls for sneaking into the freezer, and eating almost all his favorite ice cream he tried to hide in vain. No matter how mad he got, he never laid a hand on us girls. When we got in trouble, or misbehaved, mama dished out the punishment. She'd go out to the backyard, find a switch, and get them legs good."

Unfortunately, more tragedy shook the Corbin family after the untimely death of Bobby Gene. An electrical short caused a fire that burned down the huge old house very quickly. Paula and her family barely made it out with the clothes on their backs. Luckily the home was insured.

Paula and her mama soon moved into the same apartment complex that we were now about to have Thanksgiving dinner in with no ball games to watch.

Paula and I were the first to arrive. Then, Tony and Lydia Cathey, their twin girls, and an older child from Lydia's previous marriage were pulling in the driveway.

Lydia is the middle child of the three Corbin girls. Lydia and Tony owned an electrical business that Tony had built behind their house trailer. The modern business dwarfed the house trailer; Tony's tools and equipment lived better than his wife, and kids.

Paula first introduced me to Lydia, who seemed nice enough, and talked faster and louder than Paula, I thought her lips were going to catch on fire with all that friction. Then I shook hands with Tony, who I felt was quiet, and detached until he threatened to pull his belt off to beat some ass if his kids didn't settle down.

Tony and Lydia seemed to have endless problems with their marriage. Some of her problems most likely derived from alcohol abuse. Lydia started and ended her day with a beer in her hand. Tony, a typical redneck, would demand his supper be on the table when he got home. If not all hell would break loose. He didn't care if it was in front of company or not. This was his house and by God he wanted his supper hot and ready. Like clockwork, he'd finish his meal, light up a smoke, and head to his electrical shop behind the trailer. Tony only came out to administer punishment to his kids, or go to bed. I never saw him show any affection to his daughters. Not once did I see him hug or kiss 'em. That's probably why Lydia drank so much. I have to admit if Tony liked you, he would do anything to help out a friend. He was a good man's-man, but scored badly as a family man. If Tony had maintained his family like he did his company trucks, they might still be together. I don't know though, they fought like cats and dogs.

Paula told me one night, they'd had a bad fight, and Lydia tried to leave, but was too drunk to drive, so Tony took the keys away from her. She had just had her driver's license suspended for six months on a DWI charge. Boy, that wasn't going to stop Lydia from leaving, so with a six-pack in one hand and a long brown skinny crumpled More cigarette clinched between her teeth she took off on one of her kid's bicycles, wearing nothing more than a two-piece bikini. She didn't get far. She drove off the dirt road, and crashed into a sticker bush. When she woke up from a drunken stupor, she was lying in a ditch on the side of the road with scratches and mosquito bites all over her. *Damn, that must have been a pitiful sight.*

I once questioned her about drinking while we were all in the truck together. She turned to her kids and said, "Mama drives better drunk than she does sober, doesn't she?"

Talk about a rehab candidate. I wonder what could have happened if Tony hadn't taken the keys away from her and she'd passed out behind the wheel. She could have easily wiped out a whole family or someone's son or daughter, leaving eternal scars never healed by time, from an out-of-control selfish habit. Lydia was very lucky indeed. She only wiped out a patch of sticker bushes.

Mark and Charlotte Brown, with their two sons, were the last to arrive for Thanksgiving dinner. Paula said that they were on welfare, but from what

I could see, neither one looked as if they had missed any meals. Mark was a cross between a Buddha and ZZ Top band member. A real family man who has tattoos of naked women with over-sized nipples displayed on both arms.

I wonder if Mark has his sleeves rolled up or down, when singing Bringing In The Sheep where they were members of the First Baptist church of Cabot. I never knew him to ever hold down a job except for a few months as a welder building special incinerators to burn the stockpiles of Agent Orange held in a military facility in Jacksonville, Ark.

Early in our relationship, Paula would always chastise me for never wanting to go visit Mark and Charlotte. Paula would say, "Why don't you like my family? You never want to do anything with them."

So I tried to be sociable and polite, but it wasn't easy. The more I got to know them, the more I despised them; especially how they milked the welfare system. I've seen Charlotte in Knight's grocery store with two buggies full of food, all paid for with food stamps. The cashier gave her change back in cash, which she then used to purchase a couple a cartons of Marlboro cigarettes. Looking down at my buggy, with the bare essentials scattered around the bottom, really burned my wagon. There's nothing wrong with either one of them except they're too damn lazy to earn an honest buck.

I, of course, was oblivious to the circumstances, past or present, that Thanksgiving Day as we all sat down for chicken and dumplings that were umm…umm good.

Soon, two people with very different issues will have a chance meeting in a hotel room. Their combination of human chemistry, and misunderstanding between them will cause a reaction that will define the fine line of what we, as a country, perceive as sexual harassment in the work place.

CHAPTER TWO

When I met Paula she was actually working. She was a bookkeeping clerk for an electronics rental store in Jacksonville called Crown Rental. As I said, we had been seeing, or talking to each other, almost every day since we met. Paula called me one morning from work upset and crying. She said her boss was screaming at everybody in the store. I could hear him in the background over the phone.

I told her to get her things together and walk out and I'd pick her up in fifteen minutes. I told her she didn't have to take that abuse from nobody.

Paula asked me how she was gonna' pay rent and a car note. "My mama can't afford to pay for everything. She's on a fixed income."

I told Paula she could move in with me until she got on her feet and found another job.

My damsel in distress reaction to Paula's phone call would prove to be a costly move. *What is it about some men that they feel they have to be the protector of virginity?* That's an exaggerated statement in itself, but did I have some inferiority *knight in shining armor* complex? Right then and there, someone should have slapped a *dumb-ass* sticker on my forehead.

She moved in and I paid the last few notes on her car, while still hoping she'd find a job soon. For me, taking charge is a natural response. For Paula, she saw in me an opportunity of stability that she took full advantage of.

Without Apology

When we talked about what we liked in a relationship, Paula was emphatic that the man was the head of the family and makes all serious decisions.

I fell—hook, line, and sinker. I liked the thought of the old-school myth of *It's a man's world*, as though it even remotely coincides with the 21st century of the male perception. In other words, we like to think we're in control when we're really not. Down deep, all men know this to be true, but hey…look what I found? I'd come across a woman who was telling me that I should be the head of the roost. Hell, why not? It felt good, even if it was only symbolic in nature.

Months earlier, I had just got gotten out of a relationship with a strong personality, and that didn't work out. Maybe I should try the submissive type this time.

Anyhow, I felt I was in my last oat field to sew, plus on top of that, my age was hedging closer to the big three O.

Only one thing, Paula's demeanor was alluring in the sense that she wanted to be taken care of, but at the same time problematic. The best example to describe Paula's personality would be a southern Marilyn Monroe. I'm not saying they look alike. They don't. I'm talking about the mental mannerisms being similar to the Hollywood's version of the *Boop-Boop Dee Do*.

In some small demented way, I could relate to Joe DiMaggio's dilemma. Paula, to me, was a diamond in the rough. She was physically and socially engaging, but that's where the buck stopped. If I could teach her structure, then I would have a flawless diamond. And there lies the enigma of my abyss.

I started by telling her that being the man of the house sounded good to me, but in today's economy it takes two incomes to keep up with the Jones's. In retrospect, I guess I couldn't even keep up with myself, huh? Let's move on before I get too philosophically ridiculous. Anyhow, I said this needs to be a joint effort. We work together to stay together. I told her that she could take a few weeks off before looking for a new job.

Well hells bells, Paula milked two weeks into months. Then the bills for two started to catch up to the income of one. She soon found out that I had no sugar in my daddy, and I soon found out that you can lose your shirt investing in raw commodities like diamonds. Paula is, was, and always will be a raw commodity that requires high maintenance. My efforts to help her help herself would be an on-going tribulation throughout our relationship. I thought I could change that part of Paula, and mold her into what I perceived she should be. I was wrong to try, and even more than that, I never should've imposed my will on Paula. You have to take Paula as she is, an adult with a Peter Pan outlook. Paula is great within her element of freedom to spend money without having the responsibility of earning it. No matter what I did, I just couldn't afford to keep her happy. The attraction for me, besides the physical, was the gratification of being a provider, yet I wasn't quite satisfying her needs.

On the flip side, Paula could say that I gave her a false sense of security by having her move in, buying her gifts, and taking her out. Both of us wanting what the other couldn't give. When the play money ran out, and it was time to leave Never, Never land, and help pay bills, our love nest turned into a fight fest.

Paula gave into me and half-heartedly looked for work. Her resentment toward my control lasts to this day. I set a tight budget to keep us afloat until she got a job. Adding to the mix, was Ms. Corbin preaching about us living together every chance she got. I remember she would give me a stern look and wag her finger at me. (What is it about finger wagging when it's about sex?)

Ms. Corbin would say, "You're not supposed to live together unless you're married. It just ain't fittin'! You're living a life of sin in the eyes of the Lord, Mr. Steve. You know the right thing to do. I know the Lord will help you find the way. I'm gonna pray for you to do what's right. You hear me?"

All I could say that would satisfy her was, "Yes, ma'am, I need all the praying you can give me."

I told Paula that we couldn't afford to be splurging and eating out on the weekends until we got a handle on the bills. It didn't dawn on me how much she used the phone while I was at work. Heck, our first major argument was about a three-hundred dollar phone bill.

In every relationship, money issues can cause a man to get a chill in his feet, but for now I gave up the field of battle, and put our little indifferences aside.

Without Apology

It was Christmas! My favorite holiday; full of warm feelings, peace on earth, and good will toward anyone standing under the mistletoe. I took Paula to meet my parents, and to celebrate the New Year of 1990 at the Peabody Hotel in Memphis. We danced around the famous Peabody fountain in the lobby to a band playing *Auld Lang Syne*. The sounds of the party horns, the occasional bump from a drunk, confetti that glittered down from the balcony and champagne that showered when corks flew--it all seemed defiantly silent, almost subliminal except for the swish of her satin gown as we slow danced into the New Year. Who knew what the future would hold.

After the first of the year I felt as if things were looking up. Paula landed a job at a pesticide business right down the street. It was a perfect 9 to 5 job. Paula is not a morning person, but we lived so close she could sleep in 'til eight. Perfect, except after a few months on the job, the company down-sized. Paula was the last to be hired and the first to be fired, so we we're back to square one.

The frustration level for both of us took its toll on our relationship, but neither one of us was willing to jump ship just yet. I borrowed a typewriter from my parents, so Paula could work on her typing speed.

Between all the three Corbin sisters, Paula was the only one to graduate from high school. She had to go to summer school to be allowed to attend the graduation ceremonies, but she did it. Education was not a high priority in the Corbin house.

I know it's our nature to see fault in others while turning a blind eye to ourselves. So let me say that I, by no means was a perfect child with perfect parents in a perfect world. I was average in education and study habits were a chore, not a choice.

Paula got a job working in a clothing department store making barely eighty dollars a week. That was a tough pill for her to swallow since she had a spending bug stuck up her butt.

My hope was to help her land a good clerical position in a company where she could move up.

Now don't make the mistake, and assume that she is ignorant. She is not. She is scholastic in subjects that interest her. Paula just happens to be very

Stephen M. Jones, Jr.

particular with her interests. Unfortunately for Paula, what she excels at is not in textbook form. Believe me; she deserves an honorary degree in socializing.

Given my financial strain we did manage to have some fun in the spring with Tony and Lydia camping at Big Piney, a mountain run-off with white water that can get your adrenalin flowing. We'd lease a couple of canoes, and drive up this gravel road about fifteen miles to the back of nowhere, having to pay close attention while driving or else suffer bodily injury by running off the side of the mountain.

During the spring everything green had germinated and exploded to life. Limbs from young saplings reached over the rural road to slap and scratch the side of our vehicle. It didn't take long to learn to keep your window rolled up when a branch full of minuteman ants smack you on the face. After examining your ear by feel to see if it's still attached, the ant's that had slipped down your collar unnoticed bite you into a mumbo jig dance spewing superlatives.

Three quarters of the way down the road you'd better start straining your eyeballs, trying not to miss taking a right turn through a dilapidated gate that has a wooden sign nailed to the fence post. The sign was printed in red, dried-up peeling barnyard paint and in large letters that stated "Keep closed. See maw fer fee."

I mean, if you blink you'd miss it, and we missed it—damn near every time. As we got closer to the farmhouse, there was maw sitting in a rocking chair on the front porch, her face weathered like antique leather, chewing tobacco and spitting into a Crisco can.

You paid maw twenty bucks to launch your canoe on her property. Her boys, Ethan and Jr., would drive your truck back to camp. I never saw them, but I'm guessing Jr. was a big'n.

There was always a cheek crease pulled up in the cloth on the driver's side seat along with the recline position extended as far back as manufacturedly possible. I don't want to contemplate the scientific possibilities of how a crease could form in that amount of time and stay like that. Some things should be left unsolved. Beyond all that, our trucks were always parked down river where maw said they'd be every time without incident.

Paula and Lydia would be in front of the canoes. A good thing it was knee deep to a tadpoles butt in most places because neither one could swim a stitch.

Even if it seemed an adventure just to get to the damn place it was all worthwhile. I remember one curve in the creek called The Mother. Believe me, the term *mother* is short and not meant in the nurturing sense. There are three huge boulders in the middle that causes the water to flow uncontrollably rapid. Between the closer of the two is half of an aluminum canoe wedged and crumpled from impact. If you're careful, with a bit of luck and manage it just right you'll have one hell of a good ride! If you're not, then your voice will rise to be heard echoing in the distance the true complete name of the *The Mother*.

Tony and I would only take the girls when the water flow was low and slow. Paula never picked up a paddle, rather for her it was all about the meandering ride down the county side. About all Paula would do is occasionally stick her leg overboard to splash the water with her big toe. Speaking of feet, she has amazing dexterity in her feet. Paula can spread her toes and grip a rock like a mountain goat. On more than one occasion, she's picked up a rock to ping me with it. I've seen her snatch up and separate a whole basket of dirty laundry with her feet while not missing a beat talking on the phone. That bit of information has no relevancy except for you people out there with feet fetishes.

We did a lot of things outdoors, and some of them included being around water. I asked Paula why she never learned to swim.

"Mama kept us girls away from water. She'd only let us bathe in a half inch of tub water. I'm scared of deep water anyhow."

"Well, Paula" I said, "Wonder where you acquired that phobia? Looks to me like your mama, bless her heart, has put more than the fear of God in your mind."

"Oh, you leave my mama alone, Steve Jones. She can't help it if she's scared of water."

"Paula, I'm not just talking about water. She frets about everything, and so do you. I jus' don't want you to turn out to be scared of your own shadow baby. When you worry about everything, that's not healthy. The first thing I'm going to do is teach you how to swim."

Stephen M. Jones, Jr.

After the canoe trip we went back to the condo and headed to the pool. It took me an hour just to talk her into the three foot end. I never could get her to hold her nose and dip her head under water. When I tried to push the issue, she'd get hysterical, and clench me hard, digging her nails into my back like a cat on a scratching post. E-ouch!

I soon enrolled Paula into a swim class at the Y.M.C.A. I managed to somehow squeeze it into the budget figuring it was a good investment in the long run. As time went by, I learned that Paula had a lot of anxieties that she would really never be able to come to terms with. Just like her mama, she worried about everything. They were like two peas in a pod. Paula inherited her mother's insecurities. It would be much later before I realized how these insecurities would impact the lawsuit and our marriage.

Even with my apprehensions, our relationship seemed to flourish. Paula's fun-loving, energetic outlook was addictive to be around. She always had something to talk about. Paula leaned on me for almost everything and, to be honest, it made me feel good to take care of her. But damn, the way I saw it, two things hit me hard at the same time. All the bills at the end of the month and her PMS. When Paula was PMS-ing she could scream, cry, and threaten to rip your balls off all at the same time. Other than that, we were pretty much the A-typical couple, arguing mostly about money.

On a few occasions, she would threaten to go to someone that she said would take better care of her. I called her on it one night, and she jiggled her keys in my face and said, "I've got a place to go, don't you worry about me, buster."

It took me a while, but I found out that the key she was referring to belonged to a condo in Hot Springs, owned by Dan Hampton, a now retired Chicago Bear's football player. Paula said that they were just good friends. *Yeah, and frogs don't bump their butts when they hop.*

I remember when Paula and I were driving up to Hot Springs to have some fun on a weekend. We were coming up a one-way street behind the Arlington Hotel, when a big white dually truck came barreling down in the wrong direction. I pulled off the side of the road at Paula's screaming insistence. A trait that I despised, but it was either lose my hearing, or stop playing chicken and give in to this asshole.

As the driver went by Paula said in a somewhat resentful tone, "That was Dan Hampton and that's not his wife sitting in his lap."

So I smirked a little and said, "Jealous are ya'?" Paula after catching her breath from either being terrified, or caught off guard by the chance encounter quickly snapped back at me saying,

"Naw, I'm not jealous, but when it comes to my life Stephen Jones, I'll scream all I want to." (*Paula called me Steve or Stephen depending on how irritated she was with me, adding my last name for emphasis.*)

Needless to say, I noticed that she had gotten rid of the key, unless she had a spare that I wasn't aware of.

We often talked of marriage, but I kept losing the feeling in my feet. I never really regained full sensation. Her rogue irresponsibility of spending money bugged me. I did; however, take steps toward our future by getting back on track financially. I liquidated some of my assets by selling my ski boat and saving enough money for a down payment for a house. I love the great outdoors, so when I went house hunting I looked in the country. Paula wasn't crazy about living in the country. She was more of a semi-country suburbanite, if that makes any sense.

Before long, I found a little two-story house sitting on almost an acre atop a place called Billy Goat Mountain. You could stand on the front porch and see a big valley with hundreds of uninhabited acres. If you squinted over the horizon, you could almost imagine seeing the Cartwright's riding over the top of the ridge to the theme song of *Bonanza*.

I put a bid on the house, and a month later I got it for damn near nothing. It was my first and I was as happy "as a puppy with two peckers."

I started getting some feeling back in my toes. Paula's school-hood friend, Pam Blackered, worked at the Arkansas State Capitol and got Paula an application for work. A few weeks later she was called in for a typing test. Thank God I had gotten the typewriter for her so she could practice her speed. Another week, or two went by and wham, she was hired as a secretarial clerk for the department of Arkansas Industrial Development Commission, aka, AIDC.

Paula's job description varied from light typing to keeping records of gas usage on state owned and operated vehicles used in the field.

She would also walk to the Governor's office every day to gofer different documents from AIDC to be signed by then-Governor Clinton. Sometimes Paula would sit outside Clinton's office door and chitchat with his secretary and bodyguard. I believe that these trips back and forth to Clinton's office, along with Paula's artistic ability as a socialite, put her on the radar screen as a perspective candidate by Clinton's surrogate bodyguards.

These bodyguards were a special unit of State Troopers. The Governors detail, as it's called, had a shift rotation that allowed a bodyguard to be with, or near, Clinton at all times.

Paula liked her job and she had good medical benefits to boot, so things were looking up. My plan to work with Paula and help her help herself would fertilize our relationship as well.

The next step was to re-establish her bad credit. Years before I met Paula, she had taken out a school loan and never paid it back. That, combined with not paying her car note on time damn near ruined her credit. In fact, the only credit Paula had established was bad credit. I was going to change all that, or so I thought.

I got her a credit card, under my line of credit, with her name on it. I told her she would be responsible for paying the bill each month. In the long run it would help her build a good credit history, right? Wrong! All I did was give her the incentive to do lunch every day with her girlfriends. At the end of the month like clockwork, she always fell short on funds to pay her bill and yep, that's right, I made up the difference.

Paula's immaturity started to slowly chip away at my resolve again. It seemed that when I took one step forward, I took two steps backwards. The *damsel in distress* that I thought was so cute and alluring about Paula was no longer cute. *It's time to grow up baby, or I'm going fishing for a better trout.*

I seldom, if at all, brought up marriage anymore and I think Paula sensed that. I was looking for an excuse to stop cutting bait and fish. My feet weren't cold. Hell, they were frozen.

You know, looking back I often wonder what on earth compelled me to try to mold Paula into something she would never be. My efforts to conform her just lead to an eternal flame of resentment.

As an old-timer whittling on a stick once told me, "You jus' can't go 'round trying to change a woman. All your efforts will be as insignificant as a pee hole in the snow."

It used to bug the hell out of me why Paula was never responsible with money. I considered the way she was raised. The youngest of three, she was always the baby. Everybody took care of *Poohla* as she was sometimes called. Her mother and sisters cooked for her, so she never cared to learn anything other than the basics. On holidays or special occasions, however, she would borrow a cookbook and try real hard.

This still didn't explain her money-popping addiction. As I touched on earlier, I felt that part of the problem was how Paula was brought up in a religiously strict environment. Her peers were the haves and her family's religious values were the have not's. As Paula grew up, she loathed the plain hand-me-down clothes from her sister, Lydia, that she was made to wear. Paula couldn't wear Charlotte's, so her mama just took the hem out and used them as a throw blanket for picnic outings.

When Paula rebelled and broke free of her mama's religious restriction, she went hog wild in the other direction. Paula double-dipped into everything she wore. She wore it tight, short, bright, and thick.

The first couple of years into the lawsuit were a real struggle for me to get her to tone down everything, including her make-up. Boy did she resent me asking her to stop wearing pants that were so tight that the crotch produced a shape that the guys nowadays call *camel toes*. I felt the paparazzi, who were always hiding behind the next bush, would've had a field day.

Not long after I bought the little house in the woods, I didn't have to worry very long about cold feet. In fact, feet had very little to do with it. Paula became pregnant. We got the hint the following Thanksgiving when the smell of her cooking made her sick. Sometimes the best things in life are not planned.

Paula told me she didn't need to be on birth control pills because she said, like her sister, she felt she had a cyst on her ovaries and couldn't get pregnant. At times when we were intimate, she complained of pain and associated it with her maybe having a cyst. So, I pretty much believed her, but kept encouraging her to see a doctor. She always had an excuse for not going to the doctor, saying that I was always griping about her spending money, and it could be expensive to see a doctor. I told her stop with the excuses, that she's got medical insurance with the state, so go.

I should have been more responsible, and waited until Paula was examined by a doctor, but no. I hypothesized that Paula was right, because we've been having physical relations for over a year without any hiccups. So as the song says...*Don't worry, be happy*. My thought process was in the wrong place allowing my testosterone to just ponder on. When she did go, it wasn't because of pain from a phantom cyst, it was because she missed her period and I had given her a home pregnancy test.

Well, goodbye freedom—hello ball and chain. No, but really, the transition to daddy-hood was easy for me.

Even if I had my doubts about our compatibility, I wasn't willing to have our child born out of wedlock.

It was important for me to make plans to get married as soon as possible to have our marriage certificate show 1991 and the birth certificate show 1992. Only people with a keen interest on counting months would know the difference.

I know we live in a world where babies are born out of wedlock and it's no big deal. We see it flaunted by the Hollywood elite so much that it's become socially acceptable, if not socially fashionable.

Even what we watch on TV, or going to the movies can change what we perceive as immoral behavior. How do you think Hillary Clinton got elected to the senate? One could argue some of the best things in life or either illegal, immoral and fattening. Our moral behavior has changed. Case in point, a Hollywood studio can take a controversial social issue and make a movie, or TV drama out of it. You say, "So what? It's just entertainment." "Yes, but with a message."

Look, a gifted actor has the ability of transforming a hot button issue by capturing the eluding magic of creativity that tingles our senses to the point of affecting our emotions. This infectious gift we receive from the silver screen has great influence that can incorporate either positive or negative behavior. This behavior, over time, can go from immoral to socially acceptable.

I believe impressionable youth idolize superstars to the point that they want to emulate their life styles. Unfortunately, these impressions won't pay the twenty-four hour nanny service their idols can well afford.

Well Baby Bubba, this socially accepted stigma will not happen in my immediate domain. Our son would be able to answer the question, "Who's your Daddy?"

Chapter Three

I had heard about a majestic little town called Eureka Springs, Arkansas. Without ever popping the question, we drove down to make arrangements for the wedding, marked for late December after the Christmas holidays.

Eureka Springs is the gem of Arkansas. It's nestled in a valley surrounded by mountains. Most the homes are 1890's vintage, restored to their original beauty and majesty. Over half are operated as bed and breakfast. We were very much still in the Christmas spirit and seeing this place was like a winter wonderland of bygone days. It's like all the great Christmas songs played out in visual Technicolor. Eureka is a place that could easily hallmark a Norman Rockwell Christmas card.

I made reservations at a bed and breakfast house, reserving the Romeo and Juliet suite. The owner helped us make arrangements for the reception in the parlor of the old estate. The room was beautifully decorated with a ten foot Christmas tree. You could smell the fresh pine tinsel that bannered around the room with red ribbons in each corner. The tinsel was accented by tiny twinkling multi-colored lights.

The cozy warm glow of a roaring fire, crackling as it burned from within the hearth was all that was needed to make dreams come true, except maybe some chestnuts roasting. And with a twitch of an eye, there was a pewter bowl of chestnuts warming in front of the fireplace mantle. Just a few inches away, a battle-worn tin soldier nutcracker stood guard. *I don't think it gets much better than that*, I thought.

Just down the street, as the turtle dove flies, I made reservations for my family to stay overnight and reserved a day room for Paula's family since they were going home that same day.

The first kink in the chain came when Paula's mother refused to go to her daughter's wedding because it fell on a Sunday and she would have to miss her Sunday go-to-meeting services. God must love mother-in-laws. *(Except the one I have now, she is a gem among rhinestones.)*

We had to change the wedding to Saturday to make sure Ms. Corbin got back in time to get to her church meeting. I don't think God would have condemned her for missing one Sunday in twenty-five years to see her daughter get married. I thought about keeping the original date for a second by showing her the videotape of the wedding, but I realized she wouldn't watch it because it was on a TV set and God forbids her from watching the devils instrument. I was hardheaded enough to challenge her once again by breaking it down step-by-step by saying, "You listen to the radio don't you, Ms. Corbin?"

"Yep, sure do—every day."

"Now Ms. Corbin, if you hear something you don't like, what do you do?"

"I'll change the station, I sure will, Mr. Steve."

"Good, that's good" I said, "Now that's the same concept with a TV, you don't like what you see, or hear, you simply change the station, right?"

"Nope, Mr. Steve."

"What do you mean nope? It's the same thing, Ms. Corbin."

"Naw, its differ'unt." she said, "And I ain't gonna sit here and argue with you, Mr. Steve. When it ain't right, it jus' ain't right. So you watch what you want to watch, and I'll listen to what I want to listen to."

"But, but, you don't…Oh, hells-bells, Ms. Corbin. You have it your way. I just want you to know that your own daughter said you'd say it's different. I'm going to tell you right now it's no different except in just your stubborn mind."

Another problem popped up when Mark Brown wanted to give the bride away and I said double, "Hell no!" about that. Mark protested by threatening not to attend the wedding. *Hey, fine with me, one problem solved. Now there would be plenty of room in the family wedding pictures.*

The next glitch was which church to get hitched in. I wanted a very old, simple church where its doors had seen generations of newlyweds with a horse-drawn carriage. Paula wanted the famous crystal chapel called Thorn Crown, where you had to pay a pretty penny for a one-hour package. I told Paula if we wanted to get married like that we could go to Vegas.

Paula said, "I'm gonna' get married one time in my life and I don't want no little dinky church."

I started hinting to Paula that we need to lighten-up on the spending. "Look honey, I know you want a special wedding, and you're going to have one, but if you add up the cost of the reception, your wedding gown, both rings, accommodations for everybody and now the church, this is costing me a small fortune. Just those Swedish meatballs and a few other Pupus at the reception are costing me boo coos. On top of that I'll still be paying for both our rings for years. Come on honey, you mean to say you can't cut me some slack on the church? I need a break here."

Paula started to cry, saying she had her heart set on that church.

My father caught wind of the episode and paid for the one-hour lease of a thorn in my rear.

I must admit, as nervous as we both were, pretty much everything went off without a hitch. Since Paula's daddy had passed away, she was going to have her uncle give her away, but he was unable to make it because of health problems. I thought it would be nice if Ms. Corbin gave her daughter away. In the end, Paula chose Lydia's husband, Tony. That ticked off Mark and he made good on his absenteeism. That bit of resolve took the edge off the butterflies riding shotgun and made me smile a little inside.

At four o'clock in the afternoon, everyone rose as they played *Here Comes The Bride*. Paula was barely able to walk down the aisle. She was so nervous that she almost tripped over her train, and stumbled. We found out later that Charlotte had stepped on it from behind. I slipped the ring on her trembling finger that tied the knot on December 28th 1991.

The reception was a hit, except for one small detail. I didn't get to eat one single Swedish meatball. Six trays of Swedish meatballs and all that was left were those damn multi-colored toothpicks. *Who snarfed them? I had my suspicions. All three hundred pounds of her, sitting on a skinny-legged chair in the corner picking her teeth with Exhibit (A) stuck in her mouth.*

Oh well, it was time to slice the cake together for good luck, a tradition that holds as much water as fortune cookies after a Chinese dinner.

I popped the cork on the magnum Champagne bottle, and poured everyone a glass, except Paula who drank sparkling cider, and of course Ms. Corbin who would not dare allow her lips to touch a fermented grape even though Jesus drank wine at the Last Supper with his disciples.

After about an hour of traditional toasting, hand shaking, advice giving and Paula throwing the bouquet to the next unavailable maiden, things started to wind down. Especially now, since the only thing left for a cow to eat was the frozen rotunda outside.

Paula felt a little nauseous, so we thanked everybody for coming. We made our way upstairs to the Romeo and Juliet suite. I fixed Paula a hot bubble bath in the heart shaped Jacuzzi hopping that would make her feel better. I was still trying to polish off a champagne bottle I'd been coddling. So much for hot bubble baths, Paula felt worse as we both lay down on the four-poster bed. She asked me why there were mirrors on the ceiling of our bed to which I replied, "It's for couples that want to practice watching how they contract morning sickness."

As I lay there, I thought back on how my life seemed impacted on or around Thanksgiving.

It was back in 1991. Thanksgiving soon approached and we were excited about cooking a big dinner with all the trimmings in our new home. As I said before, the only time Paula was inspired to cook was on the holidays. I had to work, so I called to remind her to take out the little plastic bag of goodies inside the turkey because I had harpooned a melted bag the year before. At first she refused to put her hands inside the butt of a Butterball turkey to pull out the package. After a little coaxing, she consented and remarked, "I looked real good and this turkey ain't got no bag of innards."

"Are you sure? Remember last year."

"I'm sure...er," she responded in her twangy little voice.

"Well then, there, now. If you say so, then it must be so. I'll try to get an early out from work and be home lick-a-dee split. Hey, I'm gonna' call right before I leave, so you can put the rolls in the oven so they'll be piping hot when I get home.

Baby, I can almost smell the turkey basting through the phone. What's that honey? Nah, the flights are pretty much empty, shouldn't be a problem getting out early. Right now there's nothing going on. It's deader'n a doorknob. It's just us guys in operations watching the game. Oh.., hold on...Honey, hold on. I gotta go. Alabama's about to score, bye."

Everything was right with the world as I made it home at half-time.

"It all looks so good honey. I'll take back saying you can't cook 365 days a year to 364 days."

She quickly snapped back, "Watch it, buster."

"Oh honey I'm just teasing...could you do me a favor? Could ya' scoot your chair over just a little? No, no the other way. There you go baby. I can see the game now. No...No...No! Would ya' look at that dumb ass call the ref just made. Unfrigging believable..."

With my mouth watering and the second half of the game starting, it couldn't get any better than this. Paula handed me the carving knife to do the honorary turkey slicing. I carved several slices of white meat then went deeper for some dark meat, but my knife got snagged on something big.

"I've got it...hold on, here it comes. What the bejesus is that, an alien?"

Nope, it's just another protoplasmic bag of turkey organs.

Paula was quick to say, "I swear to God...There was no innards inside. I looked real good, I swear. Oh dear Bessie."

After that, it sort of became a family tradition, like finding the wishbone.

Paula wasn't very hungry, she said the aroma of the turkey basting in the oven made her sick to her tummy. Heck, the aroma just causes me to loosen a couple a notches in my britches to make more room for seconds. For one split moment, I hesitated and thought how odd. I wonder if she's contracted plastic bag poisoning from inhaling the fumes. But just as quickly as the thought arrived, it dissipated due to turkey overload.

"Could ya' please pass more of that giblet gravy honey?"

Later that night Paula's symptoms progressively worsened as she ran out of bed to heave ho in the porcelain throne. She hardly ate anything. I ate my unfair share of turkey, so it couldn't be from the plastic bag left in the bird. She didn't drink any alcoholic beverages so what could it be?

Paula crawled back in bed just in time for the alarm to go off. We looked at each other simultaneously, I thought out loud, "Could you be pregnant?"

She weakly responded, "I doubt it," rolling her eyes at me exaggeratedly.

So I told her, "Yeah right, I know, I know. It's that cyst you told me about that keeps you from getting pregnant. Paula, you have all the symptoms of morning sickness, so after work I'll swing by the drugstore and pick-up a pregnancy test.

Paula snapped back, "You're no doctor. I got some stomach virus, or something. That's all."

Later that afternoon, I brought home the test and Dr. Bubba administered the cup to the reluctant patient. She returned it a few minutes later at the exact level marked filled.

"Is it yours?" I asked, continuing to tease. "You didn't fill it with toilet water knowing I have a bad habit of not flushing, did ya'?"

"Oh shut up, Stephen Jones and take the cup."

I continued the examination by labeled instructions and after a few more minutes sure enough, yes sir, uh huh, a small red plus sign emerged.

"Lookie here, Paula. See that? You're on the nest."

"Well something's wrong," she said. "I told ya' already. I can't get pregnant."

"Yeah, you've told me a thousand times to Monday. Now, for the last time, stop you're foot-dragging, and go see a doctor."

Stephen M. Jones, Jr.

Paula went to a doctor referred to her by her friend, Pam. He said she was a perfectly healthy pregnant young lady. Paula never had a cyst, or anything abnormal except for a rare blood type. He also confirmed that she was eight weeks on the nest with a little *us* inside her incubator.

The doctor set the due date on, or around the 28th of July. She called me at work nervous of what I might say. I don't know why, Paula knew me well enough by now to know how I felt about having kids someday. She knew I'd stick by her like glue. Yes siree, Bob. We were adding a twig to the family tree.

Paula's morning sickness lasted close to a month and then she regained her appetite with a vengeance. Paula developed an insatiable craving for ice cream, not just any ice cream, it had to be the expensive stuff. It started off by day with a half-gallon carton of *Breyer's All Natural* and switched midstream to a tub of *Ben & Jerry's Sweet Cream & Cookies* at night.

At bedtime, Paula would prop herself up with a couple a' pillows coddling a large carton to herself. If I even tried to stick a spoon in for a little taste, she growled at me like a wild animal causing Mitzie to scurry under the bed. I had come to the realization that *Ben & Jerry* had replaced me.

Paula and I were both excited and apprehensive about having a baby; neither one knowing quite what to do. Again teasingly, I mentioned to Paula that we could explore the idea of what my tribal ancestors would do under the same conditions.

So I told Paula, "When the woman is with child and it was time for the papoose to start its journey to mother earth, the brave would lead his squaw to a secluded area in the forest. There, she would squat down with only a stick in her mouth or leather tong to bite down on. After giving birth, the mama squaw would chew off the umbilical cord, cleanse the newborn with nearby steam water and swaddle the papoose in soft deerskin. The final ceremonious event would be the belabored squaw lifting up and handing their warrior child to White Cloud, proud Indian chief of the Watwo-bubbas.

Paula sneered at me and said, "You have gone and lost your mind, Stephen Jones. This here's modern times and I ain't no squaw. If that's what you want, why don't you go find yourself a squaw in the Quawpaw district and knock her up in some backyard teepee, so she can squat nine months later in some patch a'weeds. If that's what you want, have at it, but not with me buster. When it becomes my time, I'm getting an epidural. The only thing I want natural is more ice cream. So you jus' bring me a big spoon this time. Don't think I don't know what you're doing by giving me a smaller spoon. And I want you to quit watching so much *History Channel*. That's where you get all those weird ideas from anyhow."

"Now, now don't get your tail feathers all ruffled...I was just joking. I can't believe you took me serious, Paula."

"Well buster, you need to get it through that thick head of yours, there ain't gonna be no pain for me, mister. I also know what you're thinking when you only read out loud from that baby book yore sister sent us where it says how much better breast milk is.

I can read you like a book. I know what you're beating around the bush about and I'm telling yah right now, I ain't breastfeeding either. I want my titties to stay perky. Anyhow, baby formula is jus' as good."

As Paula's tummy began to stretch, and her figure changed, I was told on a daily basis that this was all my fault

"I ain't never gonna' be able to fit into my jeans again, Steve Jones, so you kin jus' go find yoreself a knot hole if you just hav'ta feel the need, because I-ain't-interested."

"Paula you don't mean that...you're just talking out of frustration because your body is changing."

"That's right, mister. My hormones don't have you in the picture for the next nine months, so you kin forget about getting any shaky pudding."

Changing the subject and not thinking, I said, "As a rule of thumb, in the motherhood book it says you can look at your mother to see how you will fair during and after childbirth."

Paula's eyes started to get big.

"On second thought...don't look at your mama, that's just an old wives tale anyway honey. Say, look, I read that you can take some preventative action by rubbing Vitamin E oil on that cute little potbelly."

"Potbelly!" She screamed.

"No, honey, I mean—*oh hell, I put my foot in it again. What can I say?* You're going to get bigger before you get smaller. I was saving this for a special moment…here. I saw this nightshirt in that mother's to be store, and I bought it. Try it on and see if it fits." Paula came back with her fists on her hips,

"See? This is exactly what I'm talking about."

"What? I don't know what you're talking about, Paula. It looks great on you. Jus' because it says Goodyear on the belly part, is that it?"

We both bust out in laughter.

When I'd leave for work Paula would stand on the front porch and wave goodbye. I must say, she looked the part of a stay-at-home mom in her maternity Farmer John overalls along with her hair up in that infamous big red bow.

Throughout Paula's pregnancy we had many ultrasounds because of her rare blood type. She had to have a series of shots to ensure that the baby would have a common blood type. We were unsure whether we wanted to know if it was a boy or girl, but we didn't have to ponder very long. An ultrasound was done on, or about the third trimester and there it was—poking up in his sleep. At first I thought, *the baby's deformed. He's got a partially developed clubfoot.*

"What's up with that, Doc?"

Then it hit me and I said, "Look, honey, it's a boy. Right there, look. See right there…say Doc? Do they do this before they're born?"

He snickered, and answered by saying, "It's not uncommon; in fact, it's fairly normal."

Paula then blurted out, "Well, he's just like his daddy when he sleeps."

"Hush up, Paula."

"Don't like it when it's done back at yah, huh, Stephen Jones?"

We signed up for Lamaze classes and were told to bring a pillow. When we got there, I noticed that there were just two other guys in our class. The majority of the mothers-to-be were by themselves. I was in a special mood, and I said, "Where's all the daddies? Um, must be working the night shift, or something. But hey, this stuff's important, and they need to be here."

When no one said anything, I leaned over to the African-American mother-to-be on the other side of us, and playfully acting like I was talking to her baby still in her tummy and said, "Where's your daddy? Is that big ole boy working tonight?"

She turned on me, and said, "You thinks dat sum'bitch is working huh? Yeah, I no's he's working all rite. He's working on my sista now. Fow long dat no good ho gonna be jus-like-me. Now you otsa minds yo own bennes white boy."

"Excuse me... Excuse me." The instructor announced, "Please, we need to do a little more listening and a little less talking."

Paula elbowed me in the ribs and I whispered in her ear, "Damn, honey, that hurt...It sounds like soul mama should be on that illegitimate Geraldo show."

I did a little more snooping around in class and found out that over forty percent were single moms. *Damn that's pitiful, where's the responsibility of the daddies.* Meanwhile, Paula and I learned how to breathe and control the contractions when our water breaks.

After the class I asked the instructor, "Who pays for the babies being born from single moms without insurance?"

She said, "The state picks up the tab. Being a resident of Arkansas, you pay for it in taxes."

"The hell you say?"

"That's right, Mr. Jones. It equates to millions of dollars every year."

"I don't mind paying for it in taxes, but shouldn't the mother and father take some responsibility for their actions, and pay some of it back when they get a job?"

The instructor looked at me like I was picking my nose in public and said sarcastically, "So why don't you write your congressman?"

Actually, I did better than that. I ran into Senator Dale Bumpers at the Little Rock Airport on his way to Washington, DC. I explained to him that I felt that the state, and we as taxpayers, should pay for single moms to have their babies born, but have a reasonable amount garnished from both parents paycheck until the state has been paid in full. The state should make a reasonable effort to collect the people's money back. That way the residents could get a tax credit in the form of an exemption when they file each year depending on the revenue collected. I went on to tell Senator Bumpers that maybe some of the money could be earmarked for educational programs to help solve the problem of teen pregnancies.

I thought to myself, *I'm on a roll now bubba, now for the finale,* "I just don't think the state should give a blank check to people that are either irresponsible, or make a mistake. We all make mistakes Senator, but we should be responsible to pay it back. The taxpayers of the state should not carry the burden of picking up the tab."

I have to admit, I was feeling confident in my own hometown meeting scenario.

The Senator did take the time to listen to what I said, and then he responded, "Son, don't ever get into politics. You won't make it to first base. I'd never get elected with your attitude, but I like your spunk and you really seem passionate about this. Let me enlighten you. You've got to have the minority vote to survive in this state. Now, I've got a flight to catch. Hey, somebody in my group, give this young man a Dale Bumpers sticker."

He shook my hand while someone shoved a Vote for Bumpers sticker in the other. And he said while walking off, "So glad we had this little talk, son. Now remember, don't forget to vote."

"Oh, you can count on me to vote Senator," I said.

His group left me standing in a daze, holding a sticker that slightly waved goodbye in the breeze created from their passage. I'd just been shot square between the eyes by political snake oil.

In the meantime, Paula was getting close to her due date. She had a few false alarms which kept me on my toes 24/7. They always came in the wee hours of the morning, usually between two and four am. The sounds were uncanny in pitch and delivery, sort of started with a low who, mid-range whoo-whoo-whoo, then a high-pitch whooooh. This was repeated several times in intensity and volume as if a hoot owl had gone wild.

I'm a very light sleeper, so I'd jump up and help coach her in her breathing, as we had learned in Lamaze class. I made sure her contractions subsided and didn't last longer than ten minutes.

On the night of the 27th, the *hoot owl gone wild* turned into Aretha Franklin's high note.

We zoomed to the hospital lick-a-dee-split. When we got there, Paula's contractions had subsided. I thought it was another false alarm. It's what they call phantom labor, but since we were already there, I wanted to make sure Jr. wasn't trying to make his grand entrance.

Paula was able to make it to the admissions desk where I checked her in and filled out a ton of insurance forms. By the time a wheelchair came, another couple arrived and she, too, the same Aretha pitch as Paula had earlier, but this woman's water broke right there in front of us! There was this Lawrence Welk's pop sound. You know, like he did with his mouth at the beginning of all his shows along with a swoosh of air afterwards, just like that. It was as sudden, like a fish bowl being dropped on a concrete floor.

Paula felt that she could walk to the room, so we gave the wheelchair to the couple. The nurse at the reception desk said thoughtfully, "I do think you did the right thing. You were here first, but I believe they needed it a little more than you guys. It'll be a few minutes before your room is ready Mrs. Jones."

She then punched an extension on the phone, "Hey, can you get someone up here to admissions pronto with a mop before someone slips and falls? We have a small flood on the floor."

I helped Paula to her room, and stepped out to make sure the head nurse knew the name of our doctor and had called to let him know Paula had been admitted. She smiled at me, "That's all been taken care of Mr. Jones. We have a full staff on duty. Let me show you where they keep the coffee."

"That's all right," I said, "I've got to get back to my wife, she needs me. We're partners in this, you know."

Stephen M. Jones, Jr.

"I certainly hope so, Mr. Jones."

I had just turned around to head back to Paula's room when the guy's wife that we let have the wheelchair shoved a cigar into my hand, and said, "It's a girl!"

"Wow! That was quick."

"Yeah," he said. "She started labor in the wheelchair. Can you believe that? Hey, by the way, thanks for the chair."

"No problem, I just hope mine is as quick and easy as yours. Guess I'll be seeing you at the nursery."

We shook hands and wished each other well.

I went in search of Paula's room. It's funny how men take all the glory without the pain. Damn these long hallways, they all look the same in a hospital when you're in a rush. *Oh, here's the room, thank God.*

"Baby, I'm so sorry, but I went to tell the nurse to call the…"

"Excuse me, but I believe you have the wrong room!"

"Oh lord, oh no I thought you were my… oh I'm so sorry, you see my wife is having a, a baby somewhere on this floor."

"I know," she said with a smile. "Everyone on this floor is a mother-to-be."

"Forgive me, ma'am. I didn't mean to barge in on you like that."

"It's quite understandable."

She got tickled about the whole scenario. I chimed in. Her giggling suddenly turned into Who-who-who's.

"Get the whoa… out of my, my… I hate…youuu."

"I'll get you a nurse. Nurse—"

Later, the head nurse told me that I was confined to our room and the coffee stand. "Anymore roaming around, Mr. Jones and we'll put you in a straight jacket. This hospital prides itself on giving our expecting mothers a right-at-home type feeling. Look around, Mr. Jones. Does this look like a hospital?"

I shook my head back and forth.

"There's a good reason for that, it eliminates some of the stress. We don't need anymore stress on the floor, do we, Mr. Jones?"

45

Without Apology

"Yes, ma'am...I mean, no ma'am. You're just kidding about the straight-jacket stuff, right?"

"Mr. Jones, do I look like I'm kidding?"

"No ma'am."

The nurse that was assigned to Paula was busy hooking up a monitor that would track her contractions. It was sort of an earthquake richter scale, because it had a needle that would move up, and down on adding machine paper. After a while, you could pretty much predict her contractions by watching this monitor.

I called all the kinfolk and informed them we were checked in and waiting for our little miracle to appear. I had my own catcher's mitt, bets placed like Pete and ready to play all nine innings. You can betcha the hospital commission isn't gonna exile us from the game of life without a fight. All our hard work won't be denied for our little hall-a-famer.

After a while the pain got to be too much for Paula to bear. Since she had only dilated to a little more than three centimeters, the nurse felt it safe to give her a sedative, which relived the pain, but not the pressure.

Paula would say, "This is great stuff." Then she'd drift off to sleep for just a few minutes. The needle on the richter scale would start to move from a doctor's signature to peaks and valleys that would instantly awaken Paula and she'd start giving hoot owl calls again.

I was right by her side coaching her to concentrate on her breathing. Paula would look up at me and yell, "You blank-a-dee blank buster."

"You don't mean that honey. The other woman I was with earlier wasn't that mean."

She'd snarl back at me, "What? What other women?"

"No honey, woman, not women."

"Whatever. You better not be, be...and don't call me hon...knee."

The contractions subsided, and she passed out from the sedative until the next set of contractions kicked in. This went on through two shifts of nurses until a nurse used a sliding scale to make a tutee measurement and proclaimed that she had dilated to seven centimeters.

Wiping the perspiration off Paula's face with a cold towel I said, "That's a good thing, right?"

Without answering me directly the nurse said, "Let's get her ready for an epidural and inform the doctor."

"You hear that, baby? Not long now."

Unfortunately for Paula, they had to do the epidural twice. Even with my protesting, the hospital wouldn't allow me in while it was being administered, which again, almost caused me to be escorted out of the hospital. I had promised Paula that I would not leave her side. After the second epidural, the nurse didn't even bother with the sliding scale. She just reached her arm up Paula like she was reaching around for the sleeve when putting on a winter coat! After a moment of manual inspection she said, "This baby is O.B."

An abbreviated word for oblique, in other words, the baby's direction in the birth canal was in the wrong position. If Paula wasn't able to quickly correct the position by really pushing hard, they would have to do a C-section.

As it was, the baby had already been in the birth canal way too long, which causes undue stress. We looked at each other and I could see the scared, almost hysterical, expression on Paula's face. I was losing her fast.

"Paula honey, look at me. Have I always been there for you? I know you can do this. I'll be right here by your side, look at me, Paula. Let's focus, and get through this together. Come on now, let's just do it."

I kept wiping her face with a cool towel, and saw the look of determination come back.

"Okay, here we go."

I looked at the monitor to see when the next big contractions were about to hit. I held her foreword, putting my arms around her back. I clenched my hand over her hands on the push bar mounted over the bed. We gripped that birthing bar as if she and I were as one. When I felt her body tense, I gripped tighter on her hand. My head was pressed next to hers and I whispered into her ear, "Push, push, push, push."

We continued until the contractions subsided. Then we would start all over again. I felt that my own hemorrhoids were going to burst if I continued much longer. Then I noticed Paula was beet red in her face, and it hit me. She's pushing wrong. No matter how determined, she's not going to last much longer, so I said, "Paula, push like you've got to go to the bathroom. I know it sounds crude, but we're desperate here, baby. So here comes the next contraction…Push, push, push. Pooh pooh, Paula. Come on baby. Let it rip—puuush…There you go, there you go, honey. You did it, I see the baby's head, he's right here. Oh my God, he's got a lot of hair. Nurse? Where's the nurse? Hold it right there, don't-you-move!"

Paula gave me a big bug-eyed look, as if to say, "Where you think I'm going buster."

"Baby, I'll be right back. I'm getting the Doc, and a bunch of nurses."

I ran out, hollering, "Hey I need some help here. Hey…Is there anybody in this hospital who can hear me?"

"Shush, Mr. Jones, your wife's not the only expecting mother."

"But my…"

"But nothing, Mr. Jones, you keep your voice down. We'll get someone in there; you just keep your britches on. That's what got you here in the first place."

"Yes, "ma'am. I'm sorry. I just got excited, that's all."

"That's all right, now go back to your wife and calm down."

The doctor took a half an hour to get to us, and by that time, the baby had paddled his Venetian gondola back up the canal. Paula was devastated, and weak near exhaustion.

When the doctor did get there, he moved very quickly. He had Paula transferred to the birthing room. As we were being moved, my dad pitched me his new video camera. I tried to use the damn thing, but only managed to film the ceiling, but I captured some great audio.

They slipped a large wash pan under the end of Paula's bed. A new male nurse was on the other side of the bed from me and the doctor was in the catcher's position, bases loaded.

The doctor said, "All right, Paula, let's have this baby. You guys ready? Here we go, push Paula—Push. There you go, good girl."

Stephen M. Jones, Jr.

I lost it and said, "It's a girl? Isn't it supposed to be a boy, Doc?"

"No, Mr. Jones, please…refrain yourself from loud outbursts."

"Does that mean she'll have a clubfoot?"

"Stop it—your wife has to focus."

"You're right Doc…mums the word."

The doctor pulled out a pair of snipers.

"Hey Doc, what are you going to do with those?"

"It's okay, Mr. Jones, she won't feel a thing. I'm just making a little room. There, that's better now, here we go again, now rise up Paula."

Both the nurse and I raised Paula to the bar.

"Now push—that's it, Paula, push…"

In a flash, I saw a gray torpedo shoot out, and then a splat!

Oh my God, did he drop our baby? I couldn't hold my emotions back any longer, so I burst out loud again,

"What was that noise? What happened?"

"The afterbirth, Mr. Jones. It dropped into the pan below."

"Oh yeah, that's what that pan's for, huh."

I looked at Paula and said, "You did it baby. You did it!"

And she said, deservingly so, "Where's my baby? I want to see my baby."

Paula was crying and asking over and over—Is my baby all right?"

For a split moment the tension in the room was as thick as the summer air in July. But all our anxieties took a back seat when the doctor cleared his little nose passages. A newborn's cry immediately cracked the silence that brought tears to both our eyes.

A voice said, "Looks like you have a healthy baby boy."

I kissed Paula on the cheek and stammered over to our newly swaddled bundle, as a proud daddy should. I gently laid him in Paula's open arms. And so Stephen Madison Jones III was born on his due date of July 28th. We simply call him Madison.

49

Chapter Four

The year 1992 was a new beginning for both Paula and me. We started getting our house in order, and settled into the ordinary, everyday life of making a future for our family, as many young couples do. I worked on landscaping around the house, moving stones that were left in my yard by a melting iceberg millions of years prior. I used a wheelbarrow and placed the stones along the driveway to impede further erosion. I soon found out that some of these stones were just the tips of huge boulders that lay underground. At night I went to bed thoroughly exhausted and dreamt I was a lifer in the rock quarry at Sing Sing prison.

I still remember when we lived in that little, two-story house in the back of nowhere how amazed I was when we turned out the lights for bed. As I lay there allowing time for my eyes to adjust to the darkness, but it never adjusts. You could fall asleep, wake up in the middle of the night, and still couldn't see your hand in front of your face; not even a street light named desire to interfere with a good night sleep. Wrong, Baby.

When I got home from work, big daddy's moonlight job began. I sang, fed, and walked up and down the hall in a vegetative state. There…there now, he's finally sound asleep. As I gently lay Madison down and kissed his cheeks, a rooster crows, Madison's eyes pop open…"Kuh'wee" instantly followed by a silent scream that only Orca whales can hear. When this happens the baby

Stephen M. Jones, Jr.

poop is about to hit the fan. A curse of zombie sleep deprivation is placed on your soul by a childless, Creole voodoo woman named Marie Laveau.

I sought revenge. We had only one neighbor to the far left of us about a hundred yards away. They had a hen house with a rooster. Now, not to disturb their sleep, they built the hen house at the back edge of their property, which happens to be less than sixty feet from our bedroom window. So every morning, at the crack of dawn, this banty rooster would exercise his lungs for twenty minutes or so with his timeless rendition of, "Cock a doodle doo." Unfortunately for him, his singing career was cut short by a two-legged fox that was particularly fond of singing roosters, leaving the hens without a male to cluck around the house. For now—problem solved.

Most people in neighborhoods get the usual door-to-door salesman, or the black and white clad Mormons on bikes. Nope, not me…I get several invitations to join the local Klan. At first I politely told them, "Thanks, but no thanks."

Then after the third time, a wiry little bastard comes up to my door and said, "This is your final offer." Like this moron is doing me a favor.

"Yer either fer us, or agin us. Which is it?"

I betcha it was that damn new brother-in-law of mine. He must have put my name down in the hooded pillowcase drawing as a new recruit. So I told the guy, "Mister, if you'd trim some of them hairs coming out of those ears ya' might have heard me the first time. The answer is, "Double—Hell no! And if you try and burn a cross in my yard, I know where you live, so get."

However, I was warned about a cult of people that lived about a half mile behind me. They were known to come around at night with sticky fingers and take anything that wasn't bolted down.

Well by God, I wasn't about to allow some crazed Hillbilly Manson family to harm my little house on the prairie. I worked late and Paula was mortally terrified to stay there by herself anyway. On more than one occasion, she called me at work scared to death because someone was trying to beat down the front door. I rushed home to see all the floodlights turned on like some military zone in Cambodia. I believe if there was a siren, Paula would have cut that on too. That hill was lit up like *Candle Stick Park*. So after the umpteenth time of rushing home and overhearing another story from some old-timers playing checkers outside the local country store about these people they called the *Night Stalkers*, I had to see for myself. I got directions from a neighbor, jumped in the Chevy Blazer and headed for a looky-loo.

I drove down a gravel road, doing my best to decipher the crude map scribbled on a fast food paper bag torn from one end. The grease stains permeating through the paper bag made it hard to follow directions. Paying more attention to the map than I was driving, I almost ran off the road. I stopped quickly, causing a hurl of dust to engulf the truck. When the dust cleared, I looked out the side window at a dirt road that almost went vertical. *Damn*, I looked at the map, looked at the road, back at the map. *This is it. Who the hell would live up there? Well buddy-row, you like a good adventure.* If only I could reach the top without tipping over. I reasoned that somebody must have, to build this road, right? I shoved my Blazer into 4-wheel drive, and strapped in for the hayride.

As I'm moving up, feeling my tires losing their grip, I keep thinking about that little choo-choo that could. *I think I can. I think I can. I know I can.* Man, oh man, how anybody could travel up and down this road, especially with the washed out gullies a coupla' feet deep. One wrong move and I end up like ol' Jack falling down and breaking my crown.

I bet the damn thing looks like a waterfall when it rains. Nobody would make it up during a thunderstorm. Hell, I wasn't sure I was going to make it up, and it was dry as a bone. When I crest the top, I felt like I should shove a flag on top of the summit.

My triumph was short-lived as my attention was quickly drawn to a bustling colony unlike any I've seen in rural America. It was like stepping back in time to the 1930's depression era, or maybe some impoverished third world country. I felt that any minute I would pass a drab green tent with a big Red Cross symbol stamped across the top along with volunteer doctors and missionary workers scurrying around administering vaccines to fly-infested, bloated belly children.

Stephen M. Jones, Jr.

Why haven't I seen late-night info-mercials that say, "For the cost of a cup of coffee you can help children in America?"

As I slowly drove past, I noticed that some of the dwellings were made with makeshift tarps. Others were log shacks made with skinny, scrub oak timbers, the joints filled with either dried mud or clay. I didn't see any electrical hook-ups or running water.

These people were roasting big chunks of meat over open pits dug in the ground with what looked like heavy metal street drain grids as cooking grills.

Nearby were piles of tin cans stacked up four to six feet high like pyramids; some rusting and some glittering bright shards of light causing me to squint. I turned away only to glare into the face of a boy, maybe ten years old or so, glaring back as I drove past.

This doe-eyed, smudged faced boy was shirtless and wearing worn out shoes. I noticed one was a utility boot, the other a tennis shoe without laces. When I tried to reach out to give him a couple of dollars from my pocket, he wouldn't take it. He just stared back at me pulling what appeared to be deer meat off a curved rib bone with his front teeth while he tightly clutched one side, oblivious of my unworthy handout. This was late summer and hunting season was still months away. I guess when it comes to feast or famine, hunting laws don't apply to people that live like this.

Strike me dumb, believe it or not, coming up on my left were a couple of house trailers. How the hay they got those things up that *Rock of Gibraltar* is beyond me.

It is of my opinion that you can go three miles in any direction in the state of Arkansas and see a house trailer. This anomaly of fact has no statistical value, except for the fat cats that sell these low-income death traps sprinkled throughout tornado alley.

I became acutely aware that Uncle Jed and Granny were watching me as intently as I was scrutinizing the boy. The expressions told me I was not welcome. Unlike Louis and Clark, I didn't have any cheap beads or trinkets to get myself out of a jam. All I had was a half-eaten moon pie and an RC Cola.

Without Apology

It then struck me that maybe they thought I was some revenuer or lawman looking to bust up a moonshine operation.

Luckily, I made it through without any type of confrontation. The backside of the hill was just as precarious. I wanted to see how close these hillbillies were to my side of the mountain. At the bottom of the hill, I drove through a small stream and looked to my right. I stopped to notice a whitewashed, plywood structure with the door left open. Inside I could make out a table and chairs on a dirt floor with a strange blue hue emitting a strobe light effect. I rolled down my window, and goose-necked my head to get a closer look.

Unbelievably, this backwoods yahoo had a gas generator hooked up to a satellite dish. A crackling sound from behind my truck caught my attention. As I turned to see what it could be, I got nudged in the face by a big wet nose.

After a few seconds of sheer terror went by, I regained my senses enough to realize that I had just been sloppy-kissed by a horse.

I now know how the phrase, "You scared the living piss out of me" came about. That damn ol' horse caused me to find a bush so as to relieve my alter ego. As I was walking back to my truck trying to zip up, I noticed that this poor horse was dragging a log that was chained to its ankle.

I lifted Mr. Bag-a-bones hoof, interrupting the hungry flies in random formation doing aeronautical feats waiting to land back on the deep cuts caused by the chain. I was bent over inspecting the severity of the wound, when I felt the hairs on the back of my neck stand at attention. Before I could respond to my internal early warning system, a shadow, had cast over me from the midday's sun.

A twangy voice spoke out at me from within the eclipsing silhouette.

Caught off guard and confused, my subconscious formed my response, "Do I wanna what?"

I quickly realized my vulnerability and rose up from my bent over position.

The voice said, "Boy, you wanna buy this horse? Cause if'en ya' don't—get yer hands off 'em."

Stephen M. Jones, Jr.

I looked at the man to size up the situation I had gotten myself into, and it was bad. He was as boney as his horse was, wearing a used-to-be *holier than thou*, yellow-stained tee shirt with overalls and carrying a 30/30-lever action rifle. I can't believe my Cherokee blood allowed him to sneak up on me like that. If I had been downwind, I could have smelled him coming. He smelled like the combination of a wet dog, and three day old vegetable soup.

I tried emulating his accent as a sign of redneck kinship, "How yew doing? Whoo-wee…I ain't been out here in these here parts in a coon's age."

I extended my hand in an effort of homage. He eye-balled my hand leaving the other squint-eye shut, but didn't bother shaking it. Um, that didn't work, so I changed my approach to one of more authority,

"I ain't interested in buying yer horse mister, but you need to do something about the wound on this horse before it gets infected. There are laws on animal abuse."

His left eye flinched a little and I knew I had found the right approach.

He made mention that having the log and chain was the only way from keeping the horse from running off. Cause in his words, "Ain't got no fences 'round hea."

"Well, I said, "It seems a little inhumane to me, mister. You make damn sure you get some sav' on that wound."

"Yes'r, I'll get somp'in on them wounds right away. Yes'r I sho' will."

"Good," I said.

I made it back to the truck and shut the door, easing my pistol from the center console into my lap and continued listening to him ramble on.

He changed from horse selling and was now asking me if'en I wanted to buy his satellite system and invited me in for a demonstration.

I must'a taken the act too far, cause he took a shine to me. He was now inviting me in for some cold beer he had on ice. He bragged that his satellite signal could pick up all kinds of girlie movies. I smiled back at him, as his grin exposed a rickety line of tobacco stained teeth.

"Damn!" I suddenly said out loud, "What is it about oral hygiene with you people! I mean it wouldn't hurt you none to pick up a tooth brush every once in a while, would it?"

Oops...I think I just stepped all over his invite. He stood there now, not saying a word, just staring. His penetrating eyes were on me like I was wearing high heels and lipstick just before lights off at Osceola Penal Farm, with Madonna singing, *Like A Virgin* in the background.

Yeah, I thought to myself, you sick, toothless bastard; you probably have a Costco sized jar of KY Jelly kept in a dungeon cellar dug down deep into that dirt hut accompanied by his mentally challenged, half brother, Tiny, to torture my ass.

The horse was probably back up in case his food supply ran low. I wasn't about to have my scrotum made into a plug-in nightlight. So I told him, "I'll have to take a rain check on the beer and girlie movies. I'm sure I'll be missing out. You just make damn sure you take care of that horse of yours."

I waved back at him as I left, all the while keeping a sharp eye in the rear view mirror while getting the hell out of there. I could now relax my pucker muscles I was sitting on that were turning into an unbearable Charley horse.

Before I went back home, I dropped in on the local police and told them what was happening up on that ridge. The officer, with his feet propped up on his desk, laughed at my story and said, "You must be talking about old Floyd. He's crazy as a bed bug. Fella, there's some real nasty people that live up that hill and you're real damn lucky you didn't get shot."

I said, "Lucky hell! I almost got greased, squeezed and kissed by an abused horse, and all you're gonna do is say I'm lucky."

He lazily leaned up to shoo away a fly that was nibbling on a half eaten tuna sandwich with a rolled up newspaper. He gave me a look of annoyance as he picked off the infected part of the sandwich and then took a big bite. Talking with his mouth full he said that a couple of people had been shot on that ridge, "We don't even go up there without back-up."

I walked out still steamed, but thankful I wasn't put in the position to squeal like a pig.

Stephen M. Jones, Jr.

About a year later, I was at the Ye Ole Country Store when I heard that old Floyd had died of a heart attack and had to be taken down the ridge with a 4-track, all terrain vehicle. Too bad, he should've had a chain around his leg attached to a log to drag.

His heart must'a couldn't handle all those girlie movies, ya' think? *I would have left old Floyd where he died. "Buzzards have to eat same as worms."*

Chapter Five

In 1994, the airline I worked for continued downsizing by closing Sato offices on military bases. The Sato offices were considered cushy jobs. Only the very senior employees were awarded these positions. By closing the Sato offices, these very senior agents exercised their bumping rights to bid into whatever city their seniority could hold—just like I had done a few years earlier.

This caused a domino effect in Little Rock, because Arkansas was, and is, considered a retirement state. A lot of senior agents came south and within 4 four months I was on the bottom of the totem pole and given notice that I had been bumped.

I was lucky enough to sell our house for a modest little profit to a couple of interracial lesbians. One was the homemaker, the other in the military. The latter looked like she could have skated through a Special Forces obstacle course with no problem. That being said they were the nicest people to do business with. I would have rolled in the grass busting a stitch seeing the reaction of those Klan bastards as they came a' knocking with their welcome wagon pillowcases.

I had intended to move to Los Angeles the first time around to pursue my acting bug I had caught years earlier from a TV pilot I'd worked on, but decided to stay close to home at the urging of my parents. Once a week, while still in Little Rock, I was flying to L.A. for acting classes and auditions, so now it all made sense. My agent was peeved at me anyway for not being able to fly back to L.A. for callbacks. She told me, "Move to L.A. or get out of the business."

This was the incentive I needed to get off the pot, and believe me, I'm one who can sit and ponder. God help me if they invent one with memory foam seats and sports channel assess.

While Paula agreed to go L.A. she was also nervous about being so far away from her family and friends. I made promises that I later regretted, telling her that if I wasn't established in two years that we would try to move back. The other promissory mistake was that while she was in L.A. she could be a stay-at-home mom. Paula hated getting up for work and since returning from maternity leave, AIDC changed the title of her job awarding it to someone else in her absence. Her new job was the same pay, but different duties that required her not to drop off documents to other areas. In other words, she had her traveling shoes removed. Paula couldn't wait to tell her boss Claudine that she was quitting.

While on my days off in L.A. I started hunting for a house to rent. After about two weeks of searching, I found a secluded, little one-bedroom bungalow behind a main house in the hills of Glendale, California. If I recall, the lady said it belonged to an art director for Metro Goldwyn Mayer back in the 1930's.

The bungalow was painted turquoise with tropical plants, kumquat trees and a variety of vegetation indigenous to California planted everywhere. All this made it look like a Peruvian rain forest as you walked up the steep, narrow stone path.

I remember after we moved in, I'd come home every night from work to find nickel size spiders had spun webs across the stone path. The first time I ran up the path, still supercharged with the excitement of just moving to L.A., I was totally unprepared for what I found at the top of the path. The dew moistened webs stretched over my body like a cocoon. I reached my hand out to remove the wet strands of webs from my face. To my horror, there were dozens of funnel spiders crawling up my arm. I raked them off, but they were all over me. My skin began to crawl in their sequence. I couldn't take it... *Think? Oh hell, they're in my hair on my face. Stay calm, strip naked, move your ass.* So ripping all my clothes off, I washed myself down with the garden hose, while hysterically stomping the hell out of my suit that I had piled up on the porch.

For the next few weeks, I had phantom spider attacks. From that night forward, I forged a broomstick I called "Excalibur" and left it wedged in between two stones at the bottom of the terrace. I waged war by hacking through intersecting webs and smacking thousands of spiders to their doom. This therapy went a long way toward my arachnophobia rehabilitation.

The front of the bungalow had a huge bay window, eight feet by ten feet. This allowed natural sunlight in so Mr. MGM Art Director could work on studio projects at home without the use of artificial light.

However, one major drawback was the long winding stone path. I knew that moving the furniture up there would be hell. The other negative was the back of the place bordered Forest Lawn Cemetery. I kept that little secret to myself. Paula wouldn't go for it if she'd found out beforehand.

The plus side was that we could have our own little secluded tropical paradise in the middle of the city.

Since we had sold our house in Arkansas very quickly, I had to lease a house there for a month and help train the guy that had bumped me for my job. *Go figure. You get bumped and you pay for your own move. Man, got to love the fringe benefits of that.*

I had to use my three weeks vacation time to move my family, lock, stock and barrel, to California. In a little over two months, we moved from the house I sold to a one-month rental and then into the one bedroom Bungalow in Glendale, California.

To make the move to Glendale, I leased a moving truck and flat-bed trailer to haul the Mercedes from behind. I sold my Chevy Blazer, but kept the Ford Escort GT for Paula to drive to L.A. On the day we left, Paula's two sisters said their goodbyes along with Paula's friend, Debbie, who took pictures of the main event.

Boy, there was a lot of emotional hugging, crying, and down right sobbing. It was understandable, because this was the first time Paula had been out of Arkansas for any length of time.

I planned for a two-day trip. On day four we hit the mountains of Albuquerque. Little did I know that Paula's beauty sleep and make-up application would equate to us being delayed. As we started our ascent, the moving truck had a governor that kicked in. For those who don't know, a governor is sometimes placed on the engine to regulate how fast you can go. I had it floored and I was maybe doing fifteen miles an hour—tops.

To make things worse, there were miles of road construction and nowhere for me to pull off to relieve a floodgate of traffic behind us. When I was able to pull to the right, I got a convoy of middle fingers, and words of etiquette that are kept in that other dictionary of commonly used adjectives. I don't blame them, though. I've been known to have a little road rage every so often myself.

On day five we made it to L.A. at the peek of rush hour.

People who choose to live in Los Angeles have to psychologically get used to the melting pot of multicultural driving.

Here's my scale of engagement when traveling under normal conditions on L.A.'s freeways during peak traffic. Twenty miles from the destination point equals two hours. If you don't allow yourself a buffer zone and find yourself running late, you will develop a mad cow tumor on the brain that inhibits your rationalization. You'll find yourself wanting to kick the hell out of a normally sweet old lady driving next to you, because it's her fault that you're running late and her ass is too damn old to be driving anyway.

You turn to look on the other side to see Fidel Castro's cousin Don Juan, with a bucket load of his friends pitching fast food trash out the window of their chromed out, low-riding '72 Ford Galaxy 500. Oh, and let's not forget the Asian kid staring up at you with his finger stuck up his nose. These irrational prejudices completely go away as soon as you reach your destination.

After hours of being on the outskirts of L.A, losing Paula twice and half a dozen wrong turns, we made it. *Hot dig-a-dee damn. I believe in miracles!*

We met our landlady, still waiting to give us the keys. She was the typical landlord type. A thousand and one excuses why something's not working, knowing you'll soon give up on her after the umpteenth time of hearing her say, "I'll have someone out there next week."

So, you end up fixing it yourself. I'm sure some of you know what I'm talking about.

Even though both of us were fatigued from the L.A. 101 Freeway jam, I found new energy with the anticipation of showing Paula around our new pad. I thought she seemed to genuinely like the place until she turned to me and said, "Leave it to you to find a place in the middle of the city that's isolated from the rest of the world. I told you I wanted to live in a neighborhood, buster."

"I know, honey, and we are in a neighborhood. There are houses all around us."

Paula, "I don't see no houses behind us. What's back there anyway?"

"Oh, that, back there? I believe they call it Forest Lawn."

"What's that, some kind of park?"

"Yeah, yeah— that's it, kinda, sorta honey. You know…it's where people go to visit loved ones."

"What do you mean, Stephen, a nursing home?"

"Well, you're close, honey. It's where you go after a nursing home, if your unlucky enough to live that long."

The landlady blurted out, "You mean you didn't tell her?"

"Tell me what?" Paula said. "And quit beating around the bush, I know how you are, buster. You better come clean and tell me—and tell me now."

"It's just a cemetery, Mrs. Jones. So if one of you croaks," she joked, "You can be buried in your own backyard. Now wouldn't that be grand?"

Frantically using my first finger in a cutting motion across my neck I said, "Thank you very much Ms. Landlord, you're really not helping the situation. I believe I can handle it from here."

I gave her an unmistakable rising of my brows, along with a bulging eye expression.

"My goodness, she continued, rolling her eyes to the back of her head, "Why there's nothing to be afraid of, it's just dead people lying out there."

"Boy-howdy," Paula said, "That's it, I'm leaving. I'm not living next to dead folks. Nope, no way. This is all you fault. You brought me out here, you kin jus' take me back to Arkansas, or put me on a plane back home, or whatever, but I ain't staying here."

"Now, now, honey," I said, "Are you gonna let that mean ol' landlady scare you like that? We might have to give back the keys to this place and get our deposit returned."

Using my hand behind my back, I waved the landlady off.

"We just got here baby doll, and you're just tired and exhausted, that's all."

"Your husband's right, Mrs. Jones, don't pay any attention to me, and besides, it's so peaceful here. I know both of you will love it. I'll just leave the keys in the front door, and your son is just darling. I'll call you in a couple of days to see how you're getting along and of course, if you need me for anything, just give me a jing-a-ling. See you guys later."

I finally calmed Paula down, and started phase one of unloading. *I can honestly say that if I have to make another move like this one, I'll pile it up, and burn it first.*

Paula helped when she could, but mostly she arranged furniture and took care of Madison while I, like an Egyptian slave, carried the furniture and boxes up the winding path.

My pilgrimage was up one flight of stairs, then three more steps to the left. Tie open the little white gate, and take a breather. Next, I climbed up the stone path, wishing like hell that I'd never laid eyes on this place. *Oh, but you can bet I wasn't about to let Paula tell me I told you so.* By nights end, I was barely able to set the bed up and passed out with exhaustion.

The next morning, I was the early bird and took a hot shower to relieve my strained back. Since everything was still boxed, I grabbed a roll of paper towels to dry myself off with, while strutting around naked as a jaybird. Who the hell's gonna see except maybe a few dead zombies. *Oops…better keep that thought to myself.*

Paula's right though, it is secluded in the middle of the city. I went into the kitchen and did manage to dig through the box marked pots and pans to pull out the Mr. Coffee machine.

The kitchen was quite small with a three-burner gas oven. The antique was not much larger than a Coleman camping stove, probably 1920's vintage. After I poured myself some Joe, I thought our little two- seat marble table would fit perfectly in front of that back kitchen window. *Oh man—oh man;* I thought to myself, *would you look at the sunbeam streaking in.* I walked up, and threw myself into the light, throwing my arms back taking in the sun's warmth, stretching, and yawning, eyes squeezed tight.

God, it's good to be alive. My body still tingling, I heard sounds of people whispering, carried in by the morning breeze from the window that had been left half open. The sounds lapping at my senses caused me to momentarily lose touch with my spiritual tranquility to investigate. So, I lazily opened my eyes. Still trying to focus my thoughts, I found myself looking down at the beginning of an invocation of a burial not twenty-yards away. But why are they looking up at me? Finally my synapse kicks in. *Oh, hell no! Oh damn, move your naked ass away from the window, picklehead.*

I squatted like a Vietnamese farmer in a rice paddy. I did a duck walk out of the kitchen to find a moving blanket to throw over the window. *Thank God I didn't grope my grapes of wrath,* I hoped.

Phase II would finish up the big stuff, including the china cabinet and whatever drugstore nostrums I could lay my back on. After settling in, we were ready for a little R&R. I broke out the Weber for a Southern BBQ on the front patio given the fact that the backyard was full of flat headstones; it seemed the most logical choice. I threw some steaks on the grill while washing down some mixed nuts with a few bottles of *Wicked Ale*. Afterwards, we sat back in lawn chairs in 62-degree weather listening to Spanish serenades from a party in the distance.

Stephen M. Jones, Jr.

The next day, the surrounding foothills were set ablaze by some homeless person trying to stay warm in a cardboard box. After that, it rained hot gray ash for thirty days. The night's sky was illuminated by hues of bright orange in the distance. Most everyone not involved seemed unconcerned. I must admit, it was a bit unsettling having to wash ash off the car everyday. The ash covered everything like a gray, chemical snow. I'm guessing that Los Angelinos were desensitized from the LA riots in so much as the neighboring brush fires were a mere pittance of afterthought.

One of the first things we realized was the cost of living in L.A. compared to Arkansas. Since I was commuting back and forth while living in Arkansas, I knew it would be expensive. Just on weekend outings, getting our bearings cost money. Gas to put-put around was almost a dollar more a gallon. I found that interesting because we drove past a couple of refineries right off the 405 Freeway. *You know, it's beyond me how they can truck it three thousand miles away and sell it a dollar cheaper.*

The bureaucrats in Sacramento add on all these taxes to pay for their over-inflated salaries, but claim it's for the cause of cleaner air. All of which is fine and dandy until an exempt city bus pulls away from a stop and billows out a cloud of black exhaust enough to choke a coal miner's daughter. However, to be fair, I was seeing more and more buses that run on natural gas.

The grocery stores out here are a heck of a lot more expensive, too. Paula's unwillingness to breastfeed Madison because she didn't want to loose her perkiness cost a bunch. So, yes, I was on my money watch again. She wouldn't allow me to buy powdered formula, even though it was half the price of the liquid stuff. She just didn't want to take the time to mix it.

Even though the cost of living was much higher, I was still able to keep our heads above water. Speaking of baby food, I remember Paula buying chocolate *Coco Pops* at the grocery store not thinking much about it at the time simply because she has an enormous sweet tooth. I came home from one of my morning classes to find Paula trying to feed Madison *Count-Chocula* cereal. I said, "Paula, you don't give a nine-month-old cold cereal."

"I don't see why not. If I smash it up he'll be fine."

Now here's a woman who won't let me buy powdered Enfamil, but was willing to feed him chocolate cereal. Go figure. We argued for about ten minutes until I called the pediatricians office and informed a nurse and she said absolutely not. I tried to hand the phone to Paula so she could hear for herself, but she refused. *Oh, but you can bet she stayed mad at me for the rest of the day.* Paula still managed to give him chocolate milk on the sly. Maybe this is why Madison at age nine had eight cavities filled and one root canal.

Anyway, we were having more and more catfights. I had two acting classes a week and was working from 6pm to 2am. That left Paula and Madison at home alone without family, and friends. The loneliness and shear boredom was compounded by a sixty-year-old sewer pipe that burst under the bungalow. Needless to say, it smelled like a chicken farm downwind.

The straw that broke the camels back would soon come in the form of the airline I worked for. They threatened to file Chapter 11 if the employee's didn't take a two-year 15% across the board pay cut. The majority of employees fell for it and voted for the pay cut.

I was left out in the cold, now borrowing from Peter to pay Paul. Not able to meet our existing bills, I dropped one class, then the other, but was still sinking into a whirlpool of obligation. I called my airline's credit union to get a consolidation loan.

They said, "Well, Mr. Jones, if you paid off this, this, and this, we would be happy to give you a loan. Right now, as it stands, Mr. Jones, you're at high risk and at this time we can't approve your loan. I'm sorry."

I said, "If I got rid of this, this, and this I wouldn't need a loan. On top of that, if your frigging company hadn't cut my pay, I wouldn't be here today."

"We had nothing to do with your cut in pay, Mr. Jones. We're not owned by your company."

"Well then, if that's the case, don't have the same company name as who I work for, damn it." It's misleading.

I was preaching to the choir, as they say. On top of that, a day didn't go by without Paula badgering me to move back home, incorporating my parents as co-conspirators. But I held firm, with the thought that we can work this all out.

Along about this time, a bit of luck came by the way of that *old as the hills* 1920's vintage gas stove.

The pilot light on the oven went out, so I called the city to send a guy out. A few hours later, a tall, pot-bellied guy chewing on a matchstick showed up. He looked at the stove, took out a greasy handkerchief, wiped his face, folded it once then blew his nose and said, "You're lucky you guys hadn't been blown sky high. This thing is leaking gas all over. Good thing it's hot out and you have the windows all opened. Come to think of it, you're not even supposed to be living back here. There's a city ordinance that you can't lease out a guesthouse with these types of gas stoves. I'll give you guys thirty day's notice to move. You know if this thing would've blown, you and you're loved ones wouldn't have to deal with funeral expenses. Your ashes would've simply floated over to Forest Lawn Cemetery, free of charge."

"Do they pay you for your comments?" I asked.

"Nope, I give that free of charge, too."

So I snapped back, "Then I guess you don't mind if you take that chewed up matchstick out of your mouth before you strike it on all that silver and cause a spark. Hell, who knows. You might be floating right along with us—free of charge."

He smiled and said, "You're sort of a smart ass. And since you look like you work out, I bet your wife thinks the same."

Who does this guy think he is… a wife whisperer? Now I was thoroughly pissed. "You know, I seem to have confrontation with damn near anyone that comes to my door no matter where I live and there lies the quandary. Is it me, or do I just get under the skin of people in general?"

"Well, Mister, you can take it to the bank. It's you."

"Then it must be true." I said.

He smiled from ear to ear, wearing his hat half-crooked.

"Hey, I've seen that smile of yours before and judging from your accent you must be from Arkansas. Nope, Texas. (proudly) The Lone Star State."

"Really," I said.

"Well, matchstick, what's that saying about Texas, how's it go? Oh yeah, now I remember... What's the two things common in Texas? And I don't see you wearing any horns."

Shoving the paperwork in my hand, "Like I said, you got thirty days—don't make it thirty-one." Then he walked off.

The provocation worked, matchstick turned in the eviction notice pronto. He was even so kind as to personally deliver it. He seemed confused when I shook his hand and thanked him. I informed our landlady that the city had given us thirty days notice and she said, "That's not true. I've been leasing this place out for years, so you don't have to worry about a thing. You just disregard any notices and let me take care of it."

I called the matchstick guy and told him what the landlord had said. He advised me that I needed to look for another place and get my deposit back. This was the chance I was looking for to break my lease, and find a cheaper place.

Paula was damn driven to move back home, but when I found a condo on the beach for a hundred dollars a month less, she quickly did an about-face. The condo was in Long Beach, California and right on the sand. Thank God my credit was still showing good, because we got the place with no problem. I quickly went down to rent a U-Haul truck, yet agonizing over the thought of moving again. But look on the bright side, it was all down hill this time.

As I was filling out the U-haul rental agreement, I asked the representative what's up with all those illegal aliens standing outside.

"They're looking for people like you to help move," he said.

"Oh yeah, how much do they charge?"

"You can get them real cheap."

"Great. That's just what my lower back needs." I mumbled.

I drove the rental truck over to where the illegal's were standing. I looked the crowd over to find a young, strong man. You'll do, pointing to the chosen one. With a rush, the whole damn crowd tried to get in the truck. Stampede!

They must have had a flashback when being smuggled across the border. *No, they're just eager to work was all,* I thought.

I had to physically go up to each and every one. I patted them on the back in an apologetic manner and then motioned for them to get out of the truck until I reached the one I wanted. One poor fellow must have been sixty, and walked with a limp.

Anytime I start feeling sorry for myself, I think about those poor souls. Anyhow, the man I chose didn't speak a word of English, but we got along fine. You want to talk about a hard worker. He didn't stop until I broke for lunch.

I bought both of us a double cheeseburger with fries, and a Cherry Coke at the famous *In-N-Out* burger joint. Let me tell yeah, if you've never had an *In-n-Out* burger you don't know what you're missing. It's what *Haagen-Dazs* is to ice cream.

When we got to the heavy stuff and headed down that hell-a-sash stone path, my Mexican friend kept saying something in what I thought was Spanish at every tight turn. It took me a couple of trips back and forth before I could decipher that he was saying, "Goddamnie." I got so tickled about it that I almost dropped my end. At the bottom, we loaded the *U-Haul* with me still tearfully snickering.

I told him in my broken Southern language, "Try moving this stuff up hill by yourself little bubba."

He just smiled back at me and said, "No speakie English."

I smiled back and said, "Yeah, but you speak very good "Goddamnie" though, huh?"

By the end of the day, we had it all moved into our new place at Long Beach. I drove him back to Glendale and peeled out forty-dollars to give him. He handed me back a twenty saying in broken English that this was in return for him breaking a crystal bowl that he dropped earlier.

"Hot damn…you speak okay English for someone who earlier said, 'No speakie English.'"

He just smiled back at me. His honesty touched me so much that I gave him sixty-dollars instead of forty.

"And don't worry about the bowl."

I gave him an expression of appreciation, along with a farewell tight-gripped handshake. We exchanged a glance of unspoken mutual respect frozen without void of time. In a few moments, I was headed back to Long Beach. I peered back into my side view mirror to catch a last glance of my Mexican friend. I noticed that he reached inside his pack, and turned on what looked to be a cell phone to make a call. For a split second I felt a surge of anger bolt through me.

Well, shit, I thought. *This is 1993, they've just come out with the smaller version and nobody I knew even owned a cell phone.* Then I laughed out loud to myself. Either I had just witnessed the smoothest art of salesmanship to get an extra twenty, or I'm a naive gringo. Anyhow, it's just as well—a business transaction followed by a lesson well remembered.

Chapter Six

This move helped financially, but we were a long shot from being out of the woods. However, the beach was a big emotional lift for Paula. She wasn't stuck in a hot house all day, and could stroll Madison on roller blades on the bike path that runs along the beach.

It was about this time that Paula made a trip back home to visit family and friends that would forever change our lives.

I picked Paula up from the Los Angeles Airport from her visit. She seemed ecstatic in demeanor and said she wanted to talk to me when we got home.

"Is something wrong?" I asked. "Who died? What happened?"

"Boy howdy… Listen to you," she yapped. "Naw, it's nothing like that, nobody died. I'll tell you when we get home, I told ya' that already. Clean them ears out, boy."

"Well, then, there, now," I said, "Guess I'm gonna have to wait?"

"Yah betcha, buster! Have you been a good boy?"

"Why, did you bring me back something?"

"Naw, just me, ain't that enough?"

"Yep, just as long as you stayed out of those malls honey. You know we're tight on money and right now every penny counts. So try to keep your urge to splurge to a bare minimum."

"You sound like a broken record. Every time I come back from visiting, that's almost the first thing out of your mouth, Steve Jones."

"I keep saying it, because you keep doing it. You did stay out of the malls, right?"

"I don't want to talk about that right now."

"Damn it, Paula! How am I supposed to get us back on track if you keep adding to our bills? I pay one bill off and you add two more. You're going to put me in the poor house for sure."

"You best look around mister, we're already living in one. It wouldn't be a problem if you got off your high horse and we moved back home. Anyhow, you know that's what everybody but YOU wants."

"Oh, here we go—you gonna pick at that scab again."

"You know it's true, just you ask your mama and daddy," she barked.

"Yeah right, you guys are all against me because it suits your own wants and needs. You want to be closer to your friends and family. My family wants me to move back, so they can be near their new grandson. Not a day goes by that you, or my parents, don't badger me about moving back."

"Well, that's right mister and we're gonna keep on until you take us back. You're not going to be no actor. You've been out here for over six months and nobody's made you a movie star."

"It's not about being a movie star, Paula. It's a business and a craft. You don't just come out here and poof—you're being cast in a multi-million dollar movie. You've got to hone your craft and pay your dues. Pilot season is coming up soon. Maybe I can score something there. But hey, since I've dropped out of my classes because of our finances and working overtime to keep our heads above water, I don't think I'll be able to audition much. My agent hasn't called me in a few weeks. That reminds me, I need to give her a buzz."

"Well... whatever." Paula touted.

I jus' think if it's not happened yet, it ain't never gonna happen. That's all I'm saying."

Stephen M. Jones, Jr.

"You could be right," I said. "That's true, it's a shot in the dark, but I want to thank you for all your support and encouragement. I mean, you've really made it a living hell for me since I've been here."

A smug reply followed. "You're welcome," she darted back.

I grit my teeth, bite my tongue, and I'm thinking to myself, *that woman is never going to think about anyone, but herself. I have to admit, she does have the gift to somehow enlist everybody, including my family to instigate her endeavors. Well, it's not going to work on me this time.*

"So, how's your mama doing?"

"Oh, she's fine. She has to watch what she eats because of her diabetes and all."

"That's her problem," I said. "She watches everything she eats."

"You better watch it, I kin start in on your family."

"Look," I said. "Until your mama, but especially your sister, Charlotte, and that red-n-white checkered Big Boy of a brother-in-law, Mark Brown, starts taking that fork out of their mouths, that barn door ain't never gonna shrink. Speaking of big barn doors, I wonder, do toilets come in sizes?"

"You're a sick man and that's so mean," Paula said. "You've never liked my sister or Mark! All they've ever tried to do was be your friend."

"I guess it just irks me that they won't get off their lard asses to work for an honest living. Nope, that's not it either. I'll tell you what it is Paula. It's because they stole from your mama's social security and disability checks."

"My mama has forgiven them for that, jus' like she has you for bringing me out here, and as far as she's concerned, it's water under the bridge."

"Paula, don't even go there. You can't compare my actions to what they did to your mama."

"Whatever. All I'm saying is what they did to mama ain't got nothing to do with you. So you ought' a give up the ghost. It's getting old."

"Well, Paula, stop hounding me about accepting them as family and I'll shut up about it."

"Guess what?"

"What, Paula?"

Without Apology

"I'm going to start going to the sun tanning bed," Paula said, obviously eager to change the subject.

"Sorry, we can't afford it right now and besides, it causes skin cancer."

"You're not a doctor. You think you know something about everything don't ya'?"

"No, but I can tell you why you want to all of a sudden get a tan? It's because your sister, Lydia, is going to the tanning bed. Am I right? Come on Paula speak up—cat got your tongue? Say it ain't so? You know I'm right. Just go ahead and admit it."

"You think you're so smart, don'cha?" She barked.

"No, I replied with a smile. I just know that you and Lydia have this fraternal sister rivalry thing going on. So, if either one of you get something the other doesn't have, it soon evolves into an unspoken contest of who can out buy the best of whatever it is that the other doesn't have yet."

"Say what?" Paula said, with a confused look on her face.

"Oh, hell's bells, you know what I'm talking about, Paula. Let's just drop this subject. It's not going anywhere anyway.

Look, we're here. Home sweet home. Not too many people can tout about living on oceanfront property. Now, remember, I'll let Mitzie out to greet you guys when I open the door. You know how excited she gets. She'll whip you to death with her tail and then pee on you." (A sadomasochistic dog.)

Mitzie can't control herself or her bladder when she's excited. Anyhow she loved Paula and adored Madison. I don't know why? Paula didn't much care for Mitzie. Both could expect to be tongue bathed, flogged with her tail of iron, and have intermittent bursts of tinkle around their ankle. Since Madison was just starting to walk he was a sure candidate to be knocked down, licked and peed on with enthusiasm. I'd try to minimize the situation by holding him until Mitzie could control her emotional outbursts. After Mitzie did her *meeting and greeting*, we laid Madison down for his afternoon nap.

"So, Paula, you gonna tell me now what ya' wouldn't earlier, and what's up with all this cloak and dagger stuff?"

"You won't believe what happened back home," Paula said in response. "Now...listen to me first and don't interrupt. You always don't let me finish what I'm saying, before you jump right on in and I kin never finish my story."

"Well, that's because you talk so fast you're into another thought when I might want to comment about something you just said previously."

"See! See what I mean. You're doing it again." She snapped.

"Okay, okay...I'll try to keep my trap shut, so go ahead. I'm listening."

"So what I was about to say was, I never told you this before because you would have gotten mad at me, or done something ignorant, 'cause you've got such a short fuse. Now, do you remember that time I told you Bill Clinton made a pass at me?"

"Vaguely."

"Well, it was more to it than that."

"How much more?"

She was right! Inside, I could feel my temperature starting to fluctuate. Paula noted the tone in my voice and responded by saying, "I ain't going any further 'til you promise me not to get mad."

"Paula, you opened this can of worms, now finish what you started because I know there's a reason why you're just now telling me this."

"Just hold on to your horses, Stephen Jones. Hear me out first, before you get all mad at me, cause I ain't done nothing wrong. Remember my friend, Pam?"

"Who?"

"Pam Blackard. My childhood friend who helped me get on at the Capitol."

"Yeah, yeah—go ahead."

"Well ,anyway, one day, back when I was still working, she asked me if I wanted to volunteer to work the front table and give out name badges *at the Excelsior Hotel for the Governor's Conference.* Plus, she said, we get to go home right afterwards, so I was all for that! So anyhow, the day we're at the conference, Pam and I saw the Governor in the hallway talking with some people.

He looked up, saw me looking at him, and smiled back at us. We looked at each other and giggled between us, flattered that he even noticed us at all. Well, we didn't think much of it at the time until a State Trooper named Danny Ferguson stood in front of the reception desk and introduced himself as Bill Clinton's Security Guard.

He was dressed in a regular suit and all, so we said we didn't believe him. He showed us his badge and the gun under his jacket. Then he asked me if I would like to meet the Governor and handed me a piece of paper with a number on it. So I asked him,

"What's this for?" He said it was the Governor's room number and that he does this all the time because he always gets a room for dignitaries, or if he gets a call from the President and needs to talk without being disrupted. I asked Pam what she thought about it and she said that maybe he's gonna offer me a job."

I stopped Paula with my hand, waving it in her face. I couldn't stand it any longer. "Omygod, Paula, "How naive can you be...Yeah, right, I can bet he was gonna offer you a job. The kind you do on your knees."

She spoke up in her high-pitched twang, "That's exactly what he—hey, how'd you know what he did?"

"Well I guess I'm a rocket scientist Paula," I snapped.

"Oh no, you're not. It's just that you men all think alike."

"No, that's not true," I said, a bit pissed off. It's just the men you've known."

"Oh yeah" she blurted out. "That includes you, now, doesn't it buster."

"Does it now?" I barked, "I don't ever remember you performing any such particular jobs with me, unless you have split personalities and I married the traditional Paula."

"Are you insinuating that I gave Clinton a blowjob?"

Stephen M. Jones, Jr.

"I have no idea, but it sounds like that's what you're leading up to. And if that's not the case, then that was Clinton's first mistake because that's one thing that's not in your repertoire with me."

Paula screamed back at me and started to cry, "See! See how you do me? You're always trying to put me down. You never let me finish, you don't even know what happened, and now it's all my fault. Jus' because I went up to meet the Governor. What if you were in my shoes and was told that your boss wanted to meet you. Wouldn't you go? I'd never met him before and was excited at the chance of getting to meet him. Her shoulders were now shaking and she was in a full convulsive cry. I felt like a heel, I fell into the typical male ego *blame-the-woman* syndrome, without so much as to giving her a chance to finish her story. I was the Judge, jury, and accuser all at the same time.

So say something? Just don't stand there, and watch her cry. "Look honey, I'm sorry. I jus' can't believe you could be so—so…uh…uninformed as to go to this guy's room. I mean, I heard about his reputation back in Little Rock, when he was still Governor. But I'm sorry, go ahead, and finish. So, tell me what happened next?"

"Well" she said with a big sniff, "I don't remember where I was in my…my…oh, I lost my place. See what happens when you interrupt! Where was I? Oh, now I remember."

Suddenly, Paula was now completely void of emotional breakdown. I'm in complete awe! I had just witnessed an amazing phenomenon in Paula. It was like a furious thunderstorm of emotion. A flash flood of tears, and then, as sudden as it had begun, it was over. Her emotional override had just washed my resolve out to sea. Left in the wake, only remnants of dissolved mascara sketched along her face, finding the path of least resistance down to her chin, was all that remained. Not so much as a drop of moisture from the torrential flood witnessed just moments before. *Wow*, I thought, *Is she playing me like a base fiddle, or is she for real. How the hell can she turn it on, and off like that? I haven't seen that side of her before. Is this her way of ducking an uncomfortable situation?*

Without Apology

Be that as it may, I was starting to feel as cantankerously sensitive as to why she was just now telling me this. But I'd already stuck my foot in my mouth once and look what happened. *Damn, she may blow up next and I'll never find all the pieces to her puzzle.*

I don't care how long you've been with, or known someone, there's always that unpredictable learning curve that continues to flow through a relationship.

"Stephen. What's wrong with you?" Paula asked,

"Your mouth's standing wide open and you look as if you're somewhere's else. Are you listening to me?"

"Huh... yeah, yeah, go ahead. I'm sorry. I just got caught up in a moment of thought."

"Well, pay attention to me 'cause I don't wanna' have to repeat myself." Paula continued to say that she had discussed with Pam whether or not to go meet the Governor.

"We didn't see any harm in my meeting him. So I told Pam that if I'm not back in fifteen minutes for her to come get me."

I had to bite my lip to keep from butting in. So I thought to myself, *if you didn't think anything wrong about going up there, why did you feel you had to tell Pam to come get you in fifteen minutes, huh?*

"The State Trooper took me up the elevator and we walked down the hall to a room where the door was cracked open. I walked in the room, and there was Bill Clinton. He came up to me and I shook his hand. He held on to my hand and drew me close. He told me he loved the way my hair flowed down my back. The next thing I knew he put his hand up my culottes."

"What the hell is culottes?" I yapped.

Paula smacks with her lips as if she couldn't believe I didn't know.

"You know— they're shorts that look like a dress. You've seen 'em before... it's my purple outfit."

She paused for a response. So I gave her a falsetto pitch of dress recognition by forming an O with my lips and simultaneously raising my eyebrows. It was a facial expression that she perceived as a, "Yes, I know the dress you're talking about." I was lying through my teeth, I had no idea what her purple outfit looked like.

With that, she continued talking quickly,

"I then pulled away from him walked over to the window and looked out. I tried to change the subject. So I asked him what's his wife, Hillary, been doing lately."

"Paula," I said, "Would you please take that gum out of your mouth and slow down? You're throwing it around like a washing machine on spin cycle. You're talking a mile a minute."

"That's jus' the way I talk."

She then plopped a wad of juicy fruit in her hand that could choke a horse.

"You should be used to the way I talk anyhow, mister."

"You know Paula… you're supposed to chew gum one stick at a time."

"Oh dear Bessie, will ya' shut up and listen. So anyhow, as I said before you opened yer trap, I tried to change the subject by talking about his wife, soz maybe he'd get the message, but he came up to me again and tried to kiss me. I turned away…went and sat on the end of the couch."

"What the hell for Paula? Excuse me, but am I missing something here? Why on God's green earth didn't you leave the first time he tried to put his hands up your cool-aids."

"Well, I didn't want him to think I was rude and run out like that—and they're culottes. And don't you make it sound like it was my fault!"

Her voice cracked, like an unexpected bang from a firecracker thrown at your feet. "I wanted him thinking we were friends and that's all. I told him I already had a steady boyfriend."

So, I said, sarcastically, "Let me get this straight. You didn't want him to think that you were rude? And you wanted to convince him that you just wanted to be friends?"

"That's right." she said, "I thought maybe he could help me find a better job, you know him being the Governor and all."

"Well, Paula" I said dryly, "Did yah become friends?" (Sarcastically thinking in the back of my mind, *that's the term she uses when referring to guy buds, like I was when we first started going out.*)

"Nope. And you won't believe what happened next."

"Try me—I'm all ears."

I could sense in her voice that Paula was in a transition of demeanor, a finale of sorts. She was like a runaway freight train picking up speed, teetering on derailment. It was as though she was moving through a sequence of events, frame-by-frame. Then the words began flickering in my mind like a silent movie projector ending with the continuous slapping sounds from the reel still rotating out of control. I was completely transfixed on the inability to understand her thought process.

She continued her climactic experience in a nervously shaky high pitch. "When he walked up to the couch, his face was beet red. He sat down beside me, pulling his pants and drawers down all in one motion. He had a hard-on! Can you believe that? He sat their slapping it around and stuff, you know playing with it, stroking it. I was so shocked, I couldn't move—so I jus' froze.

Then he told me to kiss it. Boy howdy, I jumped up off that couch and headed for the door. I turned to him and said, "I'm not that kind of girl." But before I could get out the door, he'd already pulled his pants up and was holding them with one hand while he blocked me from going out with the other."

He said to me, "If you're smart, you'll keep this between us. Tell your boss Dan Harrington I'll call him tomorrow."

"Then he then opened the door and let me out. I was so humiliated, and still in shock. My mind was jus' numb. All I wanted to do was get away. I just ran out. I remember seeing that State Trooper sitting in a chair in the hallway. As I passed, him he had a smirk on his face like he knew all along why he'd brought me up there.

I rode the elevator down and went right up to Pam, and said to her, "You won't believe what just happened."

I told her all about what went on. She couldn't believe it. She saw how shaken I was and said that I should go on home since the conference was pretty much over with anyway. So I left, but I couldn't be by myself. I went to *Garver & Garver*, that's where Debbie works—you know my girlfriend, Debbie Balentine?"

I gave a nod of recognition and she continued by saying, "I told Debbie everything and she said, "Paula, Paula, Paula—I can't believe you didn't know about that man. Bill Clinton is known for his flings."

"And so I said Debbie, I had no idea." And Debbie said, "Jus' like you did, Stephen."

"Paula, I jus' can't believe how naive you are, but what you need to do now is to report this."

"How?" I said, "Debbie, he's the Governor."

"Well, she said, you should report him to the Police. He shouldn't be allowed to get away with that, Paula."

"I told her the police escorted me up there and besides, I jus' can't think right now…I don't know what to do. Anyhow, Debbie suggested that I shouldn't be alone either and so I left Debbie's work and drove to my sister Charlotte's to tell her, then Lydia, and finally…I told mama."

There was a short silence that I took as a way of Paula trying to see what way the wind would blow on my emotional attitude.

So I said, "Looks like I was high on your need-to-know priority list."

"Oh, no," she said, "I figured if I told ya' that you might do something. You know how hot tempered you kin be."

"Nope, " I said. "It's more likely that you thought I might break up with you, since we were, if I recall, on shaky ground in those days."

"Oh…wee-were-not, Steve Jones." She exclaimed in a slow, exaggerated tone.

"Paula, you must have short-term memory when it comes to you getting caught slipping out while I was working at night. If memory serves me right, and it does, I believe you knew your way around the Excelsior Hotel. No—You don't remember? Let me refresh your memory, Paula. I got home from work around eleven o'clock one night, and it was cold out, because I had to wipe off the frost from the truck windshield before I drove home.

"When I got home, I noticed that your car had no dew or frost on it. So, I reached down to touch the tail pipe and damn near burned the hell out of my hand. I went inside and I hollered your name at the bottom of the staircase. After a few minutes, you came downstairs yawning, looking like you just woke up. I asked you what time you got home from work and you said around six-thirty. So I acted normal like nothing was going on and we went to bed, but I woke you up at four in the morning and grilled you good, so you couldn't think to snake your way out of anything. Remember that Paula? Remember... you admitted that you went to the Excelsior Hotel to some happy hour party after work.

"I now wonder how many parties I missed out on while working late. Come on Paula, all those parties with your co-workers and no one told you of Clinton's reputation with women?"

Paula just slowly shook her head indicating, "No."

"Then why did you tell Pam to come get you in fifteen minutes?"

Water began to well up in her eyes, feeling that I was on the attack again I got angry at myself. "Damn it...would you listen to me? Here I go again...look at me, Paula. I'm dragging up the past to start an argument. It's like some bad cold I can't get rid of. The more I blow, the more it runs out, but hey, why the hell not? You're just now telling me about something that happened two years ago. All your friends, and family knew, but not me. How do you think that makes me feel?"

"Damnit Paula, it seems like we're always arguing about something, mostly it's me griping about your spending sprees. Come to think of it, I guess the reason you didn't have any money to pay your bills back then was because you were spending all of it during happy hour at the Excelsior Hotel?" *See, here I go again.*

"Did ya' ever think that maybe Clinton knew about you *way* before you ever met him in that room? Looks to me like you were leading a double life;

Stephen M. Jones, Jr.

with me by day and party girl by night. Now I know why you want to be back home with your friends."

Paula wasn't about to let that dog lay. "Let me tell you, Steve Jones, you've got some imagination. You're jus' jealous for nothing…that's all this is about."

"Really? Well let me tell you something sweetheart, you and your sister, Lydia, wrote the book on jealousy. What I'm trying to do here is find some pieces to the puzzle that you've stuffed under the sheets. So don't even go there. For instance…remember when I was working out at *Jim Bottin's* gym when some poor girl came up to me to ask about what she could do to slim down her arms. At about that same moment you were walking into the gym and saw me talking to her. Without even taking the time to listen to what we were talking about, you came up to her and chewed her out in front of God and everybody for no reason at all. I still remember her expression, with her mouth wide open, in total embarrassment. In fact, the whole gym stopped to see the fireworks coming from your mouth."

"I'm not the only one that got jealous in the gym," Paula shot back.

"What are you talking about, Paula? I don't get jealous like you do."

"Oh yes, you do!" Paula shot back. What about when you saw me talking to my old boyfriend, Mike Turner?"

"Yeah…I seem to remember we were working out---hold it, let me re-phrase that—I was working out and you were sitting on the bike watching the soaps on the gym's TV monitor. And low and behold your ex-boyfriend shows up…which is fine with me because it's a gym and sometimes you can bump into old acquaintances. No big deal, but what did pissed me off, and I wouldn't characterize it as jealousy, is that you went and got our newborn son out of the gym's daycare and let him hold our son. What you did…gave me the feeling that you were rubbing it in his face—like, "Look, Mike, this could have been ours."

"You didn't even bother trying to introduce me. You pretty much ignored me until I cleared my throat after a few minutes of standing there like an idiot. Anyway, I didn't say a word to you until we left the gym. It hurt my pride to see you do that in front of me, especially when you told me that you slept with the guy. Hell, that's not jealousy baby, that's called you having mine, and your old boyfriend's cake, and eating it too."

"Now, let me give you a first-hand example of jealousy by refreshing the memory button again, because I can dot you're I's every time you cross my T's. How about the knock-down, drag-out fight we had about the manager at the condo in Sherwood who asked me about modeling, when she found out I did some print work in local newspapers? That's jealousy. Or how about the real estate lady who sold me the house in Faulkner County? I almost lost the house because of your unfounded accusations."

"Just because I talk to the heifer in the next pasture, doesn't mean I'm going to cross the fence and eat the grass. You know you've got some major insecurity problems, baby girl. This reminds me a lot like what your sister does to Tony. She'll all but eat him alive about what he better not do when he's out of town on a job site. All the while, Lydia is having a good ol' time banging some other guy at his dumbass expense."

"I do, Paula. I do believe you knew that if you told me about this Clinton encounter back then, we wouldn't be married now. And I honestly believe that if it wasn't for Madison…"

Paula screamed at me, "How could you be so cold hearted to bring our baby into this?"

"Easy, Paula…you certainly had no problem putting our baby into your ex-boyfriend's arms, now did ya'? And don't think that I forgot about Dan Hampton's condo keys you kept on your key ring throughout our relationship. Don't gimme that *doe in the headlights* look! You know damn Skippy who I'm talking about. That defensive-tackle— the one who played for the Chicago Bears."

Remember I played chicken with that picklehead when we went to Hot Springs for the weekend. He was in one hell of a hurry leaving the Arlington Hotel, even going in the wrong direction on a one-way street. When I pulled to the side and we passed, you said that's Dan Hampton in that truck. And that wasn't his wife sitting in his lap. Remember that, Paula?"

"Yeah, I remember," she said dryly. "But I told you I never dated him. He was jus' a friend." Paula cried back.

"Yeah—right! So tell me Paula, if I am so goddamn wrong about all of this, then why aren't you all in my face and telling me to put you on a plane back home?"

She was quick to bark back, "I guess I'm nothing then. I have nothing, I own nothing. It's all yours. You have it all—I can't do nothing without your consent."

"You know, Paula, how we came together and made a baby is beyond me. *You're night; I'm day, no yin, or yang.*

"Look, I'm sorry about always being so argumentative. I know it seems that I'm being a little accusingly insensitive. I guess its human nature to bring in other baggage to booster one's point without staying in tune to the indifference at hand, but you have a way of tripping my internal wires."

"I can't believe how incredibly ignorant I must have been. Someone once told me that, 'a man was born from the womb, then after puberty, he spends the rest of his life trying to get back in.' I don't believe most men understand the long-term implications of that statement."

Paula looked confused when she said, "What in the cotton-picking world are you talking about now? I mean, you're the only one I know, Steve Jones, that can bring a load of bull into a conversation because you're so full of yourself."

Now depleted of emotional energy, I respond, "Actually, I was talking philosophical to myself out loud. I'm what you'd call waddling in reminiscent attitude. You bringing all this up now caused me to take a long look back at the road I've covered. You can't go forward without knowing where you've been. Our egos, Paula, won't allow us to stop to ask for directions."

Paula responded tearfully, "I hate it when you try to talk like you know everything."

"No, that's not true. My problem is that I know a little about a lot and a lot about nothing. Given the current set of circumstances, Paula, why are you just now telling me about this? Who did you talk to back in your neck of the woods for you to pull this dead rabbit out of the hat this late in the ball game?"

"Well," she said, with a loud sniff grabbing a paper towel from the kitchen and dabbing her nose, "on my trip back home, I went to see Debbie and she said that a co-worker gave her a magazine called *The American Spectator* and she said that there was an article about me in there."

"How do you know it was about you?"

"I know it was me, because this reporter interviewed the same State Trooper, Danny Ferguson, that took me up there. The article mentioned my first name was Paula. And Stephen, he lied about what happened up there. He said in the article that I came out of the room and I had a big smile on my face, that I looked like I enjoyed it and that I told him to tell the Governor that if he wanted a steady girlfriend to let him know. That was a bold-faced lie. I never said a word to him! He's the one who had that snide smirk on his face!"

"Think about it, Stephen. If I was so happy about what had just happened, why would I feel the need to tell that State Trooper anything? I could have told Bill Clinton myself. Danny Ferguson is the one that came up to me weeks later to ask me for my phone number. He said that the Governor asked him to get my number because Hillary was out of town a lot. I told him that I already had a steady boyfriend."

I interrupted her and said sarcastically, "Were you talking about me?"

"You don't ever stop, do ya'? Jus' shut up and listen. He said he already knew that."

"Knew what?"

"Maybe if you stop interrupting me and clean them ears out like I told ya' before and listen, you might find out. Anyhow, Danny Ferguson already knew I had a steady boyfriend and he knew your name was Steve. That scared me that he knew your name, so I told him besides that, we live together. He asked me what time Steve gets home from work? He said that the Governor could call me while my boyfriend was still at work."

"Now, damnit," I said, "That's a bold son-of-a-bitch, trying to lay his scent in my backyard."

Stephen M. Jones, Jr.

Paula gave me a contorted look.

"Sorry, go ahead, what happened next?"

"I didn't give him my number if that's what you're thinking. I told him not to ask me for it again, because I ain't interested."

"Was that the end of it, Paula? Because it sounds like you're just warming up again."

"Stephen, if I would've told you back then, you would have tried to confront him. I know you. I know how you are."

"Paula, I can tell you that, yes, it does piss me off that this butthead tried to get my number to call you while I was at work. And, yes, if I would have known then what I know now, you can bet your culottes, I wouldn't let it go. But given his position, I wouldn't have physically done anything Paula. All that would do is land me in jail. The honorable way to deal with him was outlawed a hundred plus years ago. However, there's more than one way to skin a snake."

"See how you're acting. That's why I didn't tell you in the first place. You can't stay calm about nothing."

"So is that all of it, Paula, or is there more?"

"Let's see, yeah, there's more alright. When I was pregnant with Madison, I ran into Bill Clinton with his security detail. This time it was some other State Trooper with him, not Danny Ferguson. Anyhow, I was making my rounds walking inside the rotunda of the capitol building."

I looked quizzical at Paula.

"You know, Stephen, it's that round part upstairs. From the outside it has a dome on top. You know the same building they shot that movie you were in, because you said it was modeled jus' like the one in Washington. I know you know because that's the movie if anyone blinked twice they would have missed ya'."

I acknowledged her by nodding, but gave no response to her obvious poke.

"Well, anyway, he and this other trooper were on one side and I was on the other. Bill Clinton spotted me walking the other way. You know that man changed directions to come see me. He came up to me real close and all and asked how I was doing. I said, "Just fine, thank you very much."

The Governor said, "You know, Paula, we're a lot like the movie *Beauty and the Beast*, don't you think so, Larry?"

"I guess that was the name of his bodyguard."

Anyhow he said to me, "You're the beauty and I'm the Beast."

"So I told Mr. Clinton that he didn't look like the beast."

"WHAT? What was that you just said, Paula?"

I felt like I just got stuck in my ear with a hot poker stick. I jumped up out of my chair. "Did you just say what I think you just said? You did, didn't you? What the hell's wrong with you, honey? This guy drops his Fruit of the Looms on you, and you…"

"Look, Stephen, all I wanted to do was to get away from him as quickly as possible."

"Well that doesn't make sense Paula, if you wanted to get away, all you had to do was change your direction when he did. I believe he would've gotten the message right then and there. All you did by saying what you did is keep him trying to sneak inside the hen house. On top of that by then you were already on the nest with Madison."

"He knew my boss, Stephen. I didn't want to lose my job. And besides, he wasn't going to do anything out in the open. I just wanted to get out of the situation, that's all. Why are you badgering me like it's my fault, like I did something wrong?"

"What about that picture Paula?" I said dryly.

"What are you talking about now?"

"Paula, I remember that autographed picture you brought home of Clinton. The one he signed for you to give to Madison."

"Yeah…so what about it?"

"You said that his secretary gave it to you as a gift when Madison was born. Let's see now, wasn't that after the Disney role-playing scene in the rotunda?"

"Oh shut up, that was nothing, Stephen. His secretary said that he wanted to give this to Madison."

"He's a newborn, Paula. Who gives a new born an autographed 8x10 picture of himself to a baby?"

"You're making a mountain out of a mole hill, Stephen Jones. He heard that I had my baby and he wanted to give Madison something personal, that's all."

"Sorta-like what he wanted to give you in that hotel room, huh."

"That's not fair. I didn't do nothing wrong," she cried out, tears rushing down her face again.

"Why do you want to be so cruel and mean to me? What did I do, Stephen? How many times do I have to say it? I didn't do anything wrong."

"Ah'right," I said, "I'll let it go for now and we'll move on. So come on Paula, what's the real reason you're telling me now, let's get down to the nitty gritty."

Finally she blurts, "You got problems, you know that, Steve Jones."

"Yeah, I know I do, Paula. It walks on two legs and wears culottes. Go ahead. Tell me why now?"

Still seething by my last remark, she grudgingly continued at first in an arrogant manner, only tempered as time went by. For Paula, talking is the same as what Prozac is to the afflicted.

She was saying that on the same day Debbie told her about the article in *The American Spectator*, they went to lunch at the Golden Corral in North Little Rock. And low and behold, to their astonishment, sitting a few rows away was the same security detail trooper, Danny Ferguson, who had ponied her up to see Bill Clinton.

She said that she marched right up to him and his female friend in front of God and everybody and told him she didn't appreciate him lying about what had happened in that hotel room.

Paula told me she said, "Danny, who are you to know what happened in there?"

He said, "Paula, I know nothing happened. Bill came out after you left and said he came up empty. I'm so sorry, Paula. It's that reporter David Brock. He knew nothing happened. He twisted my story to make it sound as if something really had happened. I just used your first name. I told him I only knew you by your first name. The only reason I did the interview is because there's a lot of money in this. This is hot right now, Paula. You could make a ton of money if you'd give your story to the tabloids. Gennifer Flowers made a bundle.

"This is payback time for Bill Clinton for stabbing us in the back. He said that there would be jobs for all the guys on his security detail when he went to the White house. He left us cold, Paula. So now a few of us retained a lawyer and are telling our story of who Bill Clinton really is."

Chapter Seven

After Paula's encounter with trooper-pimp, *goodie two shoes* Debbie wasted no time kicking it up a notch by suggesting they talk to her lawyer and good friend, Danny Trailer, just to see what he thinks.

Thus begins a love-hate relationship with attorneys. In my case, it's love to hate. In Paula's case, it was a faith as strong as her mother's Pentecostal convictions.

I truly believe the really nasty ones that I've had the dubious luck of having vague associations with have been on the other side of the razor wire. These guys must have gained their ambitions in the legal profession by first starting their apprenticeship as a used car dealer at Big Bob's *lemon auto sales*. Tack on four more years of skullduggery to pass the bar exam and finally being inducted into the fraternity of full-fledged bull-shiters. Some have experience in personal injury, dabble in divorce court, or teach law as so-called professors at second-rate universities. *Oh, I almost forgot. If they're really good at bullshit, they run for public office.*

These dysfunctional over-achievers slowly whittle away at our freedoms by allowing a minority of hypocrites to file suits disallowing fundamental values like the pledge of allegiance or traditional holiday activity scenes on school or government property. I believe every ACLU lawyer should be gathered up, given orange jumpsuits and sent to Al Qaeda. I'd like to see how long these infidels would last taking religion out of their government. *Hey, I snuck that personal thought in. Tick some of you off? Yeah, I thought so.*

In Danny Trailer's case he was a small cheese looking for a bigger slice. That's not to say there aren't good people with strong principles that practice the legal profession, but I found that in my long, unfortunate associations, it's been the exception to the rule.

Now, little did I know that by Debbie telling Paula of the article and introducing her to a home-grown opportunistic real estate lawyer would cast her into a mold of preconception.

So, let's recap. How did this germinate? An associate at *Garver & Garver*, where Debbie worked, showed her an article in *The American Spectator*. He said, "Isn't this your friend, Paula, that they're talking about?"

Now think about it, how do you figure that this associate knew that this was the same Paula that Debbie knew? *Bingo. That's right.* It's because blabber-mouth told everyone in her office about what had happened in that hotel room between Clinton and Paula prior to the article coming out. Yes, that's right, Debbie swings from the company grapevine. But she doesn't stop there. Oh no, not yet. She led Paula to an opportunistic lawyer after a chance meeting with trooper-pimp at a Chinese restaurant after hearing what Paula had told her. Damn, this sounds a lot like an intentionally lost draft of a Mickey Spillane novel found in a dusty attic in Toledo, Ohio.

Anyhow, looking at it from the top layer it seems logical trying to help a good friend, but peel back a few layers, and you'll see reason without rhyme, void of using common sense.

Best friend, goodie-two-shoes Deb, just took an opportunity to perpetuate an already bad situation. I'll bet that there are a lot of Debbie Ballentines in every work place, what yah think? I mean what are friends for? Some of the worst events in history were based on friendship, and good intentions. I betcha' Monica doesn't send a Christmas card to her good friend, Linda Tripp.

In a pathetic attempt of reconciliation, I tried to call *The American Spectator* to get a retraction. Every time I called, David Brock was either out, or not available. When I mentioned that this was concerning the article of the woman called Paula, I heard a scurry of activity, and muffled voices in the background. My ignorance helped them confirm that there was an encounter, but not like Ferguson said David Brock had painted the picture in his interview. So I demanded a retraction on their inaccuracy in reporting.

I immediately regretted making the call. They wanted my name, rank, and serial number, and asked a whole slew of intrusive questions that I wasn't willing to divulge. The very least of information they wanted was Paula's last name, and some type of verification. I don't know why, but I felt that we weren't ready to open that can of worms just yet, so I hung-up. Hell, too bad *The American Spectator* didn't have the same policy as the military's, "don't ask, don't tell…Unlike the author David Brock, who, after the damage was done, recanted everything when romantic relations began with Hillary's male secretary. Hillary you ole matchmaker you!

"Damn, I thought. *This whole thing is like quicksand! You slip a toe in, and the next thing you know you're up to your neck in muck.*"

I naively thought that I could straighten it out with a simple phone call. All I did was get a quick lesson in Sleaze Media Frenzy 101, another nasty profession of infestation genetically engineered to hatch a whole host of hypocrites in every nook and cranny on both sides of the political kitchen. Above all, I didn't want Paula featured on one of those sleazy daytime shows.

Unfortunately, I'd come home and see Paula glued to these same TV shows. She was drawn to the tabloids like Bill and Hillary was to a woman's vagina. Oops, I'm sorry, but it's not like I let the kitty out of the bag.

Now, at this point, I was ready to just let it blow over, but no, Paula insisted that she meet with Debbie's attorney. I told her that it was a bad idea to get involved in anything to do with Bill Clinton. I also told her that whatever she did, not to sign anything and she agreed not to.

But Paula had selective memory because she came back with a signed contract that was as thick as the name Chen is in the Los Angeles phone book.

Pissed beyond belief, I scanned over the contract. "Hot damn—Shit fire. Did Debbie have anything to do with this?"

"No, she did not!" Paula protested.

"Paula, was Debbie with you when you signed?"

"Yes."

"Then that explains it."

Paula yelped, "I kin make up my own mind, thank you very much."

So I asked Paula what kind of lawyer this guy is?

"He's a real estate lawyer. I believe that's what Debbie told me. He says he's a yellow dog Democrat."

"Oh great Paula—that means he voted for Clinton."

"What's that anyway?" Paula said.

"What's what, Paula?"

"A yellow dog Democrat."

"Geez, Louise…why me? What did I do to deserve this on my plate now?"

"Are you talking to me?" Paula asked, "Or yourself again, because I can't figure out when you're talking to me or yourself sometimes."

"Paula—Do you have any idea what you're getting yourself into by signing this? When you start casting stones, these people cast boulders. And if you have any dirty clothes stuffed in a closet, these people will find it, and hang it on display in the town square. I don't believe you understand what you're doing here."

"All's I know," Paula says, "is that Danny Trailer is gonna talk to a friend of his that works in the Clinton administration and see if they can straighten out what really happened at the Excelsior. He says he's gonna do it quietly."

"Well," I said, "if that's the case, then the way I read this contract, the word quiet must be written in invisible ink, 'cause I don't see it. I'll believe it when I see it. This reminds me of my granddaddy telling me a story about a colored man working for him on his dairy farm back in the 50's named, Arell. He said he believed that superman could fly, 'cause he'd seen it on TV with his own two eyes."

"What's that got to do with anything?"

"Well, Paula, like Arell, I tend to believe it when I see it, unless this contract is an illusion of trickery. I'm telling ya' Paula, I don't feel good about this at all."

"Oh… like, how do you know? You think you always know everything and besides, you're not a lawyer anyhow. Let Danny straighten this mess out."

"Uh huh, who all of a sudden puffed you up like a bullfrog full of bold talk?"

"I kin speak my mind when I have a mind to, thank you very much."

"Not to change the subject, but to answer your question about a yellow dog Democrat, I want to ask you if you know the difference between a Democrat and a Republican."

"Naw, I don't know anything about that stuff, you know me." Paula yapped.

"Well, basically, Paula, Democrats like big government and giving money to special interests programs. Republicans just like big business. It's like a tug'a war of ideology, which pretty much allows the American people over time an equal balance of power. Sort of like the saying, "What goes around comes around." Very seldom do they come together for the majority, but you can bet your sweet bippy there's a lot of, "I'll scratch your back if you'll scratch mine," going on. If that didn't happen, bills would never get passed through Congress. Unfortunately, they get convoluted in the process."

"Alright, now, so what does that all mean, Mister know-it-all?"

"Well, let's see, if the bill was a bee, Paula, it means that the opposing party tries to take the stinger out of the bill. No? I see you're not there yet. Let's take the word convoluted. It's like taking the punch out of that Hawaiian drink. They water it down, a shell of its former self. Understand? It looks like I'm losing you, yeah, uh huh, I'm getting that blank stare, so say something?"

"I'm not a moron, Steve Jones."

"I know you're not, Paula—I get the message. I've lost your interest. Just remember that Democrats like to give money and Republicans like to keep it. A yellow dog is someone who has had a long history in one party. Yellow dogs vote straight down party lines. They're stubborn. That's where the Democratic symbol of a jackass comes from."

"You jus' burn my hide. Why didn't you say that in the first place instead of going through all that rig-a-ma-roar?"

"Well, Paula, I like to give you examples to help you better understand, that's all honey. I'll test ya'. If Trailer is a yellow dog, which side of the yard does his family tree grow on?"

"Left side."

"Very good, Paula."

"Oh shut up! I know I'm going to regret this, but I don't understand the yellow part."

"That, Paula, is just the name they call themselves. I don't think the color has anything to do with it unless their convictions to the party are so old they turned yellow like paper, or documents turn colors over time."

"Only you would come up with a lamebrain analogy like that."

"I'm going to pretend like I didn't hear that... Nowadays, a Democrat is pretty much a Liberal. Liberals hardly ever get elected so they run under the illusion of a Democrat."

"Well, now I'm all confused again."

"I'm not surprised."

"Watch it buster." Paula snapped.

"Look, all I'm trying to do here is simplify the terminology like I did before, so we can move on. But, as always, I get caught up in my own philosophical quagmire and confuse you anyway. What I'm trying to say here is and I know you're capable of understanding, you're just not interested in politics that's all, and I can't say that I blame you.

"Let me try it this way, a Liberal is more extreme than a yellow dog Democrat on big government, which causes them to spend more of the taxpayer's money. They're part of that free love and let it all hang out—sixties generation of drugs, sex, and rock-n-roll. Your buddies, Bill and Hillary, fit into that era of round pegs in square holes."

"I don't appreciate you putting me in with them, like you're Mr. Clean. You ain't got a self-righteous bone in your body. The first week we actually started dating, you walked around naked in front of me."

"Now Paula, theirs nothing wrong with sex and rock-n-roll when it's not offending others. Besides, I wasn't the only one naked. You just stayed under the covers."

Paula let out a smirk and poked her tongue out.

"Quit changing the subject. Now, getting back to what I was talking about. Most of the time, the two parties are investigating themselves and spending more of the peoples money conducting some trumped-up congressional hearing into misappropriations. This is primarily done to rub salt into the wounds of the party that's been elected to the White House in order to gain an edge in the next election. It usually starts around the lame-duck year of the President. That's when he's in the last few years of his term in office. In the end, we the people, stay confused and they're never held accountable for the people's money. It's all smoke and mirrors, honey.

"They know the average Joe doesn't give a rip, and lives from paycheck to paycheck and only watching a slanted overview version from whatever biased news program he or she sees. The only exception to the rule is maybe a few goobers wearing coke bottle glasses while watching C-SPAN. Take for instance if you walked out on the streets like that egg headed comedian, Jay Leno, does on The Tonight Show from time to time, and asks some pedestrians what C-SPAN is. They'd probably say (in my California falsetto), " Yeah dude, I know what that is. Yo…it's like that meat that comes in a can. Like it's not very healthy to eat, but its good stuff dude." —and you know what else Paula?"

"No, I don't want to know what else, Stephen. Besides you sound ignorant trying to talk like some surfer. I've heard enough already. I don't care about all that stuff, and if you ask me, if he's the President and all, he doesn't have to scratch someone's back to get something through Congress."

"Huh…what in the hayseed are you talking about, Paula?"

"You said a 'while ago that they had to scratch Bill's back to get anything through Congress."

"Bill who, Paula?"

"Bill Clinton, silly."

"No, no, no, honey, I was talking abou—"

"Yes, ya' did. And you don't hav'ta make it simple for me. I ain't ignorant."

"But Paula, I wasn't—"

"Stop it right now, Stephen Jones! I ain't going there. I've heard enough already. I'm tired of listening; my ears are start'n a' hurt."

"Look, would you at least let me finish what I was trying to explain?"

"See how it feels to be interrupted. How'd ya' like the taste of your own medicine?"

"It's a bill, not a name, Paula, that's sent through Congress to—" Taking her knuckles and tapping on my head, she kept on, "Hello—anybody home? I already told ya', I don't care about that stuff. What we need to talk about is what we're going to do about how he tried to scratch more than just my back."

"Oh, brother you can wear me out sometimes, you know that, Paula?"

"Ditto, buster! Stephen, all I asked you was what's a yellow dog Democrat, not some long, drawn-out explanation."

"Okay, I guess I got carried away, but for your information, I wasn't talking about Bill Clinton. I'm talking about bills that go to Congress and if they get passed by the majority then they become law, understand?"

"I don't know why you're getting all tore up about something I couldn't care less about."

"You're right—I'll shut up about it. I'm barking up the wrong tree anyway. So, tell me, when did this Danny Trailer say he was going to get back to you?"

"He said he'll let me know if he hears anything. You know me... I get all nervous about everything."

"I know you do. You're just like your mama. And I also know that Debbie helped egg you on about signing that contract."

"For the last time...she did not either." Paula snapped.

"Paula, you and Debbie squawked like a pair of chickens in a Grade A hen house."

"I'm telling ya', Debbie didn't have anything to do with it."

"Yeah, right—you don't do anything by yourself. If it weren't for your best friend, we wouldn't be in this mess. I mean, who the hell has heard of *The American Spectator* magazine before all this crap happened? But no, she had to open her big mouth. And for some Godforsaken act of bad luck, you both ran into that trooper who took you up to that hotel room at some Chinese restaurant.

"And what do you do? You go up to him, and say you don't appreciate what he lied about. Well, that's all fine and dandy, can't blame you there, but you let this asshole fill your head by saying you can make a lot of money if you sell your story to the tabloids, like Gennifer Flowers. Then, you go back to your table where Debbie is salivating from the beans you were about to spill. Then you let Debbie talk you into seeing some flea-bit lawyer and now look what cha' done."

Paula knew the right button to push to try to take me off her trail, but I stayed focused.

She said, "Listen, mister, you drug me and Madison out here to California to work on being an actor, and I ain't seen nobody beating down our door to make you a movie star."

"Goddamn, Paula, this isn't about being a movie star. It's about getting a retraction. I hate that tabloid crap. You think I want our last name, and my wife, associated with all that bimbo stuff floating around. This isn't about money. I wouldn't take a plug nickel from those tabloids shows that you keep your eyeballs glued to.

"For some homegrown reason, you will always ask someone who may have ulterior motives about what *they* think you should do. I thought we both decided that you were just going to see what this lawyer thought about you trying to get a retraction. I don't know why in the hell you didn't talk to me before you went and signed that contract. Oh— I can answer that one myself. It's because you knew what I'd say. But nooo, you let your *so-called* best friend lead you down the yellow brick road to fairyland. Well, let me tell you something baby girl. We're not in Kansas. If anything—we're smack-dab in the middle of a hundred-acre forest standing in Pooh doo-doo."

"Stephen Jones, I think you need to stop reading all those Disney books to Madison before bedtime."

"You know something, Paula, it's amazing how you can change the subject at the drop of a hat."

Thinking to myself that I was spinning my wheels, going nowhere fast! I made a futile effort, and said, "Who is the one person who always has your best interest in mind and will never lead you down the wrong road? Just tell me—who?"

Paula teased, "I remember you can't see road signs all that good at night because of your nearsightedness, and we get lost because you're a man and wouldn't ask for…"

"Stop it! Jus' stop Paula. It ain't gonna work. I see what you're trying to do here. So quit trying. Hell's-bells, Paula…wake up and smell the coffee. I'm not talking about my eyesight. I'm talking about insight. Stay with me here. I'm the last person in the world that's going to steer you wrong. Look, I may get mad at you and give you crap about a bad decision, especially when we talked about this together and you went north on me, but I'll always be by your side and support you up front. You know what gnaws at me? It's that I'm your own husband and I'm usually the last one who finds out about anything you've done. You know how that makes me feel?"

"Don't get all huffy and all," she snapped back. "I can make up my own mind. And, besides you're right, if I would've called you, I know that you would have said—a big ol' NO."

"You're damn Skippy I would. Just think about it, Paula. Don't you know if you try to bring in some lawyer that this thing might not only affect just you, but our whole family, both mine and yours? Why don't you think past your nose and quit thinking about yourself for a change."

"That's it," Paula yelled.

"You got no right to talk about my nose, you're my husband and that's so mean of you." She started tearing up again.

"What? Uh oh. Here we go again. That was just a figure of speech, that's all. I wasn't even thinking about your nose. When I married you, I married all of you, and that includes that cute little beak of yours, baby."

"See!" Paula cried, "See how you treat me. That's what I'm talking about. Right here, my own husband making fun of me."

"No, I'm not, sweetheart. You bring more attention to your nose by being so sensitive about it. And don't try to turn this around on me by crying. I now know how you can cut that spigot on and off at the drop of a hat, so stop it.

"Damn it, you made me lose my train of thought (intentionally) for no good reason. Now, where was I? Oh yeah...I'm still smoke'n about that contract you say is gonna make everything alright. All I see here is percentages of book and movie deals. What the hell is that all about? This is about getting your good name restored, not some goddamn Hollywood read all about it."

She went for the jugular, "You're just jealous, Steve Jones, 'cause it's got movie deals in it."

"Is that what you think?"

She saw that she had cut me deep.

"Friggin' unbelievable. After all this...you just don't get it. do ya'? It's about your reputation. Yours and my good name. And yeah, what he did to you. He had no right. Well, Paula, you signed it. Now we'll have to deal with it. For now it's water under the bridge. Give me Trailer's number, maybe I can do some damage control. Maybe it's not too late to straighten up all this mess."

I called Danny Trailer and fished in his pond. He seemed harmless enough and assured me he was just going to quietly talk to a friend of his that works in the Clinton Administration to get some kind of quiet apology and maybe they could help get a retraction from the *American Spectator* magazine.

So I said to Trailer, "I'm assuming that Paula told you what happened in that hotel room, huh?"

"Yes she did, and it's a damn shame," said Danny said. "That man's got a reputation for stunts like that. Everybody who's somebody in Arkansas knows that...and if they don't, they're just covering up for him. Paula told me everything, including what lead to the encounter at the Excelsior Hotel. Listen Stephen, we're gonna do this thing right, and keep it quiet. I've already put in a call to my contact in Washington. Let's just wait, and see what shakes."

I just had to put my two cents in. "Well, I still don't feel very warm and cozy about all this. However, if you can get an apology or at least an acknowledgment that Paula didn't do anything unsavory as suggested from the *American Spectator*—well, hell—that just might do it. I know it would go a long way to clearing her name from any connection affiliated with this Clinton bimbo junk I've already heard too much about. Then we can let these sour grapes of an article die on the vine. Boy, I'll tell ya', Danny, I'd hate to have this cat out of the bag 'cause I sure don't want our family name out there. I don't care if my name is as common as rain. But on the other hand, nobody is gonna wipe his shoes on Paula's doormat."

"Well Stephen, there are a lot of Joneses out there. It'll take a while for them to track you guys down."

"Oh, really...seems to me that would be kinda' hard. Since they only have her first name and I'd like to keep it that way, but I wouldn't know about that Danny, not the way that damn contract reads. Now, if you can do what you say and keep it all quiet, then we can cut this dog loose to hunt in someone else's backyard."

I waited for Trailer to nibble back to my snide remark about the contract, all the time wondering if he had the used car salesman balls to do so.

"Well," Danny said, "I'm going to give it my best shot, Stephen. What I'm doing here is not a popular thing, especially me being a Democrat, but I believe what Paula told me happened. They'll believe it coming from me rather than some other guy with a political agenda."

"Good point, but look Danny, I don't give a rip about political associations, or for that matter, who the messenger is. This is about a retraction of an article that is factually wrong. Make your contact with Clinton's people, have 'em put pressure on that magazine to make it right."

"Stephen, I certainly believe Paula deserves some form of restitution."

"What was that? What a minute, Danny! Did you say she deserves a forum for restitution? Or did you say—"

"Hold on just a sec, Stephen. You're working off emotion. Listen to me, I'm going to get this thing done quietly. Do we understand each other?"

"All right, we'll see Danny...guess I've been sitting on my brain too long. It's starting to affect my hearing."

"I believe they got a name for that."

"Oh yeah? What do they call it, Danny?"

"They call them Buttheads."

There was a pause of silence on the phone. *He took the bait all right, and caught the snide remark about the contract. Let's see what happens when I set the hook.*

I then laughed out loud and he joined in.

"That's good, a lawyer with a sense of humor and a plan." With that remark, the laughter faded.

"But what you're telling me doesn't quite jive with the way this contract reads. It seems to me that there are ulterior motives at play here *Ol' Danny Boy.*"

Paula, who had been monitoring the call with radar on full frequency, gave me a nudge in protest.

Danny's tone turned defensive. "Mr. Jones," he replied, "I don't believe I know what you're talking about."

"Let's stop pussyfooting around the mulberry bush, Danny. I'm talking about a book, movie, and personal appearances in this contract you had Paula sign. That's what I'm talking about, Mr. Carpetbagger."

Paula jumped up off the couch like a bolt of lightning and mumbled something under her breath that I couldn't understand, but it sounded nasty.

I continued to say, "Aren't you putting the cart before the horse here, Danny? I mean all we're looking for here is some kind of quiet resolution."

"Look, Mr. Jones, I don't appreciate that remark and as Paula's attorney, I'm just covering all the bases and that's only if this thing deep sixes."

I almost exploded and my voice struck a high pitch, "The hell if that's so. I don't want our personal life on the front page of every tabloid right next to the woman that gave birth to a three-headed baby. You got that! And by the way, Danny, you being a real estate lawyer, where in the hell did you get that contact that Paula signed?"

That question went unanswered, only later did I found out that Cliff Jackson had given him that contract.

Danny, now very annoyed, quipped, "I'm talking to you out of courtesy. I want to remind you that your wife is my client and I'm going to do the best I can to get back her good name. This is all going to work out for the better, Mr. Jones. I'm just a small town lawyer, but I'm willing to help Paula if I can."

I paused on the phone, contemplating my next move. I was all too aware that I was surrounded like Custer's last stand. Paula standing on one side, giving me the stink eye—ready to scalp paleface, and her lawyer, from the Aryan nation of carpetbaggers, on the phone side of me. So for now, I was willing to give up the field of battle.

"Well, Mr. Trailer, I guess the least we can do is see if you hear from your contact in Washington. So with that, I'll hand the phone over to Paula now. Good talking to you."

"Same here, Mr. Jones."

I paused and eye-balled Paula who was still throwing daggers by cutting her eyes at me. I knew she was biting at the bits to smooth over our conversation, so I had to poke him in the eye with a stick just one last time.

"I'll tell ya' though, Danny—before I pass over the phone, I've always had the tenacity to call it as I see it and I see right through you like a cheap pair of pantyhose. Now, you have a good night, Mr. Trailer."

With that, Paula snatched the phone out of my hand and said, "You're such a big talker, you know that?"

Stephen M. Jones, Jr.

I walked over to sit on the couch and gave her a shrug, like what did I do? I mean I spoke my mind. I felt that this thing smelled to holy heaven. However, I admit, I had some tweaking to do on my delivery.

I probably did more damage than control, but hey, I was new at this stuff. For some good God only knows reason, I've always had the knack to put a wedge between me and most attorneys I've dealt with, but think about it, why would a lawyer put all that garbage in a contract unless, he had other motives up his sleeves, or maybe as usual, it's just me. I recognize that I have issues, having a tendency to always second-guess people in general. Basically, let's face it. I have a control problem. But when it comes to my family and reputation, I'm just not willing to give a lawyer a blank check on a situation that could have great personal impact. I believe anybody in their right mind would have done the same.

Some weeks went by with no resolve. Then Danny called, which was really a kick in the balls, to say that his friend George Cook, his contact with the Clinton administration said that the story in the *American Spectator* was all a big lie, that Paula was just another *bimbo* out for money and fifteen minutes of fame. Cook was quick to say that Clinton never knew a Paula Jones. Danny's contact, in closing conversation, said for us to do whatever you want. "As far as the administration was concerned, it wasn't worth commenting on."

After that, Danny said that he'd put a call in to a lawyer by the name of Cliff Jackson who was representing some of the State Troopers who were under attack for coming forward to talk about Clinton's sex-capades. Danny told Jackson about the incident at the hotel between Paula and Clinton. Jackson remarked, "This things got legs."

Cliff indicated to Danny that he was going to be in Washington the next week for his clients to accept an award at the *Conservative Political Action Conference* held at the *Omni Shoreham Hotel* in Washington. Jackson commented that this would give you guys the perfect platform to tell her story. All of the media will be present, and this being a Republican event, her story will fall on sympathetic ears.

105

Danny called us and with great deprecations, we decided to go. Unbelievable, right? I mean, after venomously wanting to keep a lid on this fiasco, I'm now willing for Paula to tell her story. Looking back, I had let my anger supersede common sense when Danny told me what this Cook guy said about Paula.

I remember continuing doing battle internally about the idea of going. I knew in the back of my mind that going to this event would open Pandora's box to assertions of right-wing agendas. I rationalized that we tried to talk to people who were sympathetic to Clinton first to resolve this quietly, only to get the door slammed in our face.

I still felt that Danny should have pursued a retraction from the *American Spectator* like what we had discussed by phone. Unfortunately, I allowed my personal emotion to cloud a rationale resolution, damn it. I responded with the classic southern chivalry gene inbred at childbirth.

Paula's reputation was being discarded. I felt that these people could say, and do, anything without impunity. I want to state for the record that anytime Paula was verbally attacked I took it very personal because she was my wife. I would defend my family to the bitter end. I know that sounds a little melodramatic, but those are my instincts. Bottom line—blinded by anger.

Danny had no intention of retraction. Instead of doing the right thing, he tried to milk Cook into extorting money along with some sort of lucrative real estate deal for himself. Get this…also proper jobs for both of us or else Paula comes forward.

Hell, if the shoe were on the other foot, I would have told Trailer pretty much the same damn thing Cook had said.

Let me set the record straight. I learned about that little scheme almost two years later from Paula's second set of attorneys when we all appeared in front of Judge Wright to set the trial date. I wouldn't have stood for that crap. Danny was supposed to talk to Cook about helping us put pressure on the *American Spectator* for a retraction, not some damn extortion plot. What's funny, is the way I read about it later. Danny wanted twenty-five thousand plus to get Paula a job in the entertainment business and me a better job. I laughed, because it would have been more plausible if it were the other way around. If I knew then what I know now, you can bet I would have responded differently, but hindsight's 20/20. So not knowing all of this at the time, I did a raw knee jerk reaction. *Big mistake—Should'a stayed home.*

Paula and I flew out to Washington. I found a cheap fare for Danny. I made reservations at the *Apple Tree Hotel* for a one-night stay. Paula, Danny, and I dropped off our bags at the *Apple Tree* and left for the *Omni Shoreham Hotel*. There, we met an aid to Cliff Jackson who escorted us up to his room. I can't remember the aids name, but she was quite gracious. We meet Cliff Jackson in his room, shook hands, and made introductions. My first impression of Mr. Jackson was that *his clock was wound a little tight*, probably justified, given it was the night before the big show.

He was a tall, thin man of stature with a demeanor of concentrated control. After the usual chitchat, his aid handed us a schedule of events and pointed out when we would be brought to the podium and introduced. The two troopers would accept their awards. Mr. Jackson would introduce Danny, then Danny would introduce Paula who would then tell her story.

I particularly didn't want to be on stage during the main event, but they felt I should be up there for support. I begrudgingly relented, knowing Paula would be very nervous. The aid asked us if we knew who Mr. Jackson was. I said, "Yeah, I understand that he's the attorney who represents some of the State Troopers."

"Mr. Jackson used to be close friends with Bill Clinton," the aid said.

She continued, by directing her conversation to Mr. Jackson, "Tell them Cliff, of your association with Bill Clinton. It's a great story. Go ahead Cliff."

We all turned our attention to Mr. Jackson who was standing with a hotel room glass in his hand. He had a boyish grin on his face and for a moment seemed to be in reflection.

"Well, let's see. Bill and I were friends way back when we went to school together at Oxford. We were both very young and full of political aspirations. Bill's were somewhat different from my own, but then the country was in a

Without Apology

highly controversial war. A lot of young people back then, and that certainly included Bill Clinton, had strong views about American military deployment to Cambodia. Back then, Bill actively organized and participated in anti-war demonstrations in the States and in England where he attended on a Rhodes scholarship."

"Well...to make a long story short, his name came up for the draft. I pulled some strings with some influential friends when working for the state Republican party on his behalf. This required Bill to attend the ROTC program at the University of Arkansas. Bill agreed to attend ROTC training, so this killed the draft notice, thus allowing him to avoid reporting on his induction date. Now this is the kicker—to be legally enrolled in the ROTC program, you have to also be enrolled at the university attending classes full time. Bill was not enrolled at the Arkansas law school at that time. He went back to Oxford for a second year and reneged on his promises to attend the University of Arkansas.

"Now what saved Bill's goose was when President Nixon enacted a lottery for the draft. Bill drew a high number and that assured him he wouldn't get drafted. Only then did he send a letter to Col. Holmes stating that he wasn't going to attend ROTC."

I interrupted Cliff's story. "Who's this Col. Holmes?"

"Oh, I'm sorry. He was commander of the University of Arkansas ROTC program. Oh, by the way, Col. Holmes was the only person who could change Clinton's draft status from a 1-A to a 1-D. A 1-D status meant that Clinton was deferred from being drafted."

Paula, feeling a little left out of the conversation said, "I was gonna ask you what that 1A-D stuff meant."

Cliff smiled at her and continued his story. "Since Bill didn't show up to fulfill his obligation, it left me holding the bag since it was me who had pulled some strings with my boss in the first place. After all this time he's come full circle to become a political hot potato."

" It's hard to explain to some families why their sons made the supreme sacrifice for their country and the guy who sits in the White House chose to cheat his way out of the draft. He makes a mockery of those who gave their lives for the right of all people to live in a free democracy."

"Mr. Jackson," I said. "I don't get it. I mean—that would make him AWOL when he failed to show up at ROTC, right?"

"Well, it's a bit confusing, but I like your train of thought, Stephen, but no, it wouldn't make him AWOL. His 1-A reclassification the previous year was a mute position, because in 1969 President Nixon initiated a lottery based on birthdays putting Bill outside the realm of being drafted."

"Well, whatever way you slice it, sounds to me that he should've been a fugitive of the military. You'd think that kind of stigma would've hurt his political aspirations."

"Your wrong there, Stephen. The draft rolled off his back like water rolls off duck feathers. Bill hit the ground running, he moved up quickly politically. You have to remember, back then there was a lot of indignation toward the war, so Bill came out clean as a whistle."

So, I said to Cliff, "That's a shame. Hey, now I remember who you are. You're the guy who broke the story a while back about Clinton being a draft dodger."

"That's right. I helped to make public the letter Bill sent to Col. Holmes."

"Now that you mention it, it seems like I do remember reading about a letter that said something about him not liking the Government's policy on the war back then or something like that."

"It was quite a bit more specific than that, Stephen. Bill was quoted in the letter as saying, 'Why should he be made to fight in a war that he despised and a military that he loathed.' Around that same time, Bill even went so far as to travel to Moscow. A communist country that supported and supplied the North Vietnamese that killed US soldiers."

There was a long silent pause. I cleared my throat to say, "I guess back then you were left holding the bag sounds like you're the first back he stepped on while climbing to the top."

"Nope, Stephen, I don't believe I was the first. That's why I'm representing these State Troopers, to make sure their rights don't get stepped on. Bill

Clinton used them for personal reasons and made promises he had no intention of keeping. It's our intersection of indifference that makes it a privilege to represent these State Troopers."

I stood up from sitting on the end of the bed and said, "Boy, after listening to you, Jane Fonda must have been Bill Clinton's locker door poster girl."

"Be careful, Stephen. You need to watch what you say, and to whom you say it to. There are ears everywhere."

"Thanks for the advice. I do have the tendency to shoot from the lips without thinking of the consequences. If I don't see it coming, I can be very reactionary."

Paula blurted out, "I believe the word is over-reactionary, buster."

Everyone laughed.

"All right—all right," I said "You've got me there."

In closing, Cliff said "Well, it's very late and you guys better get some shuteye, because it's going to be a big day tomorrow. By the way Paula, it was a pleasure meeting you. Don't look so nervous, all you have to do is tell your story. I'm sure you'll do fine."

"Well I hope I do alright." Paula says, "Jus' look at my hand shaking."

She puts them out to show everyone. Mr. Jackson took Paula's hands, held them firmly and with a warm smile he said, "Mrs. Jones, you're going to do just fine."

That father figure assurance is just what Paula needed and her demeanor changed immediately. We all shook hands again and Trailer, Paula and I caught a cab to our hotel.

I looked through the itinerary and saw that Ollie North, along with Vice-President Dan Quayle, would be speaking.

I said to Paula and Trailer while riding in the cab, "Hey, I'd sure like to meet these two guys. I really admire both immensely, especially Vice-President Quayle. I remember reading during the time of the Gulf War, there was a point where the military higher-uppers advised the Bush administration that they had met their objective and Kuwait was liberated. The Iraqis had abandoned their military vehicles, planes, and heavy armor tanks for fear of being annihilated. Remember that Danny?"

He nodded, and Paula just rolled her eyes.

"Anyway, the article went on to say that for months the CIA had been working with these local tribes called the Curds to help overthrow Saddam's regime. All we had to do was seize the abandoned military surplus and train the Curds. These Curd guys were pee-o'd and had plenty of enthusiasm considering their villages had been decimated by poisoned gas, compliments of that crazy asshole. Jus' like most great plans, there's always a monkey in the wrench.

"Some of Bush's closest advisors and strategists said to go any further would be detrimental to the Arab alliance. Now, I believe most strategists are void of humanity. They only factor in what looks good on paper, and forget about the human factor. You know, like the Bay of Pigs and pulling out of Saigon just to name a few. But anyway, there was one man who stood up and questioned the veracity of that human factor. He had doubts about not seizing all that abandoned military hardware. You know who that man was?"

"No," Paula said.

"But I'm sure Mr. Military genius here, is going to tell us."

"Paula, thanks for your sarcastic support, especially in front of your yellow dog attorney."

Danny just sat there quietly smiling and probably thinking at how Paula and I ever made it as a couple. Anyway I said, "That man was Dan Quayle. This is the same man who was chastised by the media because he misspelled that one simple word."

"What word?" Paula asked.

"P-o-t-a-t-o-e." I spelled out slowly.

Everyone laughed. So, I asked them.

"What's so damn funny? What'd I say?"

"You can't spell worth a flip; potato ain't got no *e* on the end of it." Paula said.

"So what," I said.

111

"Most guys are poor spellers anyway, right Danny?" I looked at Danny for male support.

"Don't look at me." Danny smiled back, "I can spell potato."

"Yeah right," I said, "that's because you're a yellow dog Democrat."

"Oh brother, Stephen Jones! Do we have to listen to more?"

"Hold your Tater Tots, baby, I'm almost finished. Anyhow, Saddam was allowed to go back and re-arm his troops to slaughter the Curd rebellion faster than you can say 'Allah be praised.'

"Don't cha' get it? Our historical American diplomacy repeats itself. You know, it's a damn shame that some Curds didn't study Native American history before giving their life for an American diplomacy of broken promises."

Catching Paula ready to part those Red Sea lips of criticism, I lightened the tone by saying, "Yes, Paula, you can add Monday night quarterbacking to my resume. Okay, here's our hotel."

"Thank God!" Paula said, "Before you go into another know-all-story."

We never got the chance to meet both Ollie North, and Vice-President Dan Quayle. By the time we got there, they had left the building.

When we did arrive at the *Omni Shoreham Hotel* on February 11, 1994, I looked up at the ominous, steel gray sky looming down on us,

and the bitter bite of cold air lapping at the corners of a stack of newspapers that had been dropped near the entrance. Umm… I thought, *Bad omen, looks like a storm's about to brew!* Damn, don't ya' just hate those premonitions!

We were quickly directed to a suite that was used as a green room. My understanding was that we were to go up to the podium right after the State Troopers were given their whistle-blowers award for coming forward about witnessing Bill and Hillary's game of mutual self-inflicted infidelities. They called it Trooper Gate. I guess Watergate set the prerequisite for future presidential scandals.

The bottom line is that these guys were miffed off because Clinton had promised to take care of the ol' boy's school when he went to Washington. Clinton had made a classic buddy mistake. Don't pluck the feathers when you flock together. Revenge, along with lucrative prospects, makes key *in-greed-ients*.

Clinton's smooth tactics of using people to get to the top was about to bite him in his cheeky Lilly.

I just had an epiphany in the middle of telling this story...*Could this all be about jobs?* I mean, think about it. The troopers just mentioned were pee-o'd because of not getting jobs! Paula, who went up to meet Clinton in the hopes of getting a better job, later Kathleen Wiley did the same, but somehow she managed to shake hands with his cabinet member inside the oval office. Then, along came Lewinsky, who reciprocated by taking dictation. All for jobs, Monica, used her leverage of indignity to arrange for Clinton to get her a job through his close friend, and adviser, Vernon Jordan. Metaphorically speaking, I guess one could say it all depends on what the word job is, is.

Again, I don't want to lose those of you who don't know the coined term 'is' is. It was a play on words used by the infamous snake oil man himself, Bill Clinton. While under oath in his grand jury testimony Bill was asked why he wasn't lying when he said, "there's nothing going on between us" when asked by a top aid about Monica. Clinton's response back to the grand jury,

"It depends on what the meaning of the word 'is' is."

Chapter Eight

We walked single file, Danny, Paula and then me. When we got to the entrance in the back, I could see that it was standing room only. I heard the presentations to the troopers. Suddenly, everything seemed to be going in three-quarter speed. It was like an all-encompassing cerebral numbness causing an F/X effect, with shrouds of backlights flashing, emulating slow motion. In a split second, I was drawn into instant recall of a vertiginous black hole in my past where bloodsucking zombies chased me around at my first haunted house experience. I instinctively had the urge to run. Only then did I realize that these were not backlights and zombies, but camera flashes.

My corneas must have oversized a thousand times before I could focus. I thought to myself, *See what happens when you make a knee jerk decision from angry emotions. You just took a big pull off a chunk of tobacco and forgot to spit. What happened to having it quietly resolved, huh?* Now, the whole world is going to know who the Paula is in that *American Spectator* article. I can see it now—Paula will appear on all those sleazy, cheap game shows with a drum roll in the background. A guy is standing in front of these three contestants with his trousers around his ankles. The MC will announce, "Will the real Paula Jones please step forward."

Stephen M. Jones, Jr.

What the hell am I thinking! How did I let myself get talked into this? Get over it! You knew once the cat was out of the bag the shit would hit the fan! Now you're having second thoughts right before the dam breaks. Get over it, Focus... Even if you don't know why the hell you're here, at least act like you do! Shrug it off, snap out of it. Repeat this three times, "Do not allow ridiculous thoughts to enter my mind!" There you go, take a deep breath; you need to be there for Paula.

You know, it's psychotic what runs through a person's mind under stressful situations.

We were told that there would be quite a few media affiliations present, but we weren't prepared for such graphic proportions. The flutter of the shutter of every cameraman must have been set on full automatic. It reminded me of the sudden sound of wings when walking up on a covey of quail.

We quickly moved up to the podium where a line of chairs toward the back awaited us. Cliff Jackson moved to the podium where there was an array of media affiliated microphones piled into position. I leaned over to Paula and squeezed her trembling hand to give her support and whispered in her ear, "I'm right here for you. All you have to do is tell it like it was. If you feel that you can't go any farther, just take a few deep breaths. Look back to me—I'll be right there, okay?"

At that moment, I looked up above my head and noticed a big furry boom microphone. A guy was on the other end of the podium holding a ten-foot pole fishing in on our personal conversation. I reached up and pushed it away and gave the guy that was holding it an, "I'll put that where the sun doesn't shine," if you do it again look.

Cliff introduced Danny first to the podium. Danny said that he had prepared a few words then he would introduce Paula. Those few words turned out to be a draft of *War and Peace*. Maybe that's an overstatement, because I wanted the whole thing over and done with as quickly as possible. So, I probably exaggerated real time, but my point was that it had consumed my patience. I was beginning to hallucinate that we were Liberals holding up Walter Mondale for President signs at the Democratic convention where Clinton had given his long-winded *put ya' to sleep* speech. I was drifting in and out of thought as Danny was reaching the end of his evocation. If only the term *fifteen minutes of fame* were true and you could melt back into the abyss of anonymity. You know, an event in one's life that's blurred by the passages of time and no one remembers it, but for some God knows reason, it pop's into your minds eye just to haunt your ass! Fortunately by then I'll be too old to give a damn. As my luck runs, I'll probably be in some retirement home all but forgotten, sitting there watching *I love Lucy* re-runs too old and too weak to reposition my bony butt because I'm sitting on my saggy useless balls, barely able to scratch the shingles on my bare head swaddled in a heavy sweater to cure the chill in my bones until sleep catches up with me again and again! I swear to God, Danny if you don't shut your pie hole soon!

Get a grip, cut him some slack. It's not everyday you go from Dog Patch USA to a lawyer being in the majors. Here we go he's about to introduce Paula. I rubbed Paula on her back as if to give her enough strength to persevere and told her, "Just go up there, and tell them what happened in that hotel room. That's all you gotta do."

And that's just what she did. Of course she was nervous, but as she continued to speak, her confidence grew. I was amazed how she drifted from passionate control to a burst of almost uncontrollable anger. She seemed to relive the embarrassing and humiliating exposer as if under hypnosis. Paula shook as she explained how Clinton reached up her culottes and tried to kiss her.

There was a combination of anger and emotional trauma in her voice. She had just told how she regained her composure then casually moved away from the window which overlooked the Arkansas River to sit down at the end of the couch. She continued to explain that she had asked Clinton how his wife, Hillary, was doing. She told the audience that by saying this, maybe he would get the message to back off, at which point Clinton in one fluid motion pulled his pants down and sat down beside her. Paula said, "I was shocked to see that the Governor was in an aroused state."

As I sat there listening to Paula trying to explain in a way that wasn't too explicitly graphic, I thought back to what she had told me. Aroused state—my ass! He was buck-naked from the waist down and was slapping his boner back and forth like a slinky toy made by Wham-O!

Paula continued to say, "He asked me to kiss it. I was so taken back I jus' couldn't think. I sat there frozen. I didn't know what to do. Then I jumped up and said I'm not that kind of girl and headed for the door."

As she said this, I looked out over the crowd of media. You could have heard a pin drop. I admired her courage to get up there and share with the world what kind of man uses his position to procure a woman with the help of the police.

How precarious Paula must have felt, not being able to summon the police for help. Unknown to her at the time, Buddy Young, the big chief of police, was Clinton's zipper man. The Governor's security detail, as it was called, was made up of hand-picked State Troopers. Buddy Young was at the top of Clinton's good ole ol' boys circle of friend's social club. With that kind of power, Clinton practically ran around the state of Arkansas as if he had diplomatic immunity.

If the women that Clinton had a sexual relationship with, or sexually harassed, tried to speak out, Buddy was there to threaten with personal harm. Sorta' like Buddy giving Bill an *all you can poke free* pass at Miss Kitty's dude ranch.

Here's a Police Chief willing to wear the badge of compromised authority. The onyx of impeccable corruption; this gem would be mounted in the crown of Clinton's administration. I mean, this guy was so obedient that Bill even named his dog after him.

So who was Paula gonna run to for help? The police? Hell, they're the ones who brought her up there. What a sad state for her to be in.

That's not to say that Paula should have bolted the first time Clinton made a move on her in that room. I guess it's easy to say what you would do in a situation like that when you were not up there. I know that those were demons I internally fought with.

I couldn't understand why she went up there in the first place. The only thing I could figure out was that Paula loves attention and I believe that she

117

was flattered because Bill Clinton wanted to meet her. I believe she genuinely thought that after talking to her friend Pam about going to meet the Governor she could use her femininity to boost her ego, and if she was lucky, acquire a better job at the state. What Paula had in mind, and what Clinton had, were quite different. I know Paula and since she was the focus of the Governor's attention, she felt the ingredients of a little innocent flirting was called for, especially aimed toward a man in his position. The recipe called for one sugar free box of instant gratification mixed with a quarter cup of self-esteem to boost sweetness. Next, two minutes to seep allowing the opportunity to brew for a better job. Blend well, and serve hot. She thought she could control the situation to her benefit. Paula didn't check the temperature setting for her recipe for innocent flirting. Her light *soufflé* turned out to be a flaming *ala-cocka*.

By her staying, when first subjected to outrageous behavior then trying to do damage control, she ignited the fuse of a well-seasoned predator. She was way over her head in shark-infested water. Even if Paula was naive in her thinking and stayed when all the signals said run like hell, that didn't give Clinton a license to drop his trousers. I mean, how does one grow balls big enough to expose himself to a complete stranger and then ask them to give you a blowjob? Maybe you have to have big balls for compensation, because the way Paula described it, a parakeet couldn't perch on his twig without falling off. You'd think—that alone would be a good reason why not to expose yourself! All and all, he's someone who is in need of some serious therapy.

I thought about his *no-shame tactic* and I've come to the conclusion that Clinton must have performed these acts so many times that it didn't even affect his moral conscience. How else could a man do such a thing void of shame? Of course that reminds me of a biblical adage, "Before thou judge, yet ye be judged"

So with that, I can't say that I haven't had my fair share of rendezvous in my hay day, but I could never expose myself to someone I just met for the first time only moments before, or for that matter, even casually know. Well, that's for a panel of Hollywood therapists to figure out, not for me to find reason behind his screwed-up childhood that probably germinated this outrageous behavior. I can tell you one damn thing—I betch'a a dime to a dollar that as a young boy, he pulled the wings off butterflies.

Don't think family values matter growing up? Then what rock do you live under?

Drifting back to reality, Paula's now just finished telling her story and was fielding questions from the press core. They asked some of the same questions I had asked, "Why did you go up there? Why didn't you leave when he made a sexual advance? Why are you just now coming forward?"

Sitting there listening, I couldn't stop myself from thinking that deep in the pit of my bowels I still had the stinking feeling that our whole purpose for coming forward was getting out of hand. By kicking it up a notch with Paula telling her story, we invited a whole host of new supporters that I wasn't sure were friend or foe. Sometimes events move so quickly that you can't distinguish the good from the bad.

So there I was, contemplating the gravity of the whole damn thing when I heard my name called, "Mr. Jones, Mr. Jones... Can we ask you a few questions? Can you step up to the podium please?"

I knew it—I knew that I couldn't get out unnoticed. You can't stick your head in front of a fan, spit and not get spat back on.

Stay strong and right a wrong. Don't make them aware what's going on with your inner struggle. Support your wife and vindicate the good name. Keep it short and to the point. As I kept talking to myself and walked the few steps to stand next to Paula, I grabbed her hand to give her a gentle squeeze of admiration. I knew it was tough for her to tell her story behind closed doors, but enormously difficult in front of the conduit to the world's conscious. To be cast into a whirlwind of uncertainty can be too much to ask of anybody.

"Excuse me, Mr. Jones."

I looked in the direction of the sound bite. A tall man in his sixties stood in a pool of reporters and asked, "Mr. Jones I couldn't help noticing that throughout your wife telling her harrowing experiences you looked very uncomfortable and if you don't mind me saying so, you look a little agitated. Do you disagree with your wife telling her story?"

Damn, the guy had read me like a blind man reading brail.

"Look," I said, "I'm just here today to stand beside Paula to support her. And if I look upset it's because of what happened to her. No man should get away with that. We're here today to get the story straight and for Paula to regain her good name."

I later learned that the reporter who had asked me those questions was a man named Reed Irvine from *Accuracy in Media*. It was one of a few Washington conservative *think tanks* that publish editorials of current events. I later lean on Reed for a good source of quick information. Reed, without his knowledge of being indoctrinated, became a member of my own homegrown cabinet of advisors. At times of crises, I would seek out Reed and others for their views and opinions. *A man who acts alone is alone.*

Once I built up my cabinet, I would choose who to call based on their expertise with the situation at hand. I learned to mentally disassociate myself from an issue that may require a very personal action or response. I asked for views from people I trusted. Then I assimilated the variables from each person I called. I tried to be totally objective from the outside looking in. This exercise of serendipity served me well, so as to keep my personal feelings out of the mix, hence no more knee-jerk reactions, or so I thought.

Although I never traveled in Reed's circles I would like to thank him for his generosity to right a wrong. I felt that he was a man of great integrity in an environment where the word *integrity* is lost in a hypocoristic inner sanctum society of news reporting. Reed was that *island in the horizon* that a survivor spots as his raft starts to crumble from the vast ocean waves slamming the unassuming against its reef of skepticism. *God, I love metaphors.*

We left the conference room in the same melee we came in, pushing and wedging our way through the avalanche of media coverage.

After the press conference, we were hustled into that green room of a suite that was set up by the Legal Affairs Council. It was an organization that

Stephen M. Jones, Jr.

I'd never heard of until Paula and I were introduced to its President, Richard Delgaudio.

Richard seemed a nice enough fellow. He was about 5'8" in stature, but whatever he lacked in physicality he made up in robustness. Richard could put more words into one breath than most people can say to each other over dinner on the first date. Bluntly, he could talk the socks off a man with frostbitten feet! His fast talking put me on guard, but his genuine hospitality gave me a sense of solace.

Paula and I hadn't even had time to get our bearings or so much as a handshake or a "Howdy Partner," when Cliff Jackson told us that a horde of media reporters were requesting a personal interview.

"What do you guys want to do?" Cliff asked.

I was uneasy about this coming-out media exposure thing. We hadn't gotten over the tingly sensation of butterflies from the first roller coaster ride, just to be asked if we wanted seconds. So I asked, "Say, is this really how things in Washington are orchestrated?"

Cliff just laughed and said, "Pretty much, Steve. You and Paula just got baptized *Washington-style*. Again, what do you guys want to do?"

Inside, I felt it was a bad move and I was uncomfortable. Outside, I felt empowered with this eager, newfound support from sympathetic ears. I thought to myself, *Right now it's about seizing the opportunity.* I had that overpowering *Moe* urge to poke the eyes of my opponent— that being Clinton.

At this point, I had not learned to control my knee-jerk reflex. I was pissed that this thing could've been quietly taken care of by a simple apology. I thought back to what Daniel Trailer told me, his long time friend with the Clinton administration had said, "You can do whatever you want. It never happened. Clinton has no knowledge of ever meeting her. It's just another one of those *bimbo eruptions*. This will be the last and only comment. There will be no further correspondence on the matter."

The more I thought about it, the angrier I got. *Who the hell does he think he is? Just because he's an elected official, he thinks he can use his power of influence*

121

Without Apology

for some morbid medieval right to any lady in waiting that he feels has that come hither look. And hey, what's wrong with a little eye for an eye, tooth for a tooth?

By the way, what feels better? To lie down and squeal like a pig. Or strike back with deliverance to keep your integrity and protect your family name. Damn those big heads and banjos. So, now my inner sanctum of neutrons had a coup to overthrow the rational regime that was echoing, Be-care-ful, remember The Alamo.

Little did I know this decision I was about to make would turn out to be the first move of a very long played-out game of high stakes Chess.

For me, I chose to play the game behind the scene. *I will become like the tip of the iceberg that ripped through the side of the Titanic, small and insignificant on the surface, but a mountain of strength below.* I looked up to Mr. Jackson, who was still waiting for our response and said, "What the hell, let's finish this ride." Checkmate.

The reporters wanted to interview me, Paula and Danny. The way Paula had handled herself at the conference, I felt that she would do fine. She was a natural in front of the cameras. I mean, she did better than I could have done given the same circumstances.

I wanted to sit in while she was interviewed to make sure she wouldn't get hurt by inappropriate questions from some rogue. *I may have not have been there for her before, in her hour of need, but I'm here now.*

So I asked Paula how she felt about giving an interview and to my surprise, she took to it like mother's milk. I told her I was amazed and proud of the way she handled herself in front of all those cameras.

She said, "It's easy when you tell the truth."

What's that adage, "The truth will set you free?"

Just then, Cliff Jackson put in an interesting thought, "Why don't you give it to the *Washington Post*, one of the most Liberal publications out there?"

So I said, "I don't know why not, I think that's a good idea. That way, they can't say it's political or bias. I want people on both sides of the fence to come together on this, whatcha' say Paula, want to give these guys a shot?"

Paula quipped, "Why yeah, I don't see why not either. We got nothing to hide. Let's talk to 'um."

Stephen M. Jones, Jr.

"How about it Danny, what ya' think?"

"Well, as Paula's lawyer, I need to be in on the interview, but I think it's a good idea to give it to the *Post*."

"It's settled then, I'll bring in the reporter from the Post," Cliff said.

After a few minutes, in stepped a tall, lanky guy in his late thirties with pen and pad in hand. He introduced himself as Evan Thomas with the *Washington Post*. He seemed nice enough at the time and wasted no time interviewing Paula with Danny. An hour later, Shepherd was finished and we had a chance to relax for a while from an extraordinary day that will live in infamy to those of us who should have known better.

We all turned on the TV for local and evening news to monitor any response. Back then, the evening news was still king, not cable. Now you'd think with the zoo of media reporters, it would have been breaking news on every channel. But no, if mentioned at all, it was a blimp on the radar screen. The media, for the most part, was a friend of Bill's, which equates to the phrase, "*birds of a feather flock together.*" It seemed that no one was ready to be the first network to provide airtime on Presidential allegations.

The nightly news at the end of their program simply made a short comment, "The annual Republican Conference was hosted today at the *Omni Shoreham Hotel*. The keynote speakers were former Vice-President Dan Quayle and the still controversial Oliver North. A woman at the conference has accused the then Governor of Arkansas, Bill Clinton, of sexual overtones. "That's the way it was today February 11, 1994." Wow, talk about lost in translation.

That afternoon the weather turned for the worse, it started sleeting and snowing. Our flights were cancelled and Reagan National was closed. I called the *Apple Tree Hotel* for an extra night but was told that there was no availability.

There we were—thrown out in the cold and nowhere to go. When Richard learned of our dilemma, he and his associates were very gracious and invited us to be their guests. The suite that was used as the green room was at our disposal. I hated to feel obligated, but Richard just smiled at me and said,

123

"Stephen, this place is already paid for and no one is staying here, so make yourselves at home."

It kinda bugged me, but where else were we going to stay? So we gratefully accepted. Paula's lawyer, Danny, stayed in an adjoining suite.

The next morning Cliff had already gathered newspapers that were represented at the conference. It was the same blip that had been reported on the tube the night before. *The Washington Post*, that we invited to a personal interview, had the story buried in the style section.

The story played it off as just another among several unsubstantiated allegations of bimbo eruptions that's plagued the administration since Clinton took office. The right-wing agenda will stop short of nothing to get at Clinton. They made him sound like he was the victim. Boy—that just chapped my ass.

Now if the right wing agenda had a leader, I never met him. However, I was starting to see how the media works first hand. Most all media affiliates are politically biased. The majority have very liberal agendas. Bill Clinton was their poster boy and by giving the interview to the *Post* we were playing on Bill and Hillary's home field turf.

That same morning, we spent time with the two Arkansas State Troopers who had been honored at the conference that the media called, Trooper Gate. One of their attorneys by the name of Lynn Davis introduced Roger Perry and Larry Patterson to Paula and me.

We talked formally at first, which is normal when you meet someone new. As the water warmed between us, the troopers started talking openly about Clinton's sexual escapades. We listened to stories of how they had witnessed and helped Clinton procure women. They said that while Clinton was Governor, he could be just as at home cruising up and down Roosevelt Boulevard in his midnight blue Lincoln Continental picking up toothless prostitutes, as well as being with some very attractive ladies. His libido had no particulars.

One trooper added, "He really liked black women…you know what they say… "The blacker the berry, the sweeter the cherry."

Paula looked confused. "What's that mean?"

Giving the troopers a look of toning it down, I said to her, "Oh it's just a term that means Clinton liked women of color, that's all."

Larry recalled once when he had accompanied Clinton to Dillard's department store to find a birthday gift for Chelsea. Bill spotted a black beauty working at the store. He wouldn't leave her alone until he got her number.

"Boy Howdy," Paula said, "It's a wonder he didn't get some disease chasing after all those women."

"Well," the Trooper said, "I ain't saying he did and I'm not saying he didn't, but what I am saying is, he didn't use protection."

Paula looked even more confused. "Protection?"

"You know Paula…a raincoat." I told her.

"Well, what's he need that for? He had his security detail protecting him. Was it raining?"

I got a little frustrated at Paula's unbelievable naiveness as Roger, one of the troopers, started snickering. So I said, "Paula—what he's talking about here is Clinton didn't use a condom. Geez … It's not like you fell off the turnip wagon yesterday. Here I am trying to be nice in my definition, and not say the word rubber."

"Oh…" she said slowly. "Well, why didn't you jus' come out and say so in the first place. Besides, you didn't use one either."

Everyone laughed. I felt a flush of embarrassment along with getting a dose of my own medicine.

"Alright Paula," I said; "Whose side are you on anyway? I'm not the one who dropped trousers on a woman I never met."

She narrowed her eyes with a devilishly teasing smile, knowing she just got my goat.

Larry went on to explain that on first-time encounters, Clinton would only have oral sex. "He'd only go all the way with women he had regular affairs with." Roger then said; "Clinton had a morbid understanding about oral sex. He believed that having oral sex, as explained in the Bible, was not adulterous. So in his mind, he wasn't cheating on Hillary."

I said, "Well, that must have been in his earlier years of tribulation, because it doesn't sound like it bothers him now. I read somewhere about him being with..., damn, what's her name, Paula? You're up on all those tabloids. You know the one who lived in the Qawpaw area. Remember? The article said that Clinton would jog a short distance from the Governor's mansion, making believe he was just going to McDonalds for an Egg McMuffin. Then he'd slip on down to her place for a little croissant and cream cheese."

"Oh, you're talking about Gennifer Flowers."

"Yeah, yeah—that's her. And then there's another one named—"

"Sally Purdue."

"Thanks, honey, very much for jogging my memory."

"You're welcome very much," Paula replied with a slight smile.

I continued saying, "I heard that Purdue was threatened by one of Buddy Young's thugs if she opened her mouth about anything."

Larry said, "We know, Steve, but the two women you just mentioned, were not one-night stands. Clinton couldn't use his Bible on them."

"Except maybe to prop up their butts for leverage," I added.

Paula said, "Oh my... Steve Jones you are so bad. Mama would never talk to you again if she heard you say that. Especially about using the good book for something like that."

"Gimme a break, Paula, there was a time, I can betcha, when your mama picked hayseeds out of her hair from some hayride...hmm, come to think about it, maybe not. Anyhow, what I'm talking about is Clinton mixing apples and oral sex in the Bible. Speaking of the Bible, I believe ol' Adam had some similar problems with apples."

"I'm not sure, Steve, but I'm figuring ya' jus' said something mean about my mama. Don't go there, buster, if'n ya' know what's good for ya'. Anyhow, that's blasphemy to say things like that and for yore information Mister, in the Bible, there ain't nothing about oral sex in the Garden of Even, so git ya' mind outta' the gutter."

"Really," I said. "Adam orally bit into the forbidden apple because of Eve, didn't he now? It's all the same."

"Nah, that's different," Paula said.

"Now where have I heard that statement before? Could it be from you're mama. Come here and give me back my rib, Paula."

"You ain't getting nothing back, Mister."

"Steve," Roger said, "You don't know the half of it when it comes to Buddy Young and Bill Clinton. We want to let everybody know what kind of person is in the White House. Most people only see the outside shell of Bill Clinton and there is so much more. The outside persona is very approachable. He will listen, with interest, on what anyone has to say, no matter who they are. He can make you believe he is your best friend, a true politician.

"Now on the inside, if you get in his way, he'll stab you in the back and leave you hanging out to dry. He is a master of disguise."

Larry, the other State Trooper said, "Clinton had a state employee by the name Betsy Wright and it was her job to shut down all the bimbo eruptions. From what I hear, it was Hillary, not Bill, who hired her. If Betsy couldn't get the job done, Buddy Young was called in as the strong arm.

"Both Larry and I have been threatened and told 'if you know what's good for you, you'll keep your mouth shut.'"

"That's scaring me," Paula said.

"Well, Paula," Larry said, "All I can say is that it's a good thing you don't live in Arkansas anymore. Plus, you coming out like this and telling your story helps you tremendously. The more high profile you are, the less likely you could have a *so-called* accident."

I noticed that the conversation was getting to Paula.

"Oh my," Paula said. "We use'ta live in the back of nowhere in Arkansas. Thank God we moved. I was so scared to be out there by myself. If we lived there now, with all this stuff going on and somebody knocked on the door at night, I'd probably pass out from fright."

Trying to take her mind off the...*someone might be out to get her theory*, I said, "Paula, why don't you give your mama a call and see how Madison's doing?"

I thought maybe she would give me some grief by my suggestion, but to my surprise, she seemed to be relieved to be out of the conversation. When she walked away, I asked the troopers to lighten up in front of her from now on.

"She can get a little hysterical about safety. A good indication that she came close to the *point of no return* is how her eyeballs became saucer-shaped when you talked about *so-called accidents*. I mean, she's still very nervous about this *coming out thing* anyway."

Roger agreed. "Yeah, you're right Steve. I could see that she was getting a little shook up.

Larry joined in, "I don't think I've seen anyone stretch their eyes open that wide without them popping out, but listen Steve, we're serious. Watch your butt. The higher profile you are, the safer you are. Believe me when I say that if the Clintons, by thinking Paula telling her story will affect their eight-year plan, then the least you can expect is both barrels loaded with character assassination. I'm giving you fair warning—they can clean your plow. Bill and Hillary will stop at nothing to get at her. And oh—by the way, Hillary is the nastier of the two. That woman sure has a mouth. When she gets mad, every other word is fuck, fuck-um, or fucker. Seriously, the woman is tough as nails and has absolutely no conscious."

Paula walked up from behind and picked up part of what Larry had just said. I could sense the concern on her face so I needed to change the subject in a hurry.

"How's Madison doing?"

"Just fine. Mama said he's sound asleep."

Still looking rattled, I said in a half jokingly manner, "It's alright, honey, you needn't worry about all these people. We'll just sic Mitzie on um."

I turned to the troopers to explain. "When you knock on our door, our dog sounds like a T-rex on the other side. She's really just a pussycat with a lot of hot air and teeth."

"Boy howdy," Paula responded, "She bit my sister Charlotte's nose and it bled for two days."

Good, I thought. *A little conflict will help get her mind off all that cloak and dagger stuff.*

So I said, "No, she did not. She jumped up and bopped your sister in the nose with her snout. There was not so-much-as a tooth mark on her nose."

"Well, even if she didn't," Paula said, "It's a good thing my sister didn't sue you."

"Is that right?" I said dryly. "It's not like Uncle Sam doesn't give 'um enough each month for sitting on their butts. You know… for some reason Mitzie doesn't seem to like your sister. You think she senses something we don't? You know dogs are like that. Most of 'em are a good judge of character.
"

Paula in defense of her sister blasted,

"No! That's not it. You're just jealous, that's all."

My facial expression contorted into disbelief as my scheme to take Paula's mind off the scary stuff completely backfired.

And I start to say, "What, I—"

Paula interrupted,

"That's right, Mister. They get by better than us with less, that's all I'm saying."

Feeling a little pee-o'd I said,

"Maybe you're right, Paula, but think about it. With them receiving welfare, along with disability money, they live the Arkansas dream. Damn. They got it all, living in that big ol' roomy house trailer."

They can sit out on the front porch taking in the cool afternoon air admiring that 77 Trans AM parked in their dirt driveway. Yee haw."

I had pushed more buttons—always taking it too far, not realizing that I was hurting Paula's feelings talking about her family in front of strangers until it was too late.

Never ever never produce a round up yell when you think you're on top. I truly believe that yelling can produce negative cogitations, just ask Howard Dean.

I tried to smooth things over by using a steamroller. So I said,

"Look, honey, I know it's your sister-n-all and blood is supposed to be thicker than water. I just hope they stand by you the way you stand by them, because I personally think they're not worth a damn.

"Hell, they've got two kids to support and all they do is sit around and graze like two cows in a field of clover leeching off the welfare system. I don't know about you, but there's something wrong with that picture sweetheart. I mean—really can you imagine…"

Paula turned away from me in mid-sentence and walked over to the troopers who, sensing our friction, had drifted to the other end of the large suite.

Now, I was standing all alone, thinking what a great job I had done changing the subject just to make the situation worse. Feeling a little awkward, I looked around and recognized an old friend of mine named Jack Daniels. I quickly poured myself a double dose of shame relief.

Eavesdropping, I heard Paula say to the trooper Larry, "You look so familiar to me."

He said, "Yep, I remember you, too, Paula. I didn't want to bring it up unless you did first. You're the one who was in the rotunda when Bill hollered your name."

"Yes, yes that's right."

"Hey, Stephen, that proves Bill Clinton knows who I am—See."

I raised my glass toward her in a half-hearted jester as if to say, *"Good for you."*

She disengaged me and easily ignored my solitary toast, giving me a dose of my own asinine medicine.

"Paula," the trooper said, "They're lying if they say Bill Clinton doesn't know who you are. If you want an affidavit of what happened in the rotunda, I'll be happy to swear to it."

While the weather closed down much of Washington, the doors of opportunity for retribution opened. There was a moment of reflection for the Clintons and us to let bygones be bygones. I had wished earlier at the press conference that we'd never come to Washington and it was all a big mistake. This wasn't exactly how I wanted to go about getting a retraction and apology. On the other hand, we tried to do this quietly through Danny's connection. Damn monkey wrench.

Let's look at the teeter totter of provocation. A friend of Paula's helped her retain a friend who knew a friend of Clinton's. Confused? There's got to be some historical irony in so far as the opportunist of a few can undermine the greater good of the majority.

For all I knew, while contemplating the voracity, was that door number one was closed and for that matter, we got downright insulted in the process. "She's a gold digging bimbo and trailer park trash."

For all Clinton knew, he was not going to allow being blackmailed, "Danny extorting for real estate profit."

Both sides wanted resolve, but misunderstood. The arson of greed ignited a firestorm of hate.

The press conference drew more media than flies at a summer picnic and then turned their backs on Paula's allegations. They cremated her story just a few hours after they killed it. That was door number two closed.

Revisiting our options, I thought, *what better excuse does one need to fly south for the winter? I'm not one to give up a fight, but looks like we landed with a thud and no bang.* Before I could come to a pondered conclusion of what to do next, door number three opened. In walks Cliff Jackson again purporting that a reporter he knew wanted to do an exclusive investigation of Paula's allegations.

"His name is Michael Isikoff and he works for the *Washington Post*."

My first reaction was negative. "Excuse me, I don't mean to rain on your parade, Cliff, but didn't we already get crapped on by the *Post?*"

After laughing at my lack of formality, he said, "But this guy's different. He wants to go to Arkansas and interview everyone who was involved in Paula's story."

Paula and Danny thought it was a good idea to at least meet Isikoff. As always, I was a little skeptical, but went along with the majority.

So that afternoon we met with Isikoff. My first impression was visual. He was somewhat short in stature with the appearance of having slept in his clothes. Michael had a sort of disheveled look and his round glasses gave him a studious demeanor.

He seemed sincere enough and said that he believed Paula's story. He, along with other staff, were prepared to fly down to Little Rock and talk to all the people involved, including Paula's sisters and her mother.

Our relationship with Izzie, short for Isikoff, would span throughout the lawsuit. As he interviewed Paula, I talked with Danny about some of my concerns.

Earlier in the week I had a conversation with Debbie Ballentine about Danny. She said that Danny and her had been friends like forever, and he had helped her with her divorce. She said they had often partied together on what she called his *party barge on the lake*. In this same conversation, she pretty much said it was a free-for-all. Kegs of beer, bags of marijuana and snorts of coke were always around at these parties.

She noticed the concern on my face when telling me this, so she said, "We had some really good times together, but I swear to God, Steve, Danny's a real good friend and can be trusted."

Debbie told Danny that he'd better take care of Paula, and make sure she's not hurt in all this. Debbie went on to say that Danny's continuous partying was one of the main reasons he and his wife were separated. Debbie finished by telling me, since the split, Danny seemed to be sinking deeper into depression and that Paula's cause might get Danny back on the right track.

Stephen M. Jones, Jr.

I said, "Well, Deb, that was then and this is now. If he's looking for rehabilitation, he can take up basket weaving, dammit. I have enough personal weight own my bunk bed without Danny bouncing up and down on it and trying to rehabilitate himself at my wife's expense."

At the time, I didn't think much about his personal life. Hell—who am I to cast stones. I mean, I'm no shepherd for sainthood, but I don't like loose ends. I've learned that your past can make surprise performances in the most inopportune way.

While listening to one of the troopers comment who the Clintons have done business with, or personally knows every lawyer in town, I noticed Danny's face turn to stone, sitting there sipping on his scotch on the rocks. I felt that Danny's services could be compromised.

Later in the evening we talked. "So, Danny, you being a real estate lawyer and all, have you ever had any dealing with one of Hillary's firms, mainly the Rose Law Firm?"

"Well, Steve-o," said Danny.

Obviously, he was feeling his scotch and water while stirring the ice with his index finger.

"Little Rock is a small city and at the moment I don't recall any dealings with that firm. I might have. I've been to so many company parties."

"Whose parties, Danny? Yours?"

"No, not mine—Roger Clinton's."

"Are you telling me that you've partied with Bill's little brother?"

"Let me tell you, Steve-o, I've partied with some real rock-n-rollers in my time, but Roger's parties were the best."

"Shit-fire, Danny, I don't give a damn about all that. Now listen—can you be gotten to?"

Looking down into his glass of amber liquor like a crystal ball, he summoned his thoughts for clarity of soul and finally said, "I believe this is a little more than a country lawyer can handle. Maybe I can help you guys find someone more qualified than me. You know something, Steve? I'm not a bad lawyer, in fact, I'd say that I'm a pretty good ol' boy and not out to harm anybody. Paula deserves an apology. Let's see that she gets it."

Chapter Nine

Izzie flew to Little Rock with our blessings to investigate and print whatever they found. We flew back home to Los Angeles to await the outcome. Izzie called us about once a week with updated reports. He asked for phone numbers, names, and addresses of people involved.

I remember that Pamela Blackard had concerns about speaking out because she and her husband still worked for the state. After some phone calls from Izzie, she reluctantly agreed to talk. The more Izzie investigated, the more confident he became that Paula was really telling the truth. I think before, he had some doubts about her depiction of the sequence of events that had led up to Clinton's outrageous behavior. Izzie knew that something had happened in that hotel room, but wasn't sure yet just what.

The timeline fit with the hotel logs and there was a private room reserved for the Governor the same day as the AIDC Conference. The witnesses, including both sisters and mother, backed-up what Paula had told them within hours of the encounter which is very interesting since Paula's sister, Charlotte, changed her story when the stakes got higher. Or, shall I say, when it was made worth their while.

A team of Clinton lawyers and investigators rained down on our past and our present. I hate to say it, but I was right about Paula's sister and brother-in-law. You know how I said that blood was supposed to be thicker than water. Not true—especially when it's your own sister stabbing you in the back for a few tokens of gold. Charlotte was Paula's Judas. I think what hurt Paula more than almost anything Bill Clinton could have ever done to her in that hotel room was that her own flesh and blood would lie on her. The fact that I told her so, just rubbed more salt in the wound. I'll talk more about family rats later.

Izzie felt that Pamela Blackard, at first not wanting to come forward was characteristic of someone telling the truth. In theory, a person not wanting to come forward because of retaliatory reasons are judged to be truthful as opposed to someone perceived as just a good friend.

After about a month of investigating, Izzie was putting the finishing touches on his story about Paula's allegations. He sent us a draft of the story that both Paula and I read. I thought it was great. It gave Paula's story legitimacy by using facts, times, witnesses, and places. Not some bimbo popping out of the woodwork for fifteen minutes of fame and misguided fortune, but a woman, victimized by Clinton, who wanted her good name and reputation back.

Izzie said the article would be out soon, maybe in the next week or so. That next week or so turned into three weeks. By then it was clear that the *Washington Post* was sitting on it. The FOB's (friends of Bill) at the *Post* weren't going to print anything that would hurt their political poster boy.

I remember hearing about widow Katherine Graham (then owner of the *Washington Post* and a personal friend of the Clintons) often being a dinner guest at the White House, which leads me to ponder, *why the hell did we go with the Post in the first place? The next time someone suggests a leap of faith, I'll think twice about it; especially when his name starts with Cliff.*

Idiotically, I thought that giving the exclusive to one of the most liberal publications in North America would change the perception that this was not about back door politics, but sexual harassment. The bastards at the *Post* just don't play fair.

I believe you can overplay you hand and I wouldn't make that mistake again. But what it did do, was plant the seed of truth in Bill Clinton's backyard garden of spin control and as any farmer will tell you, it takes time for the seed to take root and grow— and grow it did.

Izzie kept making excuses that it was caused by some inside logistic problems with his editors but after a while, he couldn't deny the fact that his piece was intentionally being stalled. Izzie said that there were both men and women at the *Post* who wanted the story out. Izzie expressed that he would take it to the open-thinkers and see if he could rally some support. A few days later, we caught wind of a filibuster between Izzie and one of his editors, Fred Barbash. Izzie and Barbash had gotten into a shoving powder-puff match. I imagined it much like a jealous outbreak in a gay bar. Example,

"Ouch... You broke a nail."

"You bitch, that hurt."

Not to say that they're gay, it's just how I imagined an established liberal editorial newsroom cat-fight to be. So don't read anything into it other than making light of a serious slant in our journalism establishment.

Anyway, a few choice words were exchanged and Izzie was suspended from work. He later went to work for *News Week* magazine. Big who-do there, also owned by the *Washington Post*. That's like passing a lateral, it's the same team.

My good friend, Reed Irvine, at *Accuracy in Media* put out a full page ad in the *Post* alleging their hypocrisy by suppressing the story. I can only imagine how hard it must've been for the hypocrites at the *Post* to have to eat crow caused by their own source. It's sort of like going to Tijuana, catching Montezuma's revenge and crapping all over yourself! It felt good for a short time to mark one up for the little guy's. "Thanks, Reed."

Around about this same time, I received a call from a Pat Matrisciana who created *Jeremiah Productions*. He sent us a VHS tape of the 1st edition of the *Clinton Chronicles*. It was a documentary of the on-going scandals in the life and times of Bill Clinton. He asked if we could meet and discuss how he could maybe help getting Paula's story out. He had warned us like the State Troopers that we could be in danger if we came out against the Clintons.

Without Apology

We agreed to meet Pat at a Mexican restaurant on Second Street in Long Beach. We got there first and ordered a coupla' frozen margaritas while waiting. Pat Matrisciana was not alone when he came up to our table. He was with a guy named Larry Nichols. Pat was tall and thin, maybe in his mid-fifties. I remember Paula remarking about how tan he looked. Larry, on the other hand, was of normal stature with a bad habit of chain-smoking Marlboros. Pat introduced himself and Larry to us.

Pat had heard about Paula from the State Troopers that were at the C-PAC conference in Washington. He wanted to hear for himself what happened between Paula and Clinton. He offered to help get her story out into the public domain. I told him that we had an exclusive with the *Washington Post*, but they were sitting on it. I expressed my frustrations with the whole damn mess and felt we were fighting a losing battle. Pat and Larry looked at each other and expressed a half-smiling smirk, as if telling themselves, "*I told you so.*"

Larry said, "Steve, Paula, I don't think you know who you're dealing with, because if you did, you wouldn't have gone to the *Post*. That's like giving a butcher a cleaver to cut your head off."

I tugged at my underwear from a flinch reflex caused by his remark, knowing he had hit the nail on the head, but that still didn't offset the sting in his words. So, by him not knowing that we had already understood the calculated risks by going with the *Post*, I looked at him sarcastically and said, "Do I know you?"

"No. Look Steve, you're misunderstanding where I'm coming from, friend, Let me explain who I am. I used to work for Bill Clinton. I was the Director of Marketing for the *Arkansas Finance Development Authority*, otherwise known as AFDA. Clinton fired me because I was not willing to go along with the corrupt misuse of state funds. I filed a lawsuit against him, and let me say, I know where you're coming from, brother. You're getting a taste of what we call *Clinton's Circle of Power*."

Larry told us that he wanted to expose how the Clintons used taxpayer's money to set up low interest loans to fictitious businesses as a way to laundry money into his campaign fund. There were supposedly some legitimate loans given out to small businessmen to cover up the slush funds coming in from the bogus loans.

"They were so greedy, Steve and Paula. They even squeezed the legitimate guys to make contributions or were told you'll lose your business loan."

I said, "Sounds like extortion to me."

"And, remember Steve, this was taxpayer money that funded this initiative. They used the people's money to line their campaign pockets."

"Oh my," Paula said, "Just think—all that stuff was happening while I was working for the State."

Still being skeptical, I said, "I never heard anything in the local papers or saw anything in the news when we were living in Arkansas about this."

Larry continued, "Well, it gets better than that. I gave a press conference on the front steps of the capitol building and all the local TV news stations were there. I told them about the corruption that was going on and about Clinton's affairs with other women. Right after the press conference, I gave out copies of the press release to the media showing them all the evidence I had gathered. Guess what? Not a peep. Not a single TV station reported it, not a single line was printed in the *Arkansas Gazette*. Sound familiar? So, yeah, I know what you're going through and so maybe Pat can help you, as he has helped me."

"What happened to your lawsuit?" I asked.

"It was thrown out by a Clinton appointed Judge. Funny thing Steve, everything that I said years ago has come true. No one would believe me back then, but now reporters are going back and looking at the court documents I filed back then. They're finally seeing that everything I said about Clinton's affairs with Gennifer Flowers and Mary Jo Jenkins was true."

"Well, Larry, looks like you've gotten some redemption from your critics."

"Oh—hell no, Steve. Let me tell you, these people who believe in the Clintons don't care about their corruptness. It's like they've got diplomatic immunity and cannot be held accountable. They give the perception that they're for the little people."

Without Apology

"Bill Clinton is very charming and charismatic. He could talk a senior citizen into signing over his social security check for a month supply of pork & beans and the poor bastard would shake his hand for it. Hillary is more ruthless, she'd hit you with a stick, cuss you out, then take your money. She wears the pants in the family."

"That's for sure," Paula said, "And Bill can't keep his on."

We all laughed at that one.

"That sounds like some of the same things the troopers told us when we were in DC," I added.

Larry continued without acknowledging what I said, he was on a roll. "But don't let them fool you. It's a productive combination between the two. That's why she stays with Bill. They're a package deal."

"I don't believe you have to sell Paula and me on that, Larry. I've never liked Clinton from the jump, but this has nothing to do with politics and corruption. It's personal. Not to change the subject, but do you work in law enforcement?"

Larry looked at me, a bit perplexed, and said, "I have no idea what you're talking about but to answer your question, no, I don't. Why?"

"Well," I said, "When you sat down, your jacket opened and I noticed that you're carrying a gun. Do you have a permit for that thing?"

"No, I don't, Steve and nor does Pat."

Pat pulled open his jacket to display the butt end of a gun.

"What's up with all the hardware? You guys expecting bad company?"

Larry said, "This is protection, Steve. My lawyer was beaten and left for dead. They broke his hip, severed his spleen and fractured his leg. To this day, he won't have anything to do with me. I've lived with death threats for the past five years. So does that answer your question?"

"Yep...Can't blame you there."

I looked over at Paula who was all bug-eyed and silent.

Pat told us that there are more than a few unexplained deaths associated with the Clintons. "A whole lot of people have been either threatened or beaten up. There was this next-door neighbor of Gennifer Flowers by the name of Johnson. He lived in the Qawpaw condos and was having some problems with vandalism. So he set up a video camera and inadvertently caught Bill Clinton going in and out of Gennifer's condo.

We got Johnson on tape telling how these Gestapo police, he felt was sent by Buddy Young, forced themselves into his flat and demanded the tape from the surveillance camera or suffer the consequences. Well, to say the least, they took the surveillance tape.

"Johnson said they looked and coordinated themselves like police officers. All of them wore suits and were nicely groomed. Johnson said they used the *good cop—bad cop* method of interrogation on him. We've also got Jerry Parks' son on tape. Have you heard of Parks?"

Both Paula and I shook our heads, as she squeezed my arm tightly under the table. It was like sitting around a campfire late at night telling scary stories with the horror flick soundtrack of *Jason* playing the whispering sounds of, "CHU-Chu-chu... CHI-Chi-chi," in your ear.

Pat said, "Jerry Parks worked as a private investigator and was hired by the Stevenson family who own the Worthen banks in Arkansas. They helped Clinton get elected as Governor and then helped in getting him un-elected the following term. Over the years that Clinton fell *in and out* of the good graces of the Stevenson family, Jerry had gathered a rather extensive file on the Clintons, including pictures of Bill at his little brother Roger's numerous pool parties.

"Some photos were of compromising circumstances where Clinton was passed out, sprawled across a bed, from over-snorting cocaine. Parks snapped pictures of many different women that Bill had affairs with. Parks' son said that the pictures he saw signified Clinton's sexual preferences had no boundaries. He even had a few shots of Hillary and Vince Foster embracing each other at a mountain cabin rendezvous. No one person has more dirt on the Clintons alternate lifestyle than Jerry Parks."

Pat continued to tell me and Paula that in 1991, Parks would become just another statistical quota of unsolved deaths that premediated the Clinton's calculated rise to power. Parks was shot five times and left for dead on a state highway. The same day of his murder, his house was ransacked and all his files on the Clintons were stolen. I'm no rocket scientist, but you've got to ask yourself who benefited from the smoking gun? It sure wasn't his wife and family.

Hold on, I'm having another epiphany, probably brought on by watching a biography about ancient Greek society on, I hate to say it, but the History Channel. Some of history's most ominous figures came to power under the same dark clouds of mysterious circumstances as Clinton. This is kinda way off in left field, which is center when talking about the Clintons.

Some historians have compared Clinton to Alcibiades, an Athenian who came to political power around 421 B.C. He was known for his womanizing and winning, at all cost, by using his intellectual strength, but he could not be trusted. Alcibiades was exiled for screwing around with another king's wife and getting her pregnant. *Go figure.* He went to Prussia, which was the nemesis of the Greeks. Sorta like Benedict Arnold did, turning redcoat in the American Revolution. Alcibiades fell from all power and ended up as only a footnote in political Greek history. Eventually, not able to control his libido, he was killed in a jealous rage resulting from a love triangle. History has come full circle more often than falling stars in the night sky.

Well, the final chapter on the Clintons has yet to be written, but talk about your Presidential legacy. The ink is still wet, especially if Hillary had anything to do with it. We'll have to see if she runs again, but who then would become First Lady? As I said, if history repeats itself Hillary may not have to worry, just be happy. A bit ridiculous, but who knows when it comes to the Clintons. I would've bet ya' a *dime to a doughnut that* she couldn't get a vote to become a Senator, so what do I know?

Maybe in Clinton's case, there is some truth to reincarnation. After all, he even looks a little like the fractured statue of Alcibiades.

Since I'm on personal objectivity, my gullibility for thinking I was fighting for a worthy cause allows for some self-cynicism. I mocked myself as a Spartan of my wife's honor. Spartans put a lot of emphasis on duty and honor which, by the way, transcended from the tale of *King Arthur and the Knights of the Round Table* to which historians agree is where Southern chivalry derived from. Damn all those damsels in distress—where would we all be today if not for damsels?

Beyond all that subjectivity, Paula and I finished our meeting with Pat and Larry with the agreement of Paula telling her story on tape.

The day that Pat brought over his camera equipment, we met Pat's wife. She was wonderfully supportive of Paula and baby sat with Madison while filming.

Pat and I talked about the location to shoot the interview. I told him that I thought the perfect place would be the recreational and BBQ area atop the condo. It was secluded because no one used it except to watch the fireworks off the *Queen Mary's* stern every 4th of July, plus it had a panoramic view of the coast of Long Beach. I also stressed to Pat not to pan to any well-known geographical or structural areas that might give away our location. Even early on, I was worried about my family's safety given the gravity of what we've been told.

It was a bright and windy day when Paula gave her story to Pat on tape. Afterward, I threw in my two bits like a story told a thousand times from some old timer, "The *Washington Post* was under the left shoe of Bill Clinton, only oozing out long enough to give him a spit shine," or some similar reactionary statement like that.

I was still seething about the whole exclusive episode. Here we give the *Post* the exclusive when other publications, more sensitive to Paula's resolve, were clamoring for the chance.

Yes, I believe our train of momentum for going public right after the C-PAC press conference was stealthily derailed by Bill's and Hill's saboteurs at the *Post*. We played right into their hands by going to them, but the internal battle still raged inside, pitting the establishment against the people's right to know. This leads me to beg the question, "Why would the establishment approve Izzie to do an investigative piece in the first place knowing that it might compromise their position? Could they have miscalculated? If so, wrong move—Checkmate."

After the shoot, Pat and his wife invited me and Paula out for dinner at a local restaurant called the *Rusty Pelican*. Pat wanted to pay us something for our time. I told him we were glad to do this and it wasn't about getting paid money, but instead it was about standing-up for my wife's reputation.

A couple of weeks later, Pat sent me a check anyway. He explained it by saying that it was a gift for me to pay some bills. He knew that we were a one-income family and could use the money. I was tempted to keep it and I did. Rent was coming due and I figured since the airline was cutting my salary by fifteen percent that I should go ahead and accept the money.

Paula told Danny about the check and he demanded his fair share per her contract.

You gotta just *love to hate* these guys. I told Danny that the check just barely paid our rent and was not some huge amount of money. "I believe it was right at a thousand, Danny. Besides that, it was in my name and to my knowledge Dan-O, I'm not your client."

Well, that pretty much set the tone with Danny and me. I mean, we're not talking about thousands of dollars here. But it sure wrinkled his shirt when I told him where he could put his fair share.

I stayed in touch with Pat throughout the lawsuit and he sent us a copy of other VHS video's called *Clinton's Circle of Power*.

One thing Pat did do was to put me in contact with retired Lieutenant Colonel Tom McKinney. I can't remember who called whom first. The Colonel as I called him, was instrumental in associating me with the *Landmark Legal Foundation*, which assisted in searching for a new lawyer. There were two reasons that I sought out a new lawyer. One, because Danny himself felt that his services could be compromised and two, my recent dealing with getting any resolve with anyone associated with the Clintons had proven to be nothing more than a mixed bag of tricks.

I also have to admit I had a great deal of animosity toward how this whole thing had manifested itself in the first place and I wasn't about to leave it in the hands of a self-proclaimed yellow dog real estate lawyer. So when Danny went looking for a lawyer that would take over, I did the same. Whether he could compromise Paula or stay onboard due to his close friendship with Debbie Ballentine, I didn't know but I couldn't take that chance. Danny could recommend a law firm that was sympathetic to the Clintons and ruin any resolve.

Within months, I metamorphosized into three distinct phases. I transitioned from quietly handling the situation to a knee-jerk reactionary to until judgment day.

I know I keep harping at it, but yes, if it hadn't been for Danny's little scheme, all this drama-trauma could have been avoided with a respectful line of communication between both parties. This was especially true early on. A quiet apology and a retraction from the *American Spectator* would have erased the whole episode. So with that bit of insight, let me line up a string of "What ifs: What if the Jones case had never happened, where would we be today? If so, there would've never been a Monica Lewinsky. Well, there would've been in the physical sense, but we wouldn't have been gagged on the knowledge about Clinton's aficionado for Monica-dipped cigars. If so, maybe Clinton would've spent more energy toward foreign affairs and apprehended Osama bin Laden when the South African government wanted to hand him over to us on a silver platter. Nope, he was too intertwined trying to plug the cracks in his personal dikes. *I mean that in the literal sense.*

What if Clinton had retaliated heavy-handed when Saddam threw out inspectors, instead of dropping a few futile bombs in sand-land? Where would we be today?

What if, when the Israelis captured Mohammed Atta prior to 9/11, they wouldn't have let him go? Oh yeah, Atta was captured, tried, and imprisoned by Israel. As part of the Oslo Agreement with the Palestinians, Clinton insisted, along with his pal, Arafat, that Israel release all the so-called freedom fighters. Terrorist—Hello?

So, under pressure from the Clinton Administration to reach a peace accord with Arafat and the Palestinians, Israel consented. They opened the gates to hell. Wake up people, see what happens if you elect someone who allows animals out of their cages to feed on the innocent.

Now Atta was free to plan, plot and implement the death of thousands of Americans.

Maybe it's just me, but I was dumbfounded how the Clintons could welcome a known terrorist like Arafat to Camp David. A man who had innocent American blood on his hands and in one clean sweep they handed him legitimacy. Talk about irresponsibility. That's like giving a child in a playground a hand grenade and pulling the pin. Go ahead, maybe in the near future we'll elect the gruesome twosome back into office and see what else happens.

What if the Jones lawsuit hadn't happened? There wouldn't have been impeachment proceedings, changes in majority rule in both houses and even worse—a war in Iraq.

I know what you're thinking, *Damn son, you're full of chili*. Not really, it's all pretty clear. If Al Gore hadn't been stigmatized by the Clinton scandals, he would have swept the 2000 elections hands down. The name *Chad* would have had no more significance than being short for *Chadwick* in the bluebloods book of baby names.

You can bet a sandal slap to the face of Saddam's fallen statue, eclipsing Iraqi freedom, that supposed President Gore would not have invaded Iraq. That's a fact.

Oh, by the way, G.W., you're welcome-except for border issues and the last-minute bailouts you kept the country safe. You scored pretty damn low on immigration in my book. Illegal's cost the American taxpayer more than one hundred and fifty billion dollars a year. That's a lot of tacos we could use to feed our own families right here in the USA. We're hungry too dammit! Now to bank bailouts and the help of your Treasury Secretary, Henry Paulson. Someone needs to give that man a monkey, tin cup and accordion, because that's where we're all headed for in the end. I mean before you could say I lost my shirt on wall street, my shorts and socks were gone too. I remember watching the stock index when congress passed the bailout. The index spun downward like miles rolled back on a clunker. My 401 turned into a 201 in days. That in itself allowed Obama and his surrogates when elected to suck the economical strength of the US dollar to depression-era currency racking up 4 trillion in debt. The big plan, I'll get to that later.

The aftermath of the Jones lawsuit still sends shock waves into current events. I wonder what Judges President Gore, (if elected,) would've nominated to the Supreme Court? *Starting to catch my drift?*

Damn, and to just think, if Obama keeps the debt in the trillions, I'm sure there'll be support to open the Lincoln bedroom back up for business by nominating Hillary. "If, if, if- you're aunt had balls, she'd be your Uncle."(Hillary.)

So with a little insight, maybe all the scenarios I just mentioned could have been thwarted and we wouldn't have been in a war in Iraq. It's amazing how friends, an unapologetic indiscretion, and a peeved off husband can start a chain reaction that could change the course of history. All this is hypothetical speculation, of course, but don't take my word for it, just ask Tipper Gore at her next bridge party, then duck for cover. I wouldn't feel too sorry for big Al. He's made millions off of pulling the wool over the eyes of green tea drinkers.

It wasn't coincidence that the Clintons didn't endorse Big Al in 2000. That would have statically sweltered Hillary's chances to run in '08 due to the fact that it'd be unlikely to have a democrat elected more than three terms. So screw Big Al, while buying time and experience in the Senate. Thus, allowing Bush a margin to win and Hillary a good shot for 08. Strategic ideology to become President has little to do with differences in politics. Politics are up front, the people's choice, but what I'm talking about is a calculated edge that can only be obtained by alliances between parties. Obama was unexpected; some of you congressmen might keep that in mind when supporting universal health care. Ops! Too late. I guess those of us who aren't mindless followers have to take it where it hurts for a while and say; "Thank you sir, may I have another," until 2012. I just hope we get rid of all the progressives on both sides of the political pulpit. If not, I'm afraid in a few years the United States will be aliened with the European coalition. That should make China happy. Hell, a few thousand mindless followers infused with Marxism ideologies could ignite a irreversible attack capitalism, and wala... "Made in the USA" will be a figment in history.

So, after talking with the Lieutenant Colonel, I took his advise and made several phone calls to a friend of his at the *Landmark Legal Foundation*. I told him of my dilemma, and that the statue of limitations on Paula maybe filing suit against Clinton was running out soon. I asked him if he could help me find an attorney for her, because I felt that Danny might locate a scapegoat in the ninth hour, losing the chance to file. I went on to tell him, "Danny said he's getting criticized harshly by his legal constituents in Arkansas for crossing over to the other side."

"Well, Stephen, because of possible political ramifications, the *Landmark Legal Foundation* can't openly represent Paula. However, we might be able to assist in finding legal representation."

"That's all I'm calling for. Just see if you can find someone we can trust."

"Stephen, I'm going fishing this weekend with some buddies. Let's see what we can catch."

"Thanks a bunch for whatever you can do, but let these guys know that we're running out of time."

"Stephen, they already know, I'll be in touch."

A few days later when Danny called and said he'd found two lawyers by the name of Gilbert Davis and Joseph Cammarata. I quickly called my friend in Kansas City who didn't seem surprised by the news, but said he'd check it out, which led me to speculate the productiveness of their fishing trip.

In the meantime, I called up the Colonel and told him the only thing I knew was that Danny told me that Gil Davis had worked as an attorney for one of the prior administrations some fifteen years earlier. Over the phone he added up the years and we both came up with the Carter Administration.

"Oh no, Steve—not Panama Jimmy. He gave away the canal and now the company that runs it is owned by communist China. You can't trust anyone associated with that humanitarian bastard."

The seeds of a conspiracy theory were about to be sowed.

"It could be a plant, Steve." the Colonel said.

"How so?"

"Well, you guys have just a few weeks left until the statute of limitations runs out, right?"

"Yeah, that's right I'm listening."

"So, if they put some bogus lawyers in there to drag their feet until this thing plays itself out, then you're never going to get Paula's name cleared."

"Colonel, I don't believe it. You know, I've felt the same way as you, but haven't told anyone for fear of sounding ridiculous. Having heard you say the same thing, I think frankly we need a vacation. There's just no way Clinton could get away with something like that, ya' think? I mean if they got caught, Clinton's ass would be in a sling. It seems to me it would be sorta' like what happened to Nixon and the Watergate scandal."

"Who says they would get caught, Steve?"

"Well, Colonel, tell that to G. Gordon Liddy. I'm sure Clinton can hit his memory rewind button and see in his minds-eye Nixon walking across the White House greens, boarding that helicopter for the last time and saying to himself, *That's not gonna happen to me, Bubba.*"

I know that would be my flashback if I were in his shoes."

"Steve, this is no Watergate and you guys are just a blip on the radar screen and nobody's going to care."

"Yeah, maybe so, Colonel, but that's how this stuff gets started. It's thought to be benign and then it spreads to the bone. I want to get into Clinton's marrow, not jump off into some wild goose chase crapola. I've been there already. All I see is us as big targets and them as flocks overhead with loose bowels. I have no intention to be crapped on all over again. Pilot to bombardier, "Let's drop our own stink bomb.""

"You're a revengeful son-of-a-bitch, Steve. I like that."

"I wouldn't cut that in stone just yet, Colonel, but I'm a man on a mission to set things right. Look, here it is in a nutshell. I think Clinton could get away with something like that if he were still Governor of Arkansas, but not President. He doesn't have a free range to graze on anymore. Now he's got all that open wild, wild west Washington tumbleweed, and his good ol' buddy elbow to the ribs—wink, wink, ain't gonna bale hay with the bureaucratic elitist in Washington. There's always someone hiding behind a boulder to bushwhack you. I think Clinton knows that, but feels he's smarter than his adversaries. That's a flaw I can take advantage of.

"From what I'm hearing, some people would like to help us see him hung out to dry politically. For what he did to Paula, I'm gonna supply the rope. Hell, listen to me, I sound like some western vigilante at high noon. Hey, *High Noon*, someone said that was Clinton's favorite movie."

"Figures, Steve. The guy who directed it was accused of being a communist."

"Really, Colonel? Sounds like you got some post cold war issues."

We chuckled together, knowing that we'd keep side-tracking each other on senseless trivia.

Continuing my subjection, I said, "I just think the consequences far outweigh any liabilities. I mean—I'm just an ordinary minded guy, but if it were me, I wouldn't be fool-hearted enough to plant a lawyer, and the only way I would contemplate that is if I were desperate, and I don't think Clinton is remotely at that stage.

"Well, Colonel, let me call our friend back at *Landmark* and see what he thinks of this big pot of brew we just cooked up. I'll let you know what I find out."

Later, those conspiracy theories were put to rest by the next sequence of events.

Paula was already in Arkansas visiting family, so she was set to meet these new lawyers at Danny's office in downtown Little Rock.

In the meantime, I developed a relationship with Christian activist, Patrick Mahoney. Patrick had contacted us shortly after Paula appeared in an interview on Pat Robertson's *700 Club*.

Although Paula was raised Pentecostal and I was Southern Baptist, neither one of us were actively going to church.

"Let me put it this way Mr. Mahoney, I have my beliefs, I just don't practice them."

Stephen M. Jones, Jr.

"Call me, Pat, Steve."

Pat had called me one night, and introduced himself. I took an immediate liking to him and found common ground on some of the issues he was passionate about. *Hey, I was looking for all the help I could muster.*

I had heard that Pat and his wife, Katie, went on a few talk radio shows in support of Paula's right to clear her good name. I found him to be a strong ally to further get Paula's story to the American heartland. While talking with Pat, we discussed the disparity between Paula and Anita Hill along with Republican Senator Packwood, who got rode out on a rail by his female constituents. They pretty much served his head up on a platter. Boy, how they stayed longest and yelled the loudest, but now, the silence has became deafening when it comes to Paula. I remember Barbara Boxer, Maxine Waters, and Diane Feinstein, just to name a few. Even Hillary Clinton got in on the action praising Anita Hill for having the strength to come forward.

"Mr. Mahoney...I mean Pat, I remember seeing mobs of N.O.W. members holding up signs protesting against Clarence Thomas being appointed to the Supreme Court especially, when all those hearings were going on. Just think—all of that commotion over a hair on a coke can."

"Yeah, Steve. I remember, too. You know that gives me an idea. What do you guys think about me arranging a meeting with Patricia Ireland, the head of N.O.W.?"

"That sounds great. You know her?"

"Oh yes, I do. Patricia and I are on different sides of the fence, but I believe she would talk to Paula. Steve, if Paula could tell her story in her own words, I believe Patricia might support her. If she does, she could be a strong ally for Paula."

"Pat, I haven't heard boo from them so far, what's up with that you think?"

"I hate to say it, Steve, but the Clintons support a lot of their issues."

"Yeah, human rights takes a back seat when it comes to political bias, but Pat, think about it—if you can arrange a meeting it might force Ireland out of the box and take a position, or if she does nothing, it's gonna undermine her whole organization on women's rights. I mean, either way it's a win-win situation. If Ireland balks and turns tail and runs, it could kill two birds with one stone, right?"

"Did you ever think about getting into politics, Stephen?"

"Who me? Oh no, hell no. I'm sorry Pat for cussing...it slipped, and you're a man of the cloth."

"Don't worry about it Steve, hell is a term the church uses frequently. I'll give Patricia a call."

Pat tried to arrange a three-way conference call with the three P's, Paula, Patricia, and Patrick. Ireland wouldn't agree to have Pat on the phone, but agreed to talk with Paula the day before she was to meet the two attorneys. I couldn't get off work until two more days, so I was stuck trying to coordinate everything from Los Angeles. Paula was to accept a call from Patricia Ireland at Paula's mother's apartment around 2:00 p.m.

Late that night, I called my friend from *Landmark* at his home in Kansas City. I expressed my concerns about the attorneys flying in, and told him what the Colonel said, "Look, I can't be there for another two days, and it's only a week left until the statute of limitation runs out."

Without me asking, well...maybe just a little hinting, along with sensing concern in my voice, he said, "I'll be on a plane tomorrow morning and sit in on the meeting with Paula."

"Great! Oh man you don't know how I appreciate that. It really takes a load off my mind. I'll call Danny to tell him that he's got company coming, plus get a hold of Paula and tell her to meet you at your hotel. Because, if you don't mind, I'd like you both to go in together instead of Paula already being there. Last time she went to see a lawyer by herself, she ended up signing a cotton candy contract."

"What's a cotton candy contract?"

"You know, a sweet deal that melts away."

"A quick sugar high, huh?"

"Yeah, that's right, so when Paula is around her *so-called* friends, things always seem to go in the wrong direction. I jus' don't want to dig a deeper hole than we're already in."

"Not a problem Steve. I'll call you in the morning and let you know where I'm staying."

"You know this means a lot to us. I won't forget it! And hey, I'm sorry I called so late."

"Don't worry about it, Steve, happy to be here for you guys. Talk to you tomorrow."

Right after I hung up, I called Danny and left a message, then Paula to make sure she'd gotten all the vitals. She agreed to talk with Patricia Ireland by phone and meet my friend from the *Landmark Legal Foundation* at his hotel the following day so they could go in together.

Paula wanted to buy a new dress. *A dress?* I thought, *What for?* What's all the hubbub about? Why would you want a new dress to impress a couple of lawyers? But hey, I'm not walking around with the biological chromosomes that require me to zip myself up from the back. Anyhow, I was too jawbone tired to argue about no mo' money. Paula never missed an opportunity to buy a *new* anything.

So, I went to bed hoping I'd covered all my bases. I lay there forcing myself not to think about the upcoming events so as to get some shuteye, of course unsuccessfully. Sooner or later, I fell asleep counting sheep with big bows on their heads.

Early the next morning, somewhere between a comatose state and half awake, the last sheep that couldn't make it over the fence awakened me. It had a tiny bell around its neck that kept getting bigger, ringing louder and louder. *Oh hell, it's the damn phone. Who could be calling me now at this hour?* I thought I'd covered all my bases. *Please God, no curve balls this early in the morning. It can't be Paula; the malls don't open before ten.*

Groggily, "Hell-ooo."

"Is this Stephen?"

"Yeah, but I hadn't looked in the mirror this morning, so I'm not sure."

"What's that, Mr. Jones?"

"Oh, it's just a figure of speech. I don't believe I caught your name?"

"This is a call from Reverend Jerry Falwell's office."

"Wow! God must like baseball."

"I'm sorry—I don't understand, Mr. Jones?"

"It's just me covering my bases, but you were right the first time, just call me, Stephen. What's Reverend Falwell's office want with me?"

The associate said, "Reverend Falwell wants to know if Paula has filed her suit already, because the statute of limitations runs out today."

Trying to get my mental bearings, I told him we had another week.

"Are you sure?" he asked.

"I'm positive. By the way...how'd you get my phone num...Oh, never mind. Doesn't matter. Tell Reverend Falwell that I appreciate his concern and thanks for the wake-up call. Goodbye."

I still think it's amazing that someone as world-famous as Jerry Falwell would call me, out of the clear blue. *Boy how events move in mysterious ways.* However, what that call did tell me is that Paula's story was getting some attention. At the time, it seemed okay to have some religious organizations sympathetic to what had happened to Paula. Looking back, Clinton had a few on his side as well.

I may not go to church like I should, and my roots may not grow as deep into the rich soul of Christianity, but I'm sure not a hypocrite about it. I wanted all the help I could get to right a wrong and there were prominent religious organizations out there willing to give us a helping hand. On the other hand, Clinton used the church very effectively, too. Having himself portrayed to the American people through the help of CNN cameos depicting both Clintons going to church professing repentance and showing solidarity had worked for them. Blubbering how he has hurt his family but never, ever apologizing to those who really deserved it.

However, very artfully he succeeded in staging the need of contrition for the more liberal members of the cloth so as to justify their public support of him. That, my friend, is called damage control when caught with his hands inside that jumbo black and white polka-dot thong of a cookie jar called *Monica's little treats.*

I mean, what's a man to do when married to a woman who's known to have a bigger bravado than he? When opportunity knocks, you take it! Right? Wrong! Not if you're the President of a nation that any precipitant action might compromise its security. (Just when you think I'm shallow, I go deep...ta-dah!)

Clinton had cleverly tapped into the churches by confessing the pain and suffering he'd caused his family. Using motivating spirituals like Evangelist Billy Graham to rise up out of hospice praising the appearance of contrition for the sake of political homage, thus dividing religious perspectives. Too bad Clinton wasn't Catholic. That might have explained a lot except for the fact that choir boys are not interns and priesthood is not a prerequisite for pedophiles. I don't know though, most denominational religious sects have had their own fair share of sex scandals, past and present. *Who knows, maybe Clinton knew he could do a Jimmy Swaggart and get some public sympathy.* Whatever the case, it worked.

In retrospect, Reverend Falwell and I had similar agendas, but for different reasons. For me, it was an eye for an eye, a tooth for a tooth sort of thing, and a demented theory thinking that I could clear my wife's good name. Apart from some loose morals and national security issues that I have already mentioned, I could give a rip about his personal infidelities. He made it personal by his own actions, not mine.

For the late Jerry Falwell's part, I believe it was the downright openness of the Clintons to rub bellies with some of the Hollywood elite that's had long agendas undermining traditional values in our family's youth. So, what if the Christian coalition bannered our plight, I was more than happy for them to pick up a shovel and start digging in.

Speaking subjectively, I believe the continuous scandals that had plagued Clinton's administration, most of which stemmed from the Jones lawsuit, caused him to evolve into a centrist more than hailing his usual liberal tenacities. Not because he wanted to, but out of necessity. He had to play ball with some of the moderates on Capitol Hill or his goose was cooked. That's the beauty of evolution—survival. The guy could change colors like a chameleon. Being the best snake oil salesman in modern politics was not enough. It's a tough sell being caught between an intern and a hard place. You had to be lucky and Bill was lucky in *capital letters*.

He had inherited a newborn economy, fresh out of recession. If it wasn't for the economy he would've been tar-babied for sure. Arkadians didn't coin him *slick Willie* for nothing. But seriously, I'm talking *right vs wrong*, not the Lincoln bedroom. Although it sounds like I'm drawing a biased analogy here, it's because that's how I felt as the lines were being drawn in the sand back in 1994. This was a non-political sexual crime, only merit less from prosecution because of the passage of time. The whole damn thing would've lain buried and not exhumed if it hadn't been for *The American Spectator* printing Trooper Ferguson's twisted manifesto of Paula being a willing participant.

Now this unfortunate manifestation of division was being spirited by political and ethical values which fueled the flames of no resolve, torching the possibility for any negotiations. "What we got here is failure to communicate."

Every time a compromise was initiated, Paula's reputation had to be tainted and dragged through the mud by Clinton's black-hearted bastards. This was the Clintons forte. Negotiate up front while their cronies ripped at your reputation from behind your back. This tactic worked well in two ways. One, it could compromise any leverage you may hold. Two, it put anyone else on notice to think twice before coming out with any similar stories of past transgressions involving the Clintons.

Hillary was like I was, but nastier. She was a player behind the scene. She was deep-six involved, so as to keep the golden egg crackless and would stop at nothing to protect the nest.

She was updated constantly and would strategize with the team of lawyers and investigators on many issues that spawned from the Jones' suit. Initially, Hillary may not have been immediately aware of Lewinsky, but she knew about it long before it became public. I would say somewhere about the same time we knew, that being late in 1997. They knew that we knew because

Stephen M. Jones, Jr.

our lines were tapped. To say she wasn't aware of the hordes of others and the likelihood that it could happen at anytime is like asking the Indian why he was riding and his squaw was walking?

His answer would be, "I have but one horse."

Like the Indian, Hillary is driven by her own political agenda and won't give up the ride for anyone. So who do you think is holding the tail and walking? Thought so.

Hillary made it a top priority to be *in the know* with the private investigators they hired. Let me name a few of whom dug into our closet and tapped our phone; Jack Palladino, Anthony Pellicano and Terry Lenzer (head of the prestigious I.G.I. agency and so-called saviour of high society when caught in low places).

In early 2006, Anthony Pellicano was arrested in LA by the FBI for possession of blasting caps and plastic explosives. Speaking of explosives, at the height of pressure for us to settle the suit, I was driving on I-5, nearing downtown Hollywood, when a loud boom went off inside my car. The cabin quickly filled with smoke and I momentarily lost control crossing two lanes and miraculously missed a concrete barrier. The acrid smell of sulfur filled my lungs. I pulled over to the emergency lane and rolled down the windows. Looking up in the rear view mirror, I noticed that the compression had caused my hair to stand on end like Don King. I almost laughed, and then thought—*the car might still blow up dumb ass*.

The Bomb Squad checked the car, but only found residue from all the smoke along with the stench of gunpowder that still lingered. Next day, I took the car to a Mercedes technician. He told me someone had tampered with the computer brain of the car that causes a shotgun blank to explode and engages the constriction of the seatbelts. Never, he stressed, had he heard or read in company alerts, of the shell engaging without a collision.

The perfect—*get Stephen out of the way*—ploy. Paula would've settled in an instant. In fact, she would do whatever the attorneys required without a questionable flinch. I was the fly in the ink—a kink in the master plan.

I told the police detective assigned to the incident what the auto technician had said. He gave me the, "I'll call you, don't call me line." Bottom line, any inquiry as to why the shell went off by itself fell on deaf ears by the LA county police. To this day, my ears still ring from that blast. So, even though I can't prove it, it's quite a coincidence for a private investigator, versed in handling explosives, to be on the Clinton's payroll. Don't ya' think? Another sleazier surrogate, retained by the Clintons, was private investigator Jack Paladino. He was hired by the Clintons back when Gennifer Flowers became an issue in the 1992 election. Paladino worked close with *Penthouse* owner, Bob Guccione, to entice Flowers to pose in one of his issues. She thought she had signed a contract allowing her complete control over the final draft, along with pictures of course, but she was wrong. Guccione using what Paladino provided, rewrote the article portraying Flowers as a *not-to-be believed, gold digging bimbo* that only alleged she'd had an affair with Clinton. So, that along with the *60 Minutes television* episode of *Stand By My Man,* all but guaranteed the Clintons a shoe-in to win the election.

This tactic worked so well—why not use it on Paula? Well, all I can say is it didn't happen under my watch.

We were well behind the Clinton's mechanized propagandist movement, still in the infancy of looking for new and improved legal representation. The Clinton's Blitzkrieg of gravediggers was already in swing in Arkansas, excavating Paula's bone yard. I may be a small fly on a big screen door, but I was willing to go the distance and find a way in to buzz some head. He sicked his dogs on the wrong postman. I think the wicked witch had it right while melting, "What a world, what a world."

I had just gotten off the phone with Mr. Falwell's office trying to shake the cobwebs out of four hours of sleep. So I cut on the tube to check-out the morning news and made myself some Joe, adding an extra scoop for a Turkish petroleum blend. News flash; President Clinton has just hired a four-hundred and fifty dollar an hour lawyer named Bob Bennett to represent him in the Paula Jones case. I wish *CNN* would get their shit straight for once. There was no case because we hadn't filed one yet. Ok bubba, let's get beyond that and focus, 'cause this was big news for all the doubting Thomas's out there. They were saying that Bennett was a heavy hitter in the arena of lawyers. Umm, so why was someone like Bennett hired if Paula's story was just another bimbo eruption glorified by the *Washington Post* to be buried in the style section? It wouldn't be, because most news affiliations are politically biased. Nah…they're all fair and balanced.

A little later, Clintontologist, Harold Ickies, was popping his reptilian head off and on news shows like a puppet with Clinton's arm up his scrawny ass fending off the four-hundred and fifty dollar an hour question from some of the more objective media sources.

As one commentator put it, "In other words, Mr. Ickies, if all this was just another frivolous accusation of sexual misconduct by the then- Governor, then why would the President hire a high-priced legal eagle like Bennett?"

His answer, "Are you better off than you were four years ago? The economy is doing great and all this is just another right-wing attack from some people who are filled with hate, and quite frankly, are jealous of the President's record."

That's right, Ickies—attack and divert, never answering the question directly. *Talk about a man who fits his name.* I sat back on the couch, sipping my brew and contemplating our next move and allowing the caffeine to soak into an overview.

Finally a few people in the media were starting to take a closer look at Paula's story and not portraying her allegation as some fifteen-minute of fame to get her picture in some sleazy magazine.

Hum…this could be a good thing, not about the sleazy magazine… that would come later, but Ireland. I'm mixing my thoughts here when I haven't fully caffeinated my brain. If I could time it just right with Paula telling her story to Patricia Ireland, maybe N.O.W. would rally behind Paula like they did Anita Hill. I mean there's more credibility than the hair on a coke can theory, right? Ireland is screwed if she plays the political gender card, but if she sympathizes with Paula and puts out some kind of press release that they're willing to protest in front of the White house- or something like that, it might pressure Clinton to settle this whole thing with an apology. Hmm, who knows? This mess might be over before it even begins and this nightmare turned day-mare would be out of our lives forever.

Oh damn, I better start getting ready for work or I'm gonna be late.

Work was a bear as usual, checking in domestic flights then international flights one right after another. Always a never seemingly end to the line out the door. Only allowed to sit down for lunch, or a toilet seat where the sanitary wax paper meets the cheeks. You'd think that 3M could invent a substance that's not only flushable but won't stick to your butt when ready to get up. *Damn those four hours of sleep.*

During all this saga, Paula was staying with her mother. After work, I rushed home to call her to see how the conversation went with Ireland.

Miss Corbin answered the phone.

"Hi, Miss Corbin. Is Paula there?"

"Oh my, my, let's see now, Mr. Steve, I believe she's still out with Lydia. They've been gone for quite a spell."

"Miss Corbin, you wouldn't know if anyone called for Paula today, would you?"

"Let's see now..."

The silence on the other end only added to my anxiety. Finally she said, "Why of course, now I remember. Lydia called then she came right over this morning so they could go shopping...And let's see now... seems to me someone else did call. Yes sir'ree some lady called. Yep, she did, Mr. Steve, but I told her Paula was out shopping with her sister. Are you all right, Mr. Steve? Sounds like you're grinding your teeth. Anyhow, I haven't seen hide nor hair of 'em since this morning."

"Frig 'um—frag 'um—frig 'um!!!"

"What's that, Mr. Steve? You're huffing and puffing so much into the phone I can't understand a word you're saying. For lands sake, what's that noise? Sounds like a muffled holler."

Taking my hand off the receiver and gaining some composure, I asked if she remembered if Paula had talked to anyone else before she and Lydia left,

"Well, lemme see now."

Again, silence on the line.

"I believe she called her lawyer this morning…uh huh…yep, she sure did, Mr. Steve—right 'for they left. Sure did."

"Thank you, Miss Corbin, good talking to you, gotta go now."

"Mr. Steve, if you can't control your nerves, you're gonna be on high blood pressure medicine 'fore your time. You hear me?"

"Yes Ma'am you're so right, Miss. Corbin. Maybe I can borrow some of yours 'til I can get me some."

"Oh, lordy no. You can't do that, you'd hav'ta get your own. As it is…I can't afford mine anyhow."

"I was just kidding, Miss Corbin. I'd like to talk more, but I've got to call Danny. You know…Paula's lawyer, before he leaves his office. Do me a favor and tell Paula I called. I'll call her back, that way you won't have a long distance charge."

"Oh lordy yes, Mr. Steve, me being on a fixed income and all. Thank ya' fer thinking about that."

"No problem since it should be on my nickel anyway. Bye for now, Miss Corbin."

I called Danny and he said that Paula had called and asked if it would be okay for her to go shopping. She wanted to buy a new dress for tomorrow's meeting. Danny said that he and Patricia Ireland both had called Paula but her mother said she was out buying a new dress. Danny said that Patricia was really put out because Paula thought buying a new dress was more important than speaking with her. I asked Danny of Ireland's demeanor about Paula's story and he said skeptical.

Danny then asked Ireland for support from the N.O.W. organization and Ireland said she wasn't convinced about Paula's story.

I told Danny that's exactly why I wanted Paula to talk to Ireland. Woman to woman, not lawyer to activist. That's like mixing oil and water.

The best laid plans, screwed up by a damn dress. I guess Clinton could say the same thing.

Paula and I had a big blowout over her missing Ireland's call. I was very clear to Paula that it was important to talk to this woman and I thought she felt the same. After I tried to explain what a big deal it was to have missed Ireland's call, Paula really didn't see what the big fuss was about.

Her comment made little sense to me. "That's what lawyers are for, Steve. To talk to people like that."

The only thing on her mind was looking good in her new dress. Something's wrong with this picture. I wanted redress and Paula wanted a new dress. Again, I took a pause in that fact. *Was this all about me or Paula?* Because it seemed that I was more outraged than she was. We're on the verge of sacrificing personal freedom for the greater cause; that cause being reputation and self-esteem. The only thing you take to the grave with you is your reputation and *no* amount of money can buy that. So that was it. I think I wanted an apology from Clinton more than Paula did. She had my name and her reputation was a reflection of my own.

Chapter Ten

The next day things went a little better. My friend from the *Landmark Legal Foundation* met Paula and they met the Virginia based attorneys in Danny's office downtown. I made sure that I would be there by conference call. I wasn't going to get into something this time without testing the water first. I took my lunch break at work the same time as the meeting and had ten dollars in quarters for the slot on the pay phone. Remember, back then cell phones were not the norm.

I was having difficulty hearing everything that was going on. Paula again told her story of what had happened between her and Clinton. She was constantly being interjected by one of the lawyers saying, "Count one, intentional infliction."

A few minutes later, "Count two, defamation of character."

Paula continued again when someone said, "Can we get him on outrageous conduct?"

Another voice, "Maybe."

"Count three—denying her equal rights under the Constitution by sexual harassment and assault."

"Paula, how was your work environment?"

"Well, let's see. I know when I came off maternity leave, I didn't get my same job back. AIDC renamed my job classification and gave it to another girl, but she did exactly the same thing I had done. My new position was a nowhere job. I got paid what I was making when I left, but it was at a lower pay scale. What I mean is that I got the same pay as when I left on maternity, but my pay raises were at a lower scale. I would've gotten more money if I'd had my old job back. Am I making any sense here?"

Someone said, "Good, we can use that, a hostile work environment. We can tweak it later, but I think we got something we can put on paper."

At this point, I could feel the pace of resolution picking up, but I still didn't know who these guys were. So I asked about the lawyer's background.

Like clockwork Paula interceded. "Oh, Stephen, you're not a lawyer. That's what *they* get paid for, to lawyer."

"Paula, that's funny, because I'm all ears to know how you've already paid for their services."

Silence.

"That's what I thought! Now look honey, all I'm doing is making sure everything is okay. Last time you went to talk to a lawyer to ask advice, it brought us to where we are now. I just want to make sure we're doing the right thing here. You're right, I'm not a lawyer, but I do have enough common sense not to step into a bigger hole than we're already in. I'm not sure that you understand what's about to happen, Paula. I'm sure everyone at the table will agree with me. Bottom line, is as soon as you file this suit, the shit is gonna hit the fan."

My friend with *Landmark* said, "Stephen put you mind at ease, I've already talked to these guys and they're on our side. We've got a lot of common ground here. I don't think we have to worry about them working for the other side."

I guess Gilbert Davis sensed my concern and said, "Mr. Jones, this is Gil Davis. Let me assure you that we're here today because we feel the same way you do. We believe Paula's story and we believe we can resolve this matter in a way that I know concerns you too. That, Mr. Jones, is restoring Paula's good name. If it will make you feel better, I can tell you a little background about myself. I served under the Nixon administration as a federal prosecutor."

"Joe and I have been paying attention to Paula's story in the news. When I read that she was looking for new representation and that the statute of limitations were about to expire, I talked to Joe about it and we put a call through to Danny's office."

"Danny sent us a copy of the complaint that's to be filed by this Friday, May 6th. We thought it needed some work and because of the limited time we had to work with, we felt it necessary to be here in person. Personally, this is the sort of David and Goliath case that I like. I fought a big company for a farmer that lasted more than a few years and won, so I don't need the money. I get a sense of personal satisfaction fighting for the underdog."

Paula put in two cents, "Was it a lot of money?"

"Let's just say we won big time."

"Oh my," Paula responded.

Gil continued, "We're just country lawyers, wanting to do the right thing for you, Paula."

"Mr. Jones, this is Joe. Joe Cammarata. I want to tell you that after listening to Paula's story of the trauma that Clinton put her through, I want to take this fight to his doorstep. I think we've got a case here."

The operator's voice interrupted us. "Please deposit two dollars and fifty cents to continue."

"Crap! Listen, I'm about to run out of quarters, but I'm going to be flying in tomorrow morning. Good talking to everybody, I'll see all of you in person, hopefully tomorrow. And, Paula, don't forget to pick me up at the airport at 10:29 in the morning."

Again, that same raspy voice repeated, "Please deposit two dollars and fifty cents now."

"Hey operator! Why don't you kiss my…"

The operator turned my call into an automated message that said, "If you would like to make a call, please hang up and dial your operator." And then there was a loud click as my call was disconnected.

"Ass!"

Without Apology

Paula and Lydia met me at the airport Thursday morning. I drove Lydia's truck directly to Danny's office downtown. Lydia told us to call her when we were ready for her to pick us back up.

Danny's office was on, or close to, the top floor in a high-rise building. Actually, I was impressed with his office. I imagined some rinky-dink office in the shady part of town, but this was nice. He had a big office with a view of the city. Behind his desk was a little icebox stocked with new and improved cold pouches of *Hawaiian Punch* that you shove a straw through. The straw was even cellophaned to the side of the pouch. All self-contained, snazzy.

On this hot day in May, everyone in the office was sipping punch that we had all grown up with. There, I met my friend, and his red-headed colleague from the *Landmark Legal Foundation* who then introduced me to Joe and Gil.

My first impression was Laurel and Hardy, void the stupid expressions. Gil was a big robust man and Joe was of average height but thin as a rail. That's where the comedic similarities ended. When Gil spoke, it was with an air of authority and self-assuredness. Joe had an aggressive, pit-bull mentality that was probably rooted on the playgrounds in central New York where he grew up.

I liked Joe right off. His passion and heart seemed similar to my own. He took an aggressive outlook, while Gil took a more diplomatic approach. Whatever you called it, their professional personalities seemed to give them balance. Gil had been there—done that and was ready to do it again. Joe couldn't wait to go there, and just do it.

After everyone had shaken hands and the introductions were finished, we got down to business.

Gil said to Paula, "Before we get started, we need you, Paula, to sign a contract for our services. It was handwritten by Joe at the last minute."

I spoke up and asked to read it before Paula signed. Sure enough, it was handwritten. I read through it noticing that it was on a contingency with the exception of, if there ever was a fund set up on Paula's behalf, that the contract would revert to an hourly rate. I questioned this over Paula's objections of—"Here we go again! Why can't you jus' let me sign it S-t-e-p-h-e-n Jones! They're the lawyers here."

"Mr. Jones," Joe said, "By Paula signing this, it won't cost you a red cent. It's never going to come out of your own pocket."

I said, "Look guys, I'm still a little worried about this fund thing I'm reading. What's that all about? I mean, if the fund doesn't cut it, who pays then?"

My friend from *Landmark* took me aside and led me down the hall to a room that was a legal library with three or four rows of bookcases cram-packed with moldy smelling books.

The smell drew me back to elementary school where I had feverishly read *Curious George* books in hot rooms without air-conditioning. Only an occasional breeze from an open window would scour the Mississippi heat lapping at my senses. Shaking the thought out of my head just as quickly as it had entered, he said, "Some lawyers call this the gray room. Nothing written is in black and white!"

"That's comforting to know," I replied.

"Look Steve, this is how it's going to work. As I told you, *The Land mark Foundation* can't be upfront with this case if it's filed because of the ramifications we've already talked about. What we *can do* and I've already talked to Joe and Gil about this, is to financially back you guys if there's no resolution and the case moves forward. What this means is that Paula, and you Steve, won't suffer the burden of having to pay legal fees. You have my word on that."

"Well that makes me feel a lot better, but I'd like this resolved before we get to that point."

"I think we all do Steve. Now, are you ready to go back in and get started?"

When we walked back in, Paula seemed a little nervous. I think the gravity of the situation had finally started to sink in, and now she was getting cold feet, where only moments before she was had been all gung ho.

She was at the window high above, looking down at all the hoards of news crews gathering around the front of the courthouse.

My friend whispered in my ear, "Why don't you and Paula go in the library so you can discuss this alone?"

"Thanks. I believe that's what we need to do."

I took Paula by the hand and we went into the gray vault of smelly books. When we got inside, Paula commented, "Boy, Danny needs to get some mothballs to put in this musty room."

"Paula," I said, "Have you ever smelled mothballs before?"

"Well of course I have, silly. My mama has them everywhere."

"So how'd you get their little legs apart?"

Confused, she replied, "Say—what in the world are you—she stopped in mid-sentence, realizing it was a joke. Oh, you're so bad."

"I'm just trying to take the edge off of a serious moment." I took both her hands and asked her, "Are you sure that you want to do this?"

"Oh I don't know, Stephen, all those people out there and they're out there because of me and they look so hot and all."

"Well, not exactly Paula. They're out there sweltering because of who he is and what you said he did to you in that hotel room. And yes, to see if you're going to do anything about it, so they can splash it all over the headline news. People eat that crap up. I betcha' those bastards in the Clinton administration sure wish they had handled it differently now. If they think they can label you like all the rest of his one-night-stand bimbos, they've got another thought coming!"

"Stephen, I'm so scared to do this. I don't know if I can or not."

"Look Paula, if you remember, I didn't want anything to do with this to begin with, but whatever you decide to do, I'll be right by your side all the way. Just know if you do it, we'll be doing it together."

"What about Debbie? She's my friend and I don't want to hurt her."

"Paula, what in the bejesus are you talking about?"

"Well, don't you tell a soul, but she said she had this affair with a State Representative, or Senator, or someone like that, and she thinks that if I file, people will find out about it."

Stephen M. Jones, Jr.

"Paula, I think you need to worry about your own backyard. That's where you can bet your sweet bippy they'll be. And if you remember, it was Debbie who brought the *American Spectator* to your attention in the first place. If it wasn't for your friend, we wouldn't be where we are now. So I'm not too concerned with poor little Debbie's romps being brought out of the closet."

"I know. I know," Paula said. "But she's still my friend."

"I know you think she is, Paula, and maybe she says she is, but she uses you. I wish you could realize that. I'm the one who's married to you. It's your reputation we're fighting for. I'm telling ya', if they think they can bulldoze your reputation into some landfill they got another thought coming. Don't ya' see? That's the only reason I'm here, so please believe me when I say I don't feel sorry for any collateral damage Debbie helped create." I hesitated just a bit to let what I had just said soak in. "Paula, do you honestly think, as you refer to Debbie as your dear, dear friend that she will loose any of her privacy? Oh no, it'll be us, if you decide to file this damn thing. God, I hope she could catch some slack. It'd serve her right, putting a bug up your ass about this whole mess in the first place, but as I said, Clinton's dogs are gonna be too busy digging around in our trash cans to give a rip about paying any attention to Lil' Debbie's cream-filled escapades. And if I know her, she will continue to leech a free ride at our expense.

"Look, the bottom line is you've got my name. And now your a part of me, as I am you. I'll always be there for you. I hope you know that. Let's get this thing resolved together. I'll be you're backbone when you feel you can't go on, but if you want out, honey, now is the time to do it, because there's no turning back until it's resolved. You've got to promise me, Paula, that you'll finish what we start here today. Even when it gets a little hot in the kitchen and it's gonna get hot. So you need to decide if you want to do this thing together or let it go."

"Are you gonna be there for me, Stephen?"

"All the way and then some, baby."

"Well...all right then, I'll do it. And I promise I won't back out when it gets too hot!"

"Are you sure?"

"No... I mean yes, I'm sure! Oh I'm so nervous I don't even know what I'm saying. You know me, you know how I am."

"It's okay to be nervous, Paula, probably for me more so than you."

"That's a big ol' lie, Stephen Jones. You're never nervous about anything."

"That's because I hide mine on the inside and you wear yours on the outside is all."

"Name me one time when you were nervous—just one, Stephen Jones?"

"When Madison was born and you struggled in labor through two shifts of nurses. I was bad nervous then, Paula."

Touched by the moment, her voice became a little shaky, "Yeah... you're right. I guess you got me there."

"Okay, Paula, you ready now to go back in together and start setting some things right?"

She nodded her head and I grabbed her hand as we walked back into Danny's office.

As soon as we got into his office, Paula said, "I want to file against 'em."

Joe Cammarata already had his jacket off and sleeves rolled up working on the complaint.

Paula signed the same handwritten contract that Joe had prepared earlier.

Danny said that he had a whole pile of messages from Clinton's new lawyer, Bennett.

Gil Davis added, "Good! Let's keep 'em sweating a little longer, we still have lots of work to do. Paula, is there anything else that happened in that hotel room or how the State Trooper sent you up there, that you might have left out?"

"I don't think so," she said.

Gil continued, "I believe we have enough to file on the State Trooper that took you up there. By mis-using his authority as a law officer and procuring you for the then-Governor for a sexual encounter is against the law."

"Oh my," Paula said, "I never thought about that."

Joe countered, "I know that what I'm about to ask you could be a little uncomfortable Paula, but was there anything distinguishing about the President's anatomy?"

Paula looked a bit doe-eyed. "I don't understand yer question?"

So I said, "Paula, he's asking—and correct me if I'm wrong, Joe, what Joe is wanting to know is, if there's anything about Clinton's pecker that stands out to you as being different? Joe needs to know this so he can help you prove that what you're saying is true."

There was a slight chuckle and a giggle, coupled with an immediate clearing of the throat passage, indicating an apparent effort to refrain oneself at my iniquitous explanation to Paula's perplexed indifference. It seemed appropriate at the present time to drop the formalities.

Paula, now clearly understanding Joe's question, started talking, "Well, as far as I could tell, his thingie-wangie was about maybe—four inches long and around the size of a quarter."

Elaborating, as she made an okay sign with her hand to demonstrate. I looked around the room to see if everyone was like me, tight-lipped and trying very hard not to distract Paula's serious description.

Joe furthered his line of questioning by asking Paula, "Was the President's penis in a state of arousal or uh… uh… was it flacid? That means not aroused."

Paula, "Oh, he was aroused all right! He was playing with it. Flopping and bopping it around."

"Paula," Joe said, "Were there any distinguishing characteristics, like birthmarks?"

"Um…let's see. The only thing else I can remember is that when he took his hands off himself, it pointed way over to one side." Paula using her index finger outstretched, demonstrated, "… and it was leaning to one side like this."

"Paula!" Joe blurted out, "You're pointing to the left. Did it lean to the left or the right?"

"It was left."

The whole room howled.

Paula, a little taken back, asked, "What's so funny?"

Wiping a tear from my eye, I said, "He's politically correct."

The crowd went wild!

Paula still mystified, "I still don't get it."

Joe then said, "It's the Leaning Tower of Pisa."

Another howl followed by a moment of composure. Joe grappling with restraint, asked, "How far over did it lean, Paula?"

"It looked like it touched his leg! He had to pull it over to keep it straight."

There was now silence. You could hear a fly buzzing its way through the room.

Joe looked at Gil, "You get what I'm thinking."

"Yeah, something like that's not normal."

Not knowing when to stop, I commented, "You can say that again, it confirms he's crooked."

Gil said, "Exactly! But not in a joking matter, Stephen. More importantly, it means that Paula can identify a distinguishing characteristic on Clinton."

As if the Grinch stole Christmas, a big smile creased my face.

Paula chuckled, "Oh, now I get it. It's because he's a Democrat, and it leans left."

Smiling back at Paula I said, "That's right, honey, now you're catching on."

Gil sitting behind Danny's desk twirling his *Cross* pen between his fingers like a baton exclaimed, "Now we've got some bargaining power to get this thing settled and this includes everyone in this room. Do not discuss this with anyone. We need to keep the lid on this tight."

Later that day Joe and Gil talked to Paula's mother and her sisters. Both sisters admitted that Paula was very upset the day of the incident.

However, Charlotte's story changed after we filed, saying that Paula had told her, "Whatever happens, it smells like money."

That's interesting to note because Charlotte's deadbeat husband, Mark, along with their two sons had posed for a picture with the then Governor Bill Clinton when he was campaigning for re-election. Mark's mother had personally worked on his campaign in her district. A few weeks after we filed, Paula's sister, Charlotte, suddenly had diamond rings on every finger. Mark was in the local coffee shop pulling wads of hundred-dollar bills out of his pocket. *All of this from a family on welfare? I don't think so*, I thought.

The Pro-Clinton *Arkansas Gazette* was hot off the press dishing out negative articles toward us about Charlotte's new version, not mentioning that she had changed her story. *Where's the fair and balanced?* I had a better chance spotting the planet Pluto with a pair of binoculars.

The Clinton cult was hard at work to divide and conquer. Paula felt betrayed by her own sister.

Paula asked, "How could my sister lie about what happened! Ain't blood supposed to be thicker than water?"

"Not when it comes to money honey. I hate to tell you that I told you so, but if you remember, you couldn't understand why I didn't like Mark and Charlotte in the first place. You had to practically drag me, kicking and screaming, when we visited. Oh, I can see what you're thinking and no, it's not because they lived in a trailer, either.

"You know what's so damn funny, Paula? Don't you find it ironic that you're the only sister who lives in a real house and Mark and Charlotte, who live in a trailer, are in cahoots with the same bastards that label you as trailer park trash?"

That comment went unchallenged.

Michael Isikoff called also saying that Charlotte had changed her story from when he had interviewed her last. So I told him to call and tell that to the biased bastards over at the Arkansas pig and whistle *Gazette*. "There so far up Clinton's ass, they can tell you if he had scrambled or poached eggs for breakfast."

Izzie replied, "I could call them, Stephen, but as you know, it won't change any minds over there."

"I guess you of all people, Izzie can relate."

Paula's new attorneys also talked to both Debbie Balentine and Pam Blackard, making sure what Paula said had coincided.

Everything seemed to come together for a good chance for negotiation. So around mid-afternoon on the fifth of May, we all huddled our chairs around the desk where Gil Davis sat.

Gil asked, "You ready to do this, Paula?"

With a nervous nod from her, he put in a return call to Bob Bennett.

Now that everything was set in motion, it all seemed surreal that it had to come to this point of Fahrenheit.

The call connected and both men talked.

Gil must have known Bennett, because from what I was hearing, it sounded as if they were reminiscing old times and asking each other how their families were getting along.

Not yet astute on the carnal knowledge of the usual discharge of salutations before getting to the raw meat at hand had caused me slight perplexity.

Then Gil told Bennett that we would be filing the case today. All of us were posed at every corner of the desk, each tweaking their necks forward in an effort to decipher Bennett's response from Gil's reaction.

Gil chuckled, and then said, "Well on the contrary, I think we do have a case to file, Bob."

They seemed to go back and forth on the merits of the case like two old bull elks vexed in a prelude of destiny over territory. Then Bennett changed the dynamics and Gil gave a concerned glance at Paula. He put his hand over the receiver and told Paula that Bennett just told him that there were naked photos of her floating around. Gil then asked Paula pointblank, "Are there any photos of you like that floating around?"

All eyes now focused on her, I could only guess what emotions must have surged through her at that moment of intensity as I squirmed on the armchair of the seat she was sitting in, waiting for her to answer.

Stephen M. Jones, Jr.

She batted her big blue eyes, exaggerated by the double-layer of mascara and said profoundly, "Why no, I've never posed naked for anybody."

Gil took his hand off the receiver and said, "I don't know of any pictures, Bob, but I'd be interested if any do exist."

Without taking a breath, as if *tit for tat*, Gil charged in, "My client says your guy has a distinguishing characteristic on his penis that she can identify."

After a substantial silence, Bennett without responding, asked Gil, "What would it take to get your client not to file."

Gil said, "She doesn't want money, Bob. She wants her good name cleared. A statement from your guy clearing her name is all it's going to take."

There was a long, distinct pause before Gil spoke to Bennett.

"All right. We can do that. Let me get the fax number for you."

Danny, on queue, scribbled the number on a stick'em pad and handed it to Gil.

"I'll be looking forward to your call later this afternoon."

Gil hung up and said, "Bennett has to talk to his client; he said he'd call us back."

Later, Bennett called back and each side wrangled back and forth on an acceptable letter exonerating Paula's good name.

The first draft was faxed and passed around for all to read. After reading the page length draft, I felt that it was unacceptable. The architectural structure of the draft was quite illuminating. My gilded apprenticeship marveled at the master of spin, if only for it's purity of creativity. It was my first taste of what was an early American snake-oil based portrait of what is—is. In its purest form, Clinton denied ever meeting her or acknowledging that anything between the two of them had ever happened. What I read was that it was all a big mistake, a hoax of circumstance and nothing asserted in the *American Spectator* between Paula and Clinton ever happened.

On top of that, it was full of legal jargon that made every statement a gray area for interpretation. I felt that Clinton's statement should be condensed to a paragraph of matter-of-fact, crystal clear words that were beyond a shadow of doubt in meaning.

It took great resolve not to bang my head repeatedly on the desk top out of frustration. You could say, take out *that* word and delete *that* statement with Bennett's camp grudgingly complying to agree only to get it faxed back with a different set of words with the same damn gray meaning! This sort of pretentious bull went on for hours, back and forth, until we whittled it down to one paragraph.

The statement was not an outright apology, but exonerated Paula's good name from participating in any implied sexual escapades with Clinton. The statement said that Clinton had no recollection of meeting Paula in a room at the Excelsior Hotel, but he didn't challenge her claim that they had met there.

Clinton went on to say that Paula did not engage in any improper or sexual conduct. "I regret the untrue assertions, which have been made about her conduct, which *may have* adversely challenged her character and good name."

Now, I went round and round the mulberry bush on the words they had inserted—"May have?"

Both Paula and I wanted it out.

"Look, Stephen, we're going to have to give a little and take a little. As it reads, I think Paula is getting everything she wants. The President is going to have a hard time explaining this statement."

"Maybe," I said, "but this last line where he states that, 'He nor his staff will have any further comment,' is bullshit! You know damn well his popinjay cronies will be out there in droves. I'm not a lawyer, but is there any way we can get some kind of gag order on this thing?"

Paula, like clockwork, incensed on my involvement said, "Finally, you admit yer not. Why won't you learn to leave the lawyer'ing work to them? They know more about them kind' a things than you do."

"Look, honey, I'm just trying to make sure they don't trash you anymore than they already have. I believe you need to quit worrying about the impression and just see that I'm thinking about you and covering all the bases, so you don't get hurt anymore—that's all."

"I know you, Steve Jones, you're just trying to act like a lawyer and you're not!"

"Paula, I just said that I wasn't, but what I am acting like is a husband who cares about stopping some of the raw sewage that these people are capable of spewing."

Once again, silence filled the room until Gil finally broke it by saying, "Sure, why not. We'll put in a tolling agreement."

I looked at Paula and shook my head. Then I said, "You have no idea what you're dealing with. I've tried to explain it to you, but you seem to resent me every time I make a statement or ask a question. I may not be a lawyer, but I do have enough common sense to ask a question or pose a thought that may or may not help. Hell, I don't know, Paula, but if it helps shield you from getting hurt, then I'm going to do it."

"It's just the way you say things, Stephen. It's your tone. You come off sounding controlling and I don't like that. It make's me feel like my word don't count."

"Yes, Paula, you're right. Sometimes I can sound controlling but to be fair Paula, you told me from the beginning that you wanted a man that took control and made the decisions. If you remember, this was not my idea. You claim that prize all by yourself, sweetheart. You sought out a lawyer and I was brought in after the fact. So don't be too fast to cast stones my way. Unbelievable. Here I am trying to protect you—and here you are pinging me in the head for it. I think I need a shrink to figure that one out."

Joe broke in confirming a tolling motion, "Let's toll the damn thing and go a step farther, Paula. Instead of one of Clinton's spokesmen reading the statement, why not have the President read it himself."

Paula said, "Now—I like that idea."

Glancing my way to see the stone hit me square between the eyes. Gil said, "Let's put it in writing and call 'em up."

After a few minutes the new amendments were fresh off the press.

Gil asked Joe, "How long has it been since Bennett said he had to consult with his client?"

"Forty-five minutes," Joe replied.

"Okay," Gil said. "Is everybody in agreement with the statement as it reads now?"

Everybody nodded.

"Paula, you're the client. Are you okay with this so far?"

"Can I read it one more time?"

Joe reaches over and handed the statement to Paula.

She read it out loud, and then said, "My...oh my! He's gonna have to read this to everybody on national TV. Well, that'll suit me just fine."

"That's if Clinton agrees to it Paula," I added.

"We've got Bennett on line one," Danny said.

We all huddled around Gil, taking our same positions as before as if each had been personally assigned.

Gil asked Bennett if he could speak to his client. Gil put his hand over the phone and said softly, "Clinton's in the room."

Joe looked over to us with the expression of "Hot damn—it doesn't get any better than this."

Paula seemed animated and was at the edge of her seat, so I just said, "I guess we got his attention, huh?"

That resulted in an elbow in the ribs, with me moving off her armchair to stand.

Gil told Bennett that we need Clinton to read this personally and not some White House spokesperson. Gil put his hand over the phone to relay that Bennett said he didn't know and to hold on. Bennett came back saying that Clinton would read the statement.

I said, "Wow, I thought he'd balk on that. That's great."

"Shush" Paula said, now out of elbow reach, but still close enough to get the full on stink eye.

Gil pitched the curve to Bennett, "Bob, the final stipulation is that we want a six-month tolling agreement in the statute of limitations. We don't want you guys taking pot shots at us in the press after we settle this thing. We want to be able to re-open this case if you do."

I don't know what was said on the other end, but it seemed ugly. I thought to myself, and not out loud for obvious reasons, *hmm, that last compromise must have pulled a hair in Bennett's shorts* because he could be heard screeching from beyond the phone's range of clarity. Instantly, we knew how they felt about that.

Gil pressed on, "We need to close the deal or file the case before five o'clock when the court clerk closes. What's it going to be, Bob?"

Reluctantly, both sides gave a little and took a little that day in an honest effort to find some type of common ground. Bennett said the tolling was a deal breaker but Clinton consented to reading the statement on national television. We agreed not to attach the tolling to the statute of limitations. On Clinton's word of good faith, we agreed to leave the last line as it was.

The statement, verbatim that Clinton was to read, is as follows:

<u>Clinton's Statement</u>

I have no recollection of meeting Paula Jones on May 8, 1991, in a room at the Excelsior Hotel. However, I do not challenge her claim that we met there, and may very well have met in the past. She did not engage in any improper or sexual conduct. I regret the untrue assertions which have been made about her conduct which may have adversely challenged her character, and good name. I have no further comment on my previous statements about my own conduct. Neither I nor my staff will have any further comment on this matter.

A formal draft was to be witnessed and signed by both parties the next morning.

Gil sent Billy, his paralegal, to give a press release. Billy was still in school working hard toward taking the bar exam. By virtue, Billy was more than willing to deliver (sacrifice himself) a statement to the hordes of press.

Like a sweatbox, the front of the courthouse was embodied with heat vapors, rising up from the concrete jungle. Sadistically, I enjoyed the view!

I think everybody in the office pretty much grilled Billy on what to say before being lead into the lion's den. We looked down and watched the spectacle from high above. Billy was easy to spot, his red hair stuck out like a burning bush.

With their sights locked in, the press encircled him like a hungry pack of wolves. Billy read a short statement saying that we may file something tomorrow, which lent truth to earlier speculation that negotiations were ongoing.

Amazingly, one reporter was using Billy's back as a writing pad.

Billy survived, but looked like he'd been chewed up and pooped off the side of a cliff.

Afterward, we went to a restaurant to celebrate the end to a close call and unwanted publicity. The restaurant, called *Juanita's*, must have been a favorite hangout of Clinton's, because pictures of his mug were plastered all over the place. Paula, Joe, Gil, and myself got a booth close to a television that was hanging on the wall. It was our first chance to see what was reported. We didn't have to wait long. I was starving, so I was head-deep into the chips and salsa when Joe said, "Son of a bitch. Those assholes lied."

I said, "What—what'd I miss?"

I looked over to Paula, then Joe, who was fixed on the TV that was now showing the clip of Billy reading the statement we had given the press earlier.

Joe said to Gil, "You know what this means, we've got to file this thing now. They broke the agreement and the goddamned ink's not even dry!"

I clamored for an explanation, "Will someone please tell me what the hell just happened?"

Gil said, "Stephen, they just reported that a White House spokesman said that we weren't going to file because Paula's family was against her and she didn't have a case."

"You got to be kidding me? What a frigging nightmare!"

"That's it then, Paula was quick to add. We're filing—right Gil?" Paula had always drawn her strength by leaning on others.

"That's right Paula, first thing in the morning. I'll fax Bennett's office and tell him the deal is off—we'll be filling."

The fax read as follows:

Confidential

Dated 05/06/94 A.M.

To: Robert Bennett, Esq.

Bob,

I appreciate your efforts to resolve this dispute amicably.

We must have a tolling agreement.

Sources at your client's office are cited by numerous press reports as giving spurious reasons for the filing delay. This illustrates to me that the "no comment" provisions are very difficult to rely upon, if they stand by themselves without sanctions.

My client would relinquish her claims without hope of resurrection if your client's staff, in an understandable effort to cast the ambiguous language of the press release in a favorable light, comments on it publicly, or for background.

Other problems exist, including your client's refusal to make a direct acknowledgment that he was in the hotel suite with Paula, and that he definitely knows her. Further efforts to resolve these matters seem fruitless since the tolling agreement is unfortunately a "deal breaker," as you have said.

Therefore, the complaint will be filed today.

You should be receiving a fax of the complaint with this

message. Please advise if you will waive service.

Gil Davis

Later, I would find out that an aid for Hillary was the White House source that had leaked the story that broke the deal. *Bet ya' wish you could take that mother of all screw-up's back, huh Hillary?* I wonder where we'd all be today if she would have stuck to the gentleman's agreement of no comment. I guess Hillary's no gentleman.

So…on Friday, the sixth of May, we filed a four-count complaint charging William Jefferson Clinton with sexual misconduct by assaulting her on May 8, 1991.

In tandem, we filed against his cohort Danny Ferguson, the State Trooper who had conspired against Paula to deny her rights under Arkansas Civil Law.

Any money made from the lawsuit after legal fees, were to be given to a charity of our choosing.

CHAPTER ELEVEN

This is as good a place as any to air out a few grievances. I want to clear the air from some less than credible authors and one in particular, Jeffrey Toobin, who said that my motivation for this lawsuit was all about money and political hatred. "Well, Mr. Carpetbagger, it was never about money for me. I can't speak for Paula, after we separated she allowed herself to be exploited for profit in the same manner as Gennifer Flowers.

She posed for *Penthouse*, the very same magazine we had sued to protect her privacy. Paula said she did it because she was desperate for money. *Victim to the very end, huh Paula?* I find that hard to believe when her share, after attorney fees from the Clinton settlement, was a cool quarter million. So you can imagine how I felt after five years of battling for her good name and reputation, just to hear that she posed for *Penthouse*.

She disgraced everything that I had tried so hard to protect. That's something she'll have to explain to our two sons someday. I'm sure she'll blame everyone—but herself.

While history may cast a dim light on Paula's less-than-honorable mentions, I truly believe that my driving force behind the shroud of circumstances was true, honorable, and yeah, maybe a little vengeful. *Hell, I'm only human!*

As the case ensued, so did my perception. It wasn't so much about Paula's reputation, but my own—both intertwined by vows. I saw in Paula my own vulnerability to protect and honor her.

Looking back, there were many times when we were offered large sums of money to go on TV talk shows. Yeah, we sure the hell could have used the money, but you see, that would have undermined what the suit was all about.

I also believe, with all my heart, that it would've damaged any other woman or man's chances for redress in our courts by what is perceived as sexual harassment in the work place and not as some frivolous joke to be thrown out, but taken seriously.

If Clinton had gotten away without any consequences then precedence would have been set and the bar standards would have been lowered. Every flea-bitten lawyer from Paducah, Kentucky to White Plains Minnesota would make a mockery of sexual harassment in the work place. So it was important for me not to accept money for those very reasons and, of course, the implied stigmatism that goes along with it.

Clinton's lawyer, Bennett, was just itching for us to exploit the lawsuit for money, so he could legitimize his slanderous accusations that the lawsuit is "tabloid trash, with a caption."

What decent human being wants to earn a buck by exploiting an embarrassing, sick sexual encounter years after the fact? If I could wash my hands of the whole Pompous Pilot matter with immunity from judgment, I would. Unfortunately, I can be quite reactionary and it's not in my nature to lay with the sheep. All I can tell you is while Paula and I were together, I would have never agreed to do anything that would embarrass my family for the sake of money. I'd like to believe that I hold myself to a higher standard than that. By all accounts, that's what the lawsuit was about to begin with.

After the settlement, I was in contact with numerous women's organizations that wanted Paula as a spokesperson at their next meeting, some of which were willing to pay for her time. I thought this was great for two reasons. Paula could be an inspiration for other women who felt trapped and abused in a hostile work environment. And, the longevity of the suit put a

Stephen M. Jones, Jr.

financial strain on our family. Clinton's close friendship with Al Checchi, owner of the airline I worked for the past eighteen years, had me terminated.

To me, accepting money for a speaking engagement seemed a legitimate cause. But there was one problem, Paula chose a different path.

As for political hatred, it's true, I was never much of a fan when it came to the way Clinton governed the state of Arkansas, but I wouldn't characterize it as a caricature of *hate, Mr. Toobin*. I think of it as *the proof is in the pudding* syndrome. Arkansas was one of the poorest states in the union with the highest crime rate per capita given its size and population. Little Rock could rival the gangs of Los Angeles. Let me tell you, there are plenty of homeboys of all races involved in gangs south of the Mason-Dixon line. Instead of taking a hard line to clean up the streets, Clinton ignored the growing problem so as to not offend his political standing with the minority.

Since I'm big on environmental issues, it bothered me that Clinton eased the dumping restrictions so his buddy, Tyson, could monopolize the poultry industry thereby making the Arkansas River one of the most polluted rivers in the US at one time. Tyson repaid Clinton with big donations to both Governmental and Presidential elections.

Although I was no Clinton supporter, my dislike was a difference of opinion of what he had done in a hotel room with Paula. So with that said, I like to think of myself as having conservative values, with some liberal tendencies, when it comes to some social issues. My driving force was purely a personal vendetta of honor. The political differences was just icing on the cake.

Where do you think the term throughout the lawsuit of restoring Paula's reputation and good name came from? That didn't pop out of the sky like a fuzzy UFO sighting. That was me, behind the scenes burning the ears of Paula's lawyers wanting to restore my wife's reputation that I thought had been tainted by untrue allegations.

That was Clinton's big mistake, putting his cronies out there like Paul Begala and the biggest asshole of them all, James Carville, who with his one comment about dragging a hundred dollar bill down the street of a trailer park, drove the stake deep into the heart of any early negotiations. As far as I was concerned, that one comment, along with the continuous personal insults, caused me to want nothing less than an apology for Paula.

I let it be known that in the course of this case that James Carville, with his Roswell good looks, should take heed not to have any coincidental encounters in my cornfield. Of course, knowing now what I didn't know then, I might owe James a dollar's worth of regret seeing how he knew Paula better than I did. Although where I'm from, a man doesn't make personal attacks on another man's wife without any consequences.

Getting back to the subject of sour grapes—for a disingenuous author like Jeffrey Toobin, in his book to suggest that I was out to sue Clinton for money, is a damn lie. It was true in his book that I was outraged when the *Washington Post* politically quashed Paula's story. I expressed my feelings on film for Pat Matrisciana in his documentary, *The Clinton Chronicles*. Toobin retained a copy from Clinton's legal team that had subpoenaed the unedited version.

In his book, he portrayed me as having to make six takes for the camera, walking over to kiss Paula as staged. Well, yeah, that's because it was! He used his knowledge that I've been in a few movies by demeaning my mannerism as a method actor, when Toobin damn well knew that I was taking directions from Pat off camera to shoot it over and over until he got exactly the shot he wanted.

As I said—true, but twisted to frame me into his version of the bad guy out for blood money.

In fact, the only time I ever talked to Toobin was when Paula's spokesperson called us and handed her cell phone to him. I had trouble understanding half of what he was slurring, because Toobin was slap-happy drunk from being out to *Margarita Ville* trying to schmooze up to Paula's spokesperson so as to get a personal interview. Which, by the way, is what most of the sneaky ones do. They try to infiltrate into your family as an "*I feel your pain*" type of person and I'm own your side, to either print some exclusive news breaking revelation, or lure you on some television show to boost their ratings.

After a while of living in a vacuum of existence, I learned that there was an advantage to all this unwanted intrusion. I could give them a little taste of their own medicine or I could bring them into the fold, that being after they had proven to be either friend or foe. If friend, I could leak out information that would benefit our position, just like the Clintontologist. "If you can't beat-um, join-um."

On the flip side, if you were foe, I would dissimulate information. For example, Greta Van Susteren, while on *CNN*, would pretend to be a friend.

She once talked to my son when he accidentally picked up the phone. Paula noticed Madison talking on the phone for a few minutes.

"Who's he talking to?" she asked me.

"I don't know? I thought you answered and gave the phone to him to talk to Nana!"

I put the phone on speaker. It was Greta, just talking away with Madison. Greta had this bad habit of calling up minutes before going on the air, so she could say something like, "I just spoke to the Jones's and they say "X, Y, and Z" on whether a sitting President can be sued."

Now keep in mind, I had just gotten off the phone with her telling me that as a lawyer she felt that a sitting President could be sued, but on her show; however, she completely contradicted what she had told me just moments earlier. As I watched her show, Greta reminded her audience that being a lawyer herself, she took the position that the Jones' case should wait until the President leaves office. *I'll be damn! Just can't trust anybody at face value anymore.*

So that's why I evolved into a *show me* kind of guy. I think Greta should've renamed her show at *CNN* to *The Two Faces of Greta."*

"Hey Greta! That's exactly why the Supreme Court Justices sit on the highest bench in the land and you earned an honorary degree in deceptive journalism.

Well, after that little charade, I used her solely for dissemination. That being said, I immensely respected the lead reporter on her show, Bob Franken. I found him to be honest and most of all, a man of his word. I can't in all honesty say the same for Greta. Now that she's with *FOX* news, I see that they hold her to a higher standard of what's fair and balanced.

As for Jeffrey Toobin, I flatly turned down the interview that he wanted to do with Paula. I can smell stink and this guy stunk. I saw right through him like a cheap pair of pantyhose stretched over the face of a dime store robber. It's almost funny, the harder disingenuous drunks try to talk straight, the more they ramble and reveal their face card.

I remember how he was massaging our ego by telling me what a sorry son-of-a-bitch Clinton was, and how much of a family man, with traditional values, he was. Boy, ain't that a bird dog! Yep, Toobin's family would've been real proud of *Daddy Dearest* that night.

As I said, I knew our dirty laundry would be hung out and dried along with statements taken out of context for disingenuous effect. Hell, I didn't want personal baggage out there anymore than Clinton did, but by God I wouldn't stand by and be blatantly chastised by some short pudgy *Alice in Wonderland* character trying to steal a headline by looking in rabbit holes. I understood that HBO was going to work a deal with boozer boy. A miniseries based on his book, but many people had threatened libel suits, so the project was dropped. It's this kind of narcissism of cynical bias that spawned my biggest reason for writing this book. I wanted my side of the story told and I wanted closure. This book is not a pro Paula, anti-Clinton, (well maybe a little) or for that matter a pro Stephen book. God knows, I made my fair share of mistakes and said things out of anger, but hey, that's the composition of reality.

Paula and I went through the gamut of human emotions for five long years. I think those feeling were justified, given the set of unwanted circumstances that were thrown our way. You're reading this book the way I perceived it on a humanistic level from inside the glass, not outside looking in through a hexagon of broken colored facets with hidden agendas. Let the chips fall where they may. I think there was enough room for everyone involved to make mistakes. The story is as much of a cultural tragedy as it is a source of historical value.

Well enough of that, I just want people to know how tremendously hard it was to allow personalities (just to name a few), whom I'd never met before, say or write falsehoods about anyone and not respond because of the greater cause. See—see how I get when I write and drink a good bottle of red wine bursting with oaky-vanilla and fig tannins' at the same time. Maybe I need more wine and less memories. I know what you're thinking. Well, there's a big difference between drinking for effect and connoisseuring.

After a chaotic week, we flew back to Los Angeles after filing the case against Clinton and Ferguson.

I took great strides to keep the media from finding out where we lived. Even with a name like Jones, I knew it was just a matter of time until they found us.

A few weeks went by and Paula was offered a host of media appearances. All talk show circuses were turned down including one that offered Paula seven-hundred thousand dollars to take a lie detector test on national television. Paula was willing to take the test, but the attorneys were not as willing. I scrutinized the offer only because it could have paid for legal fees without strings attached from the *Landmark Foundation* giving minuscule credence to Hillary's right-wing phobias. To boot, the money was badly needed for investigative work that was on hold for lack of funds.

The attorneys were worried about what questions would be asked, who was going to perform the test and under what conditions. I'm sure they didn't want egg on their face if Paula didn't pass the test on national television. The fact that we would have been blasted from the Clintontologists for taking money, no matter how justified, sealed the deal not to accept the offer.

However, Paula was all gungho to do the show. "I'm not afraid of taking no dang lie detector test. It'll prove to everybody that I'm telling the truth!"

In the interim, the attorneys did set up a lie detector test with a retired FBI agent. Paula spent several days in Washington with him. When she had finished, the attorneys arranged a press conference to announce that she has passed the test with flying colors.

While commuting back and forth from LAX to DCA, Cindy Hayes, Paula's first spokesperson and fundraiser, put together an interview with a reputable news reporter named Sam Donaldson.

Without Apology

Paula's attorney Gil, a close friend, hired Cindy Hayes. If you watch C-SPAN, Cindy's husband was the guy who standsup and reads the new bills to be voted on in Congress. I guess someone has to fork over the pork!

Anyway, this move by Gil to hire Cindy changed the hand-written contract to revert from a contingency to an hourly rate. I wasn't too keen on that clause in the beginning. I knew it would eventually come back and bite us in the butt.

As for hiring Cindy, I was totally against Paula signing the power of attorney contract that she sent to Paula. It gave Cindy the power to hire and spend any amount of money raised on whatever she deemed fit, for one year.

After an augment with me reminding Paula what had happened when she went off half-cocked and signed a contract with her first attorney, Danny Trailer, she signed it anyway out of spite. It sooo pissed me off that she could be so incredibly irresponsible that I pretty much washed my hands of the whole mess for a few months. I sat on the sidelines to watched the *"I told you so"* flare ups.

Cindy's salary, along with her family members she hired along the way, was in the thousands. The few times there was money raised, it was gone lick-a-dee-split.

After Joe called me and asked if I would call my friend at the *Landmark Legal Foundation* to pay for legal fees because they hadn't been paid in a while, I got off the sidelines ready to rumble.

I requested bank account statements from the fund. Cindy did her damn'est to stop me by canceling two of my requests. I finally got Paula to personally sign the request and faxed it to the bank demanding copies.

It took just a glance over the statements to conclude that nothing spent had helped to defer the cost of the lawsuit. Every time money came in, all of it was sponged up in salary or used to purchase electronic equipment that certainly came in handy in supporting Cindy's *Mama-Mia's Pesto Plus* business she ran out of her home.

To be fair, Cindy did use some funds to reimburse herself and rightfully so, for clothes and new make-up for Paula.

Cindy wanted to change Paula's image into a softer look. Cindy tried to stop some of the personal attacks by changing Paula's wardrobe to what Paula described as a *plain Jane look. However,* Paula went along with the new makeover, but she wasn't too pleased at the way Cindy wanted to change her hair and make-up. I'd been trying to get Paula to tone down her make-up for years which only led to the layers of resentment.

Sam Donaldson gave Paula plenty of airtime to showcase her new look. The first of two interviews with Sam Donaldson had great reviews, interjecting national attention to her story.

In the interim *Time Magazine* put Paula on their cover that Sam paraded around with during his personal appearance on *The Tonight Show* with Jay Leno. The only comedian that can stump his chin instead of his toe. The next night, Sam appeared on David Letterman. After those appearances, Leno and Letterman, overnight, would have new material generated from the Jones' suit for years to come. Pretty much both sides of the fence got their fair share of being the butt-end of their jokes.

Things were moving along, except for the continuing rumor of naked pictures of Paula that kept floating around. My friend Rev. Patrick Mahoney called. He said rumor was that *Penthouse* had pictures of Paula, and was putting them in their upcoming Christmas issue.

I turned to Paula, while still on the phone, and told her what Pat was saying.

"Now Paula, are you sure you've never posed for anything that they could use against you. Look, it doesn't matter to me. That was in your past and I didn't know you back then. Lord knows I've done some things myself. So, honey, listen to me. You need to tell me if you have pictures out there so we can do damage control before this thing gets out of hand."

"All I know is I did some pictures in a bathing suit for a photographer in Cabot, Ark. but that's all I did."

I held the phone out in Paula's direction. "Hey Pat, did you hear that?"

"Yeah, Steve I did, but I'm telling you—my sources say they've got something, along with an article, and it won't be pretty."

"All right Pat, I'll call the attorneys to see what they can find out. Thanks. See ya'...you, too, Pat. Bye now."

The next morning, I called Joe and told him what Pat had said. Joe told me he'd check it out and call me back. He did and said the rumor was true. Bob Guccione, the owner of *Penthouse*, was doing an article with pictures of Paula from some unknown source.

Later in the week we found out that Paula's brother-in-law and some old boyfriend had agreed to do an interview with *Penthouse*. I asked Joe if this was the guy that Bennett was referring to when he said that there were naked pictures of Paula out there.

"I'm sure it is Steve. Bennett mentions it and now *Penthouse* has the real deal. That's the way these people work."

"Well Joe, Paula's right here and she says the only pictures she's ever posed for were in swimsuits. She did say a few were on the skimpy side, but none were naked. She said the guy who took the pictures was some photographer, who she never dated, so the old boyfriend must be false or maybe someone else."

"Paula told me that her sister, Lydia, did some pictures in the buff a long time ago. Maybe they got the wrong sister. What do we do now Joe?"

"We slap an injunction on them."

"Can we do that?"

"You bet we can, I used to practice in New York, that's my old stomping ground."

That's exactly what Joe did. He filed an injunction that stopped *Penthouse* in its tracks. It was unprecedented in the courts history to have ever stopped a porn magazine from going to press from printing unauthorized pictures of a non-celebrity type. If this injunction was upheld, Guccione would stand to lose millions.

This caused several offers to come Paula's way. A jeans company offered her fifty-thousand to do a print ad, with a press conference holding up the check. Cindy Hayes accepted this offer to help fund Paula's legal battle. Uh-huh. I couldn't see any difference between this offer and the seven-hundred thousand dollar offer, except it was a hell of a lot less.

We badly needed money for investigative work. The money that came in from the *Landmark Foundation* wasn't nearly enough to wage war on all fronts. That's the reason I was told why Gil had hired Cindy Hayes.

By fund raising, she would be able to offset any expenses. The way I saw it, the damn thing looked like a cash cow for somebody. As far as I know, not one single dime went to the lawyers or to pay for investigative work. Go figure.

Cindy thought she could do damage control from any negative fallout from the *No Excuse* jean ads, by giving half to a charity. It was still spun that we were out for money by the Clintontologists. The twenty-five thousand we tried to give to a Little Rock women's shelter was refused because the head of the shelter was a F.O.B. Talk about a two-faced hypocrisy from a fundamental humanitarian organization. We then gave it to a Virginia-based women's shelter that was overwhelmed by the generosity.

The court date was set to enforce the *Penthouse* injunction in New York City. Paula and I flew in a day early to attend the proceedings.

Joe's father, who was still living in NY, invited us to a 17-course dinner in historic Little Italy. Over dinner, Joe thought it best that Paula not appear in court. He summarized that Guccione's lawyers could very easily call her to the stand and ask her about the Clinton lawsuit including the sealed distinguishing physical characteristics. So the next morning it was planned to quietly drop Paula off at a deli across the street from the courthouse escorted by an ex-FBI agent, turned investigator.

Joe, myself and Billy would attend the court proceedings.

Joe picked us up from our hotel in one of those extinct, big fat yellow cabs that was an icon of New York. Once inside the cab, discussion fell back to the purported article and pictures that would be challenged in court.

"Well, all I can say, Paula, is they must have something, because they're not the type of magazine to use bathing suit shots."

Without Apology

"When are you going to get it through your thick skull, Steve Jones, that I didn't pose nude for anybody?"

Joe reined in the conversation, "Stop it—Paula. They sent me a copy of the issue."

Joe pulled the magazine out of his briefcase. The picture of the woman on the front was the spitting image of Paula in revealing lingerie, but not her. In big captions it said, "See Paula Jones totally nude."

Joe had ear-marked the pages and opened the magazine showing one of several pictures of Paula on a bed with her boyfriend wearing only a thong.

Paula responds, "Ooh...those."

Needless to say, I was floored. I guess I wasn't prepared to see my wife lying in bed, posing spread eagle, next to her ex-boyfriend right before going to court to defend her honor. As much as it hurt to see her that way, I grew angry by her response. Holding back all my emotions, I blankly said, "Paula—do you know what you've done?" Not allowing her to respond, I continued. "You've just undermined everything."

She burst in, "Once again, Steve Jones, I have no idea what you're talking about. And I don't know what-you-think-you're so upset about, these pictures were taken before I even knew you."

"Paula, it was never about that. You're damn right I'm upset. I don't want to see you and some guy at the ninth hour pop up like a jack in the fucking box after you said nothing existed! Not to mention our family's *coming soon to a news stand near you* embarrassment of one leg going north, the other south and a piece of transparent dental floss stretched across your shaky puddin' making a happy face. But for the sake of argument, let's forget about you lying to me from the jump, making me look like a total fucking idiot, telling everyone and their mother that there's no nude pictures and focus on the here and now."

"Think about it. In one clean sweep you've lost any credibility that you had with your attorneys. How can Joe or Gil walk into any courtroom and fight for you when they don't know if you're telling them the truth."

Paula shot back, "I took a lie detector test, didn't I?"

"That, Paula, was just about what happened in the hotel room. I'm talking about *why* we're here today. Why in the hell couldn't you come clean about this weeks ago? I told you it didn't matter if something happened in your past, as long as we can deal with it before something like this happens."

Grasping the veracity of her predicament, she looked at Joe and softly said, "Honestly, Joe, I forgot all about these pictures."

"Bullshit—Paula!" I blurted.

"You just don't forget about doing something like that unless you're some porn star and you've been corn-balled so much you can't remember the day of the week."

"You got no right to talk to me that way, Steve Jones!"

"You got to be kidding me, Paula? I'm your husband and I have no right! Everybody who's been in your corner, with their necks stuck out for you, just got them chopped off, but I have no right—fucking unbelievable!

Joe said, "Look, we're almost here. We can debate this later. We've got an injunction to enforce."

The investigator was standing near the deli as we dropped Paula off with him. Joe then had the taxi driver pull up in front of the courthouse. Joe and I walked silently up the never-ending steps.

I noticed many of New York's finest standing in union to keep the clowns from getting rowdy. I guess they got a heads-up from the local media telling everyone the circus was coming to town.

I was so pissed at Paula that when a reggae guy, with matted dukie hair screamed obscenities at me, I reached out and shook his hand.

"Right on, Bro."

He looked at me like I had lost my mind. He was half right, I had just gotten the wind of trust knocked out of me and was still reeling on what to do next. I felt like wet linen hung out to dry, flopping in the indignant breeze of self-analysis.

Hells-bells, I'm too deep to climb out now, so I'll keep digging. Maybe I can poke my head in the sand and nobody will notice. I wonder if some jerkster will come up while we're at a family restaurant asking Paula to sign a copy of his

Penthouse issue. Damn these thoughts in my head. Anyhow, fat chance that will happen.

Well it did!

The media cameras were not allowed inside the court room; however, there were plenty of sketch artists sitting in the jurors' booth making sweeping motions on big sheets of paper.

Billy and Joe's dad met us inside the courtroom. I couldn't help noticing the gleam in the eye of Joe's dad showing how proud he was of his son. At that moment, I wished that I could have felt that proud about someone or something of value.

I looked around and saw at least four or five well-dressed, uptown lawyers representing *Penthouse*. A loud, strong voice, that could be heard all through the room, said in an authoritarian tone, "Please stand for the honorable Judge Leisure."

After all the preliminaries, Joe asked the court's indulgence to allow Billy to serve as his aid; briefing Judge Leisure that Billy will soon be taking the Bar exam. The Judge asked Billy where he was going to law school and he seemed pleased that Billy was serving as Joe's apprentice. If you could have heard Joe that day, you would have thought we were going to enforce that injunction. He went *point by point* explaining that Paula's brother-in-law didn't back up any of his accusations in the written article that accompanied the pictures.

Penthouse attorneys gave no evidence that any sexual encounters stated in the article ever happened, all hearsay.

Joe emphasized they were lies and that *Penthouse* couldn't produce one witness to say otherwise. Ending his surmise, Joe said that because Paula was a victim in a separate complaint, that there were people with ulterior motives wanting to defame her good name by exploiting her private life. The law has protections to prevent a publication to print defamatory, unsubstantiated accusations about ordinary people.

The Judge took a recess and would render his decision upon returning.

Stephen M. Jones, Jr.

Joe and I stood in front of the men's urinals discussing the possibilities. "Hey Joe, I'm not sure what's going to happen, but I think you pulled it off. I mean, the other side didn't say squat. All they did was produce that scumbag who wrote the article and he didn't say much about anything as far as I could tell."

With a smile on his face he walked to the porcelain sink to wash his hands and said, "You liked that, huh?"

Knowing that he felt the same and appreciated the compliment, I said, "Yeah, Joe, you pretty much told 'em you came ready to kick ass and chew bubble gum and that you were all out of bubble gum."

We both laughed and it felt good to laugh right about then. It relieved some of the tension built up from earlier.

Billy and Joe's dad were waiting outside the large courtroom doors when the officer stepped out to say that the court is soon to be in session.

Joe said, "Well, is everybody ready?"

I commented, "Yeah, I'm ready for a second helping of whatever you're gonna dish out, Joe."

We all took our seats just to stand back up as soon as we sat down when the bailiff announced the Honorable Judge Leisure. As we sat back down, I noticed the thick binder he laid on top of his bench. It didn't take me long to know the direction the decision would take when he opened his statement with, "If I had known then, what I know now, I would not have allowed an injunction in the first place."

He was talking about article 21, which stated that if a person is in the public eye or of a celebrity status, then a publication can write or print anything they choose as long as the publication shows a reasonable effort to obtain what *they* think is the truth. Meaning, even though it may not be true they can still print it.

So I'm thinking, *who the hell says she's a celebrity. Just because she's suing the President doesn't give them a license to print lies.* Then there's this echo inside my head saying *how do you know they're lies?*

After what happened inside that cab ride how far are you going to go to protect your wife's reputation, Bubba? She's going to make a monkey out of you yet. Yeah, but this happened before I met her, and she's my wife. The echo diminished with a "you'll be sorry" epithet.

I snapped back to reality as the Judge started to read from that thick decision on his bench. He quoted past suits as far back as Rachel Welch vs *Playboy* 1960 something to present day celebrities that have sued, and lost under entitlement slash article 21.

The more I listened, the madder I got. That big old son-of-a-bitch of a Judge already knew what his decision was before Joe even opened his mouth. There's no way all that paper work in front of him was just prepared in a ten-minute recess. Why did that damn Judge facilitate a courtroom façade of due process when he already knew what his decision would be?

To me, it was the same salt in the wound that Paula had given me earlier. I couldn't stand it any longer. I got up in the middle of his epitome of judgmental due process and walked toward him with purpose. Judge Leisure looked up over his reading glasses, but continued to read as I continued my stride.

The change in the tone of his voice told me that he was a bit unsure of my motives. That in itself gave me solace, knowing that he wasn't sure what the hell I'd do next.

As I got to the end of the front pew I looked him square in the eye, turned left and headed toward the large double-chambered doors. If a man could give a *go to hell look*, I sure gave him my best shot.

Unfortunately for me, it wouldn't be the last time this Judge would rule against me. Years later I filed a breech of contract against Abe Hirschfeld on behalf of Paula.

You might remember, but if you don't, let me bring you up to snuff. Toward the end of the lawsuit, Hirschfeld offered Paula one million dollars to settle with Clinton. Since our legal liabilities, after years of doing battle, were in the three million dollar range it seemed like a good idea at the time. If we could settle with Clinton, the Hirschfeld money would go a long way toward paying off what we owed.

Stephen M. Jones, Jr.

The way I saw it, Hirschfeld got a million plus in the way of free advertising. He was on every talk show, holding up a personal check, spouting that all we had to do was settle the lawsuit and he'd pay Paula a million bucks.

Hirschfeld, "No strings attached, settle with Clinton and take the money. I want to help get the country back to business." In his words, he felt that the lawsuit was interfering with world business by too much monkey business. We opened dialogue to see if he could put his money where his mouth was.

Seemed simple enough, right? Reach for your ankles hambone! Nothing in this world comes that easy, at least not for me.

We accepted his offer, but at the ninth hour, he attached a string. It was imperative that Paula fly down to Washington on Halloween, of all days—of all days. What a bastard! The press, like a witch on a stick, flew with that.

He wanted Paula to stand along side him at the Mayflower Hotel for a national press conference to accept an enlarged check, probably the size of his prostrate gland, or the deal was off.

The official check that Hirschfeld had displayed on all the cable news shows is the one he handed to Paula. She was told by Hirschfeld's attorney to give the check back to Hirschfeld when the cameras stopped rolling, because it was only symbolic.

The money was to be wired two days later. The contract was simplistic—settle the lawsuit with Clinton, indemnify him of any further liabilities and he would pay one million dollars.

Within two days after the signing of the contract, Hirschfeld would wire the money into a trust account in Dallas, whereas it would stay until the lawsuit was settled. Problem was, Hirschfeld never wired the money. He got away with all that national publicity for free.

So, where's the connection with Judge Leisure you ask? Okay. When Paula and I were smack dab in the middle of getting divorced, the IRS concluded their four-year audit.

I told the divorce Judge that the Clinton case was never about money for me, but Uncle Sam didn't see it that way. He wanted me to pay for the taxes

199

on the Paula Jones fund. I had just gotten my job back after two years (I'll get to that story later) and my first pay check was garnished and my accounts were frozen by the IRS. In my own defense, I said that Paula should pay since it was her lawsuit and she received all the settlement money to the tune of over two-hundred thousand dollars. All I was asking for was enough money to pay the taxes from her lawsuit.

The Judge rubbed his chin in thought about it and said, "I'll order it to be split. You pay half and she pays half."

"Well, hell's bells Judge! Why should I pay anything?"

"Because, Mr. Jones, you were married at the time of the settlement and California law splits everything down the middle."

"Well, Judge, if that's the case, then my half of the settlement can go on the taxes."

"Nope" he said. "Can't do that either."

"Why not? What's the difference?"

"The incident between Clinton and Paula happened before you two were married. So the settlement is for her pain and suffering that may, or may not, have occurred."

"So, what you're saying is that she gets the money and I have to pay half the taxes?"

"That's right. You can fight it in court, but my decision will stand."

"Sounds like a bag of farts to me, Judge"

Only in a perfect world—since I was working and Paula was not, the IRS garnished the full amount from me, including penalties and interest, to the tune of thirty-seven thousand dollars, not half. Think Paula paid her half? Nope, notta.

After asking about the Hirschfeld offer, the divorce judge, feeling generous, threw me a scrap and said that I was entitled to half of any recovery from the breech of contract she had with Hirschfeld, if I so choose to pursue a case.

"Wow, Judge, that's awful kind of you, thanks for the dog biscuit."

Having no other *ways to my means*, I hired an attorney in New York and sued the old bastard for breech of contract. I served him while he was in

Stephen M. Jones, Jr.

Rikers Island State Prison for allegedly trying to hire a hit man to kill his long-time business partner, Stanley Stahl, who died of natural causes a few months later. A bizarre twist of events to say the least. It was as if I was running around in circles in an endless field of cow poop.

As luck would have it, the Judge who was assigned to the New York case was none other than the Honorable Judge Leisure. After four more long years of legal battle, Judge Leisure threw out the case on a baseless decision late in 2004.

I think Leisure was going through the motions, thinking more about retiring to his favorite fishing spot than making a fair decision. I mean, why would you throw out a case after four long years of hell dealing with Hirschfeld's antics in court?

Hirschfeld would hire, then fire, an attorney and then make himself pro se.

This circus act continued through five different attorneys. For those of you that don't know the term pro se, it means defending oneself in court without a lawyer.

By allowing Hirschfeld his constitutional rights, he had made a mockery of the judicial system. His supposed ignorance, plead right into the court's loophole.

Case in point, once out of the blue, while Hirschfeld appeared in court, he blurted out to the Judge asking him if he knew what the five points of the Jewish star represented. Historically, there is some debate between five points and six. The Star of David has six, double triangle. *Obviously, another side show of diversion.* I think even the Clintons could have learned a trick or two from this flim-flam man. Personally, I don't know what the five points mean in religious terms, but I can tell ya' that in the business world, the six points are: Screw-you-by-all-means-necessary.

While I sued him, he was also being sued by his own son, Levy, over control of his estate, who was simultaneously being sued by Hirschfeld's daughter. On top of that, Stanley Stahl's business benefactors were suing him along with the State of New York for back taxes. *And I thought I had problems.*

But my point is—he knew how to work the courts. By the time we'd requested documentation or subpoenaed a witness, the lawyer was no longer representing Hirschfeld. Extensions were as common as in Hollywood hairdos. Judge Leisure was sick and tired of dealing with the case, so he pitched it, simple as that. *Dammit, I couldn't win for losing. I was pitching horseshoes once and got hit in the head. I wonder if that's got anything to do with my luck?*

Hirschfeld has since died and I'm sure he's in a place that suits his deeds. As for Judge Leisure, I'm sure he has long-since retired, sipping on a fruity drink someplace with a piece of sacrificial pineapple impaled by a paper umbrella and wearing a different kind of robe.

Other than Paula and my attorney, nobody until now, including that old fat fart himself, knew I filed that case.

Now, let's go back in time to the previous court room scene. Upon my departure, I opened the large, double doors leading out of the courtroom, grasped the backside of the latch and slammed it closed as hard as I could. The echo rumbled through the big chambered hallway like far away thunder. The sound was a bit louder than I had imagined, so I expected to get an immediate response from the officer standing inside Leisure's courtroom. A few seconds went by, nothing happened. I waited a little longer, but no one came out to address my behavior, so I went back into the men's room to relieve some tension.

After about ten minutes, court was adjourned. Joe came over and asked me not to give any comments to the press while I was still having trouble compartmentalizing my coyote ugly attitude.

"Stephen," Joe said, "I can see it in your face. Loosen your tie before you explode or something. Now listen to me...Hey! I'm serious here, don't go flying off the handle and say something you might regret later. Let me do all the talking. This is not over yet, you'll see. Just don't say something in anger."

"All right, Joe. We'll do it your way—for now."

We walked out and Joe made some superficial comments, but that was underscored, because Paula was spotted in the deli across the street. Like

Stephen M. Jones, Jr.

wildfire to dry grass, word got out and the media ran scurrying toward her. Joe and I pushed hurriedly through the crowd.

It must have looked like a scene from the *Keystone Cops*.

The investigator muscled his way through, with Paula in tow. Joe tried in vain to hail a cab as the reporters gave chase falling over each other trying to catch up.

All of us must have run at least two blocks, dodging open street venders selling everything from *Coney Island* hotdogs to not so fresh fish. The combination of smells, along with an exerted heart rate, made it impossible to hold your breath and run at the same time. Joe finally hailed a cab. We quickly piled in sitting silent, except for our loud craving of heavy breathing chastised in a internal rhythm; humpty thump.

Paula's excited twangy voice popped like a pierced balloon, "Hey Joe, so tell me…tell me all about it. What all happened in court?"

Chapter Twelve

We weren't the only ones in the Big Apple. Paula's old boyfriend, Mike Turner, who posed and sold his personal stash of pictorial memorabilia of Paula and himself for fifty grand, with the help of Hillary's black helicopter patrol, was on promotional tour for *Penthouse*.

Coincidentally all of us being in town at the same time, I think not. *Starting to get the picture now of how the Clintons work?*

Turner was there to do an interview with the tabloid show *A Current Affair*. He was enticed to sell his stash with the help from the Clintons attorneys and P.I. Jack Palladino.

Remember Bob Bennett telling our attorney, Gil Davis, that there were nude pictures of Paula? Defaming one's character by using a porn magazine worked so well when the Flowers scandal broke, that Hillary thought it would work on Paula. Big mistake. They underestimated my fortitude in their smear campaign. *Know your enemy, learn what they do and do it better.* I was starting to catch on, but what price was I willing to pay? Time will tell.

This guy Jack, you know, the same investigator that I had mentioned earlier that the Clintons hired to work with *Penthouse* to disclaim Gennifer Flowers accusations he was a hard fish to catch.

Stephen M. Jones, Jr.

I tried in vain, on several attempts to serve him. Palladino operated his investigative services out of San Francisco. He had no office and his address was a post office box. I hired an investigator to pose as a client. Each time we set up a meeting he no-showed. Our phones were tapped early on and so he was always tipped off. I even switched to a digital cell phone, when advised by G. Gordon Liddy that they can't tap into digital. However, Palladino seemed to always know when I sent my guy to San Francisco.

Over the almost five- year legal battle, I had our phone lines cleaned several times, but if the Feds are involved, they just simply go to the central station, flash their badges and slip in what they call a *torpedo* into your line. When they do that, you don't get the tell-tell signs of echo's or delay effects that are typical of wiretaps.

In the beginning of the suit, they tapped into our line from the condo where we lived. On the second level in the garage of the condos was a switch box. Inside the box were all the phone lines to all the tenants. There was a padlock that I noticed had been cut with a bolt cutter. I had the phone company called and the representative showed me our line. He pointed out the crimped wire that he said looked to him like it had been tapped.

"See the little tooth marks on the wire here, Mr. Jones?"

"Yep, sure do."

"Now, look at the other tenant lines. See any of those marks on any of those lines?"

I inspected each one, but didn't see any that had been crimped in the middle like ours was. Next, I had him replace the crimped wire with a new one. I had a new lock put on and monitored the switch box every few days.

On the third day, I found that the lock had been cut. I inspected our wire line and found that it had the same crimped marks as before. Needless to say, that burned my wagon, dammit. I went out and bought a lock that could not be cut by bolt cutters, and I also switched the labeled unit numbers with my unit just to confuse the son-of-a-bitch. That defensive measure lasted a little longer; however, they just picked the lock. I changed to a combination lock, they picked that, too. Bastards. I had spent many a night, hiding around the back side of the garage, waiting for the guy to show up. Somehow they knew when I was trying to stalk them. Looking back, I guess it was a good thing I never had a face off. I'd probably be in jail today because it would've been ugly.

Harold Ickes, who answered to Hillary, was the Clintontologist who worked with all the investigators. He managed the sewer flow. If you had diarrhea, and the Billarys wanted to know about it, Ickes was your man.

As I saw it back then, there were two main differences between Paula and Gennifer Flowers. One being Flowers had consensual sex with Clinton; the other was that Gennifer Flowers willingly posed and got paid for her story, which in turn ruined her credibility. Those were two key factors back then that could turn the tables of public opinion on our side. The Clintons just stubbed their toe in the middle of the night by trying to make Paula a harlot by using her past. Most people don't like to see a victim exploited by power and position. And Paula, I was starting to learn, plays victim better than anybody I know.

A Current Affair was to kick off *Penthouse's* December issue of Paula by shooting a promo trailer for their upcoming exploitive episode. Mike Turner and a *Penthouse* spokesperson were outside the Penthouse building.

Joe got wind of the interview and right in the middle of the interview he walked up to Turner and asked, "Are you Mike Turner?"

Turner acknowledged that he was by reaching out to shake Joe's hand. Then Joe said, "Here you go, this is for you. You're being served with a lawsuit, compliments of Paula Jones. Oh, and you work for *Penthouse*, don't you? Thought so. Then here's another one for you."

Damn, just to imagine the look on Turner's face when Joe served him those papers gave me a good feeling. Vengeance is golden in small doses. We sued *Penthouse* and Turner for twenty million.

A few days later we got a call from Joe. "Hey, Stephen, guess what? That asshole Guccione wants to talk to Gil and me at his house in New York. Maybe he wants to settle?"

"I don't know Joe, maybe." I said with little enthusiasm.

Joe seemed kinda' excited about going to see the guy that wears a bad *toupee*. Where I'm from we call them squirrels. Probably, because it looks like one sitting on top an old fence post. Anyway, week or so later, both Joe and Gil went to see what squirrelly was up to. Joe said that Guccione had given them a private tour of his palace. I asked Joe if he was wearing a bathrobe.

"No man, that's the other guy."

Joe said that Guccione must have been real proud of his wealth, because he pointed out one of his prized possessions; a Baby Grand piano in 18k gold leaf that had originally belonged to Judy Garland.

I was getting impatient and couldn't stand it any longer. "Okay—okay, that's all beautiful and nice, but what did the asshole want, Joe?"

"He wants to pay you guys eighty thousand to do an interview about how the Christian right jumped the boat when they got wind of Paula's pictures. He says you can still sue him, that this is a separate deal."

"Wow, Joe, he's a bold son-of-a-bitch. You have to appreciate the calculating mind of a prick like that. You tell Guccione where he can shove that eighty grand. Up the north end of a south bound mule—that's where!"

"I've heard that saying before, Stephen, and I think you got it backwards. I believe it's shoved up the south end."

"Hell, Joe, I'm from the South, if there's going to be any shoving it has to go North. Now, we being good friends and all, I'll let you hold the tail."

We both laughed at that one.

"I figured as much," Joe said. "Oh, and by the way, we hired a research firm to find out which state we can sue him in. Since *Penthouse* is distributed in all fifty states plus internationally, we can sue them where we have the best legal advantage."

"Sounds good to me, as long as it's not going to interfere with the Clinton case, I'm all gung-ho, Joe.

However, sometimes the best laid plans, with all the right intentions, get dumped.

Paula and I flew back to New York for depositions on the new *Penthouse* case. They were held in the law offices of Guccione's lawyer.

I sat outside with the secretary in the foyer traumatizing myself into magazines. Having flashbacks—remembering back when Paula introduced our new son to Turner in the gym where I was working out. I sat there, foaming at the mouth, snatching through blurred pages. Taking my anger out on the secretary, I said, "What's up with these magazines?"

She looked at me questionably. I continued, "I mean, you've got all the business and *Architect Today* magazines, but you don't have your own client's *Penthouse* magazine out here. Oh, I wonder why."

I don't know who I was more pissed off at, Turner or Paula.

I kept a sharp eye out for Turner. Something inside me wanted to confront him. To let him know what he had done was sleazy and pretty damn low-down.

Paula, Joe and Gil were down a hall inside a conference room. I found out later after they took a short break, Turner was brought in through a back door.

The way it was supposed to work was that after Joe and Gil took Turner's deposition on video, Guccione's lawyer would take Paula's. That never happened.

As I was sitting there, scouring through magazines, Guccione called in to talk to the secretary. My ears started burning. I pretended to seem interested in reading an article and stopped turning pages.

"Well, Mr. Guccione, they've been in there a while now," the secretary said. "Hold on and I'll put you right through."

A few minutes later, the phone rang again.

"Yes, Mr. Bennett, just one moment… he's been expecting your call."

She rang the attorney in the conference room, "Mr. Bennett is on line one."

She paused for a moment, and then said, "I'll put him right through, Sir."

I waited a minute longer, walked up and asked if I could have a sticky tab off her desk. I wrote down that Bennett had called and that the call was forwarded inside the conference room. Then I folded it and glanced up at the secretary who was scrutinizing my intentions with an ice-cold stare. She knew that I was reacting to her conversation with Bennett.

"It's too late now, honey, cat's out of the bag," I said. "I know how you feel. Your boss is going to be peeo'd. If it's any consolation, don't expect much on Secretary's Day. Now be a good little girl because I've got an errand for you."

I grabbed the stapler off her desk without asking and snapped it shut on the paper, piecing it tight with the wired barb. I handed the note to her and asked her to give it to our attorneys.

She did so, as if being dragged down the hall to have a tooth extraction. I stood there watching her slow dance her way down the hall. She turned and looked at me half-way down to see if I was still standing there.

Sarcastically coaxing her, I said, "Yep, I'm still here and I know the conference room door is not the one you've got your hand on. It's the next door over. There you go, that's the right door. Good girl. Now go in there and get it over with—scat."

She opened the door and disappeared.

When Joe and Gil wrapped up Turner's deposition, we had an emergency Powwow to re-think our position. I begrudgingly agreed to everyone's suggestion to drop the suit to preserve the Clinton case, with the option to pick it back up later.

It was of the opinion that Bennett, by way of Guccione's attorney, was going to demand that Paula, in her deposition demand, to tell them the distinguishing characteristics of Clinton that had been sealed with the courts. That was our negotiating ace in the hole. Joe and Gil didn't want to give that up. By the way, in a deposition, they can ask you very broad questions and you have to answer. No *ifs, ands, or buts*, unless you're the Clintons and then words take on new meanings.

Instead of taking the back door out, Turner strutted right past us like a banty rooster thinking he had a big pecker. He pushed the down button on the elevator, turned, and gawked back at us with a hyena grin Well, by now you know me. I wasn't going to stand by and let that chicken poop fly the coop.

"Hey, Turner," I said, as I started toward him. "Don't think for a moment that this is over for you?" I leaned into his ear, up against him hoping he would try to push me away.

"It's not over by a long shot, baby Bubba." He shot back, "I know you."

I whispered, "No you don't."

A short, round attorney came up, stood next to Turner and then called out to Joe and Gil. "He threatened my client. You'd better get some control over your client." I turned toward the attorney, touching my forehead against his. He recoiled against the elevator. I said, "They're not my attorneys. I'm on my own."

Ding! The elevator door opened.

"Saved by the bell, you boys have a nice ride down. I'll be seeing you, Turner."

I stood there eye-balling them until the elevator door closed. Both Joe and Gil were not too pleased, to say the least, at my actions. *Hey, he should've used the back door.*

On the condition of dropping the suit Turner, had to give up his stash of pictures and love notes.

Joe and Gil took separate cabs to the LaGuardia airport, basically because all of us couldn't fit in one. Their flight to DC was about the same time as our flight back to LA.

Paula was saying her goodbyes to Joe and Gil while I grabbed our bags. I shook their hands and thanked them, then said, "I'll take the pictures now and anything else Turner provided."

Gil said, "No Steve, we might need them later."

"And if you do, Gil, you know where to find them."

"Well, Steve, you're not our client."

"That's right, I'm not! Paula, tell your attorneys that you want your personal pictures back."

"I'm sorry, but I do want my pictures back," she said, rather meekly.

Stephen M. Jones, Jr.

"Give them back the file, Joe" Gil said.

I said in a monotone voice, "Thanks boys…can't say it's been real fun, but we all have a plane to catch."

After they left, I opened the manila folder. My eyes fall on a cocktail napkin which read in red lipstick, "I love every inch of you Mike. Love, Paula."

I closed it and sucked in a cold blast of winter air as if to freeze my internal burn. "Here, I believe this is yours. I'd keep up with it if I were you."

Paula gave me a pity look, but said nothing.

"Oh hell Paula, I don't know. Burn them! No, you can't do that—you might need the goddamn things. Oh, do whatever you want to do with them. I just know I don't want to see 'um again."

Paula started to cry, "Stephen, why don't we just drop the whole thing? I'm just so sick of it all."

"Look Paula, it's not like I didn't tell you what to expect from these people. Your past is your past, but no man likes to be slapped in the face with it. I told you before, be honest and upfront, so we can nip it in the butt, but no…you had to wait to the last minute. Thinking what? That somehow these pictures that the Clintons dug up were going to simply disappear. "No, baby." I wiped the stream of tears from her face. "They're going to be front page. That's how the Clintons operate."

You know me, Paula, do you really think I'm going to let those bastards roll up a copy of *Penthouse* and beat me over the head with it just so you can drop the case now. I think not."

Back in LA, things didn't get easier. A local news station was reporting that Paula had gotten paid by *Penthouse* to pose in the upcoming spread.

Bad enough seeing my wife, with an old boyfriend, in a porn magazine, but to say that she got paid was the ultimate in family embarrassment. My own grandfather, who took me hunting and fishing as a boy, said that Paula belonged in a brothel. It took me a few years before I would talk to him after that comment.

So when I saw a local news clip, where it said that she got an undisclosed amount of money for posing in *Penthouse*, it was the straw that broke the

211

camel's back. I called the station and told them that I wanted a retraction. They pretty much said, "It's our story and we're sticking to it, so sue us."

The guy had a point. I can't sue every Tom, Dick, and Harry. That's what got me in the mess I'm in now. I've got to weigh all options, avoiding the knee jerk reaction when bozo news stations make false allegations.

I called a local attorney in the yellow pages to find out exactly what the state stipulations were. I called Bugliosi and Associates, thinking to myself, *I wonder if he's the same guy who prosecuted the Helter Skelter gang?*

When no one answered, I left a message. Half hour later, Vincent Bugliosi called back. After a few preliminaries of confirmation identification questions, I asked him what Paula's legal recourse would be if the local media continued to report false accusations.

Mr. Bugliosi told me pretty much what I expected, "Steve, don't sweat the little stuff. It'll burn itself out if it's not true. You going after them just adds fuel to the fire."

"Yeah, I know, but it still puts a strain on the family when this trash is spread by so-called *legitimate* news sources. Just think about the average guy who brown-bags it to work every day—like me, comes home, flips on the news and takes it for gospel. That needs to be changed, Mr. Bugliosi. People need to know that some news organizations have agendas and don't always tell it like it is."

"Well, Steve, that's the way it is. You can't change the world in a day."

Quiet honestly, Mr. Bugliosi was more interested in Paula's suit against Clinton. So, I told him that all we wanted was a simple apology without going into graphic specifics. Pay off our legal fees and it would be over.

Mr. Bugliosi spent over an hour trying to convince me to drop the case without an apology. He told me how this would hurt the Democratic Party and the country as a whole. He told me that he was a personal friend of Bob Bennett and he would be happy to facilitate a call to Bennett.

"Mr. Bugliosi, there has to be some accountability on Clinton's part. Paula just can't drop the case to save the Democratic Party. What about her rights? Although there is merit in what you say, it's not fair to her."

"This case, Steve, if it goes to trial will divide the country. I don't think either one of you want that kind of shroud hanging over your lives forever."

"Mr. Bugliosi, with all due respect, I don't think it's fair to put that monkey on Paula's back. I think it squarely belongs to Clinton. He can have this settled tomorrow if he wants to."

"Steve, he's not going to do that. He's the President of the United States."

"It's true, he is, but that doesn't make him above the law. We seem to be going around in circles and I do appreciate your advice on how to handle false reporting and yeah, if you want to call Bennett and tell him how we feel, that's great, too. But let me be clear, any negotiations have to go through Paula's attorneys. I'm not an attorney, although Paula seems to think I try to act like one."

I looked over at Paula knowing that she heard me. She, in turn, stuck her tongue out at me.

Smiling back at her and wanting to wrap things up with Bugliosi, I said, "Having you talk to Bennett on our behalf would be unethical would it not?"

"Steve, you're misunderstanding my approach."

"Really! Let me ask you a question. Your friend, Mr. Bennett, on a recent interview was asked what he thought of the Jones' lawsuit. And his answer was philosophical. He said, "I once had a dog that chased cars, now I don't have a dog."

"Mr. Bugliosi, what do you think Bennett's approach to the commentator's question was?"

"Sounds to me Steve…like he's got a dead dog."

"Sounds to me like a threat, Mr. Bugliosi. So if you talk to him, you tell him that if one hair on my family's head is harmed over this lawsuit, he won't get a second chance."

Funny, I never heard back from Mr. Bugliosi. I wonder if he ever gave Bennett my message.

Chapter Thirteen

The media finally found us in Long Beach and they pretty much made our life a living hell. We tried as much as possible to have a normal family life, but it's hard when you have cameras hiding under every nook and cranny.

We were living at a gated condo and when the media camped out there, it was hard for the other tenant's as well. They were trying to go about their business, but they were constantly being harassed about information about us.

The simple things, like going to the market got to be a *cat and mouse* game. I got to be pretty good at avoiding them.

I remember once when the winter rains flooded out the ground level and drenched all our carpets. We were sleeping on a mattress in the living room allowing the fans in the bedroom to dry out the water- soaked carpet. About one o'clock in the morning, this bright light came shinning through the sliding glass patio door. At first, I thought it was a search light from a police helicopter scanning the beach for anyone up to no good. As I peeked out, to my surprise it was a woman reporter with camera rolling—taping an action news interview. The cameraman must have been using the headlight from a union pacific locomotive. She started out by saying in a suave voice, "I'm standing in front of Paula Jones' California beach bungalow."

I shook my head and laughed to myself. If that woman only knew the truth, I don't believe she would've used those same words to describe our lifestyle. We were piled up together on a mattress, along with one big farty hound trying to get some shuteye.

It seems that the more you try to avoid them, the more aggressive they become. I wanted to try to keep a low profile, but after *Penthouse* it was open season. Not only was there the usual media, but the paparazzi and independents were bounty hunting as well.

This one guy must have been there for weeks at a time. Paula and I actually felt sorry for him. He was out there rain or shine. One time we needed to go out for something so I waited until he put down his camera and was stirring his Starbucks brew. We hopped in the car and raced out the security garage. I looked back in the rear view mirror to see him knocking over his coffee grabbing for his camera only to get a shot of our tail lights. It's the little things in life that *make or break* the rest of your day. I tried to find humor in our captivity; however, this guy's tenacity finally paid off.

I snuck out to the beach to let Mitzie do her business. She was in her full-hunch-poop position when I saw him running toward me, kicking up clouds of sand, holding onto his video camera that was bouncing around on his shoulder like a sack of potatoes. I tried in vain to pull Mitzie, but could only manage to get her to budge a few feet. I grabbed her tail trying to hasten her progress by shaking her butt trying to dislodge that damn log that wouldn't fall. Mitzie acknowledged her displeasure by displaying all upper and lower teeth, crocodile style.

"Don't you give me that look, you old fat and sassy…" Before I could pull the plastic doggie bag out of my pocket, the camera guy was on us. I could see the red light above the camera lens flashing turn green knowing that his camera was rolling. I looked down at Mitzie in disgust. She looked up at me as if to say, *I'm finished when I'm finished*.

"All right—all right, you got me; just don't film me with my dog in contractions."

In between his heavy breathing he smiled and said, "Shit happens."

We struck a deal, he didn't film my dog in a compromising position and I allowed him to get the shots he needed for the tabloid he was working for.

Time rolled by as Clinton's lawyer kept stalling—buying time until after the 1996 elections.

Joe and Gil had subpoenaed Betsy Wright, remember? The Clinton's bimbo eruption equalizer, but she was conveniently out of the country. People seemed to think that Bill hired her, but au contraire, it was Hillary.

We were short on funds for investigative work, so I tried to gather as much second-hand information as I could get and give to Joe. One source was a reporter named Ambrose Evans-Pritchard with the *London Telegraph*." We sort of scratched each other's back. He wanted travel dates of Vincent Foster to Geneva before his suicide. In return, he offered me the name of a police detective that might help with our case.

After I collected some information on Foster, I called Ambrose for my back scratch.

"So, Ambrose, who's this police detective?" In his over the pond accent;

"Steffen, you're going to love this, his name is Mark Brown."

"You're shitting me, right? He's got the same common name as my fat ass brother-in-law, Damn, it just gets better and better."

"Careful, Steffen, you're name doesn't exactly exude an uncommon attire, ol' boy."

"So true... I'm about as common as *God gave sense to a goose*. So, Ambrose, what can you tell me?"

Ambrose told me that Brown had done some investigative work for Pat Matriciana. So I called Pat and he gave me Mark's number. Mark and I hit it off pretty well. I told him if we could manage to locate some money in the fund, that we might possibly be able to use his services.

Mark told me he was one of the detectives who had worked on the Mena, Arkansas case where some kids had witnessed a drug shipment being dropped near a train track from a plane. They rode their bikes and got there before the bad guys. Unfortunately, the drug dealers caught up to them. The kids were found cut in half by the train. At first it was pronounced a suicide, but later changed to murder. Mark told me when the investigation started to connect the Dixie Mafia with possible payoffs to Bill Clinton, the case was shut down. To this day the murders are unsolved. *I'm wondering, is it just me, or is every death associated with the Clintons pronounced a suicide.*

It's interesting to note that this same drug organization was part of the big picture of money laundering for the CIA Iran-Contra re-supply operation. Reagan-appointed CIA Director Richard Helms was one of twenty convicted in the Iran-Contra cocaine for guns scandal. Oh, and who was the Vice President and former Czar of the CIA when all this went down? None other than George Bush, Sr.

Now you don't think that George Sr. was in the dark when all this was going on, do ya'? Helms testified to Congress that the CIA had successfully completed over sixty-thousand assassinations. I think I just found the lost Inca treasure of why the Clintons and the Bushes are so chummy. *And you thought it was all about good will and disasters.* All this flim-flam sounds a little like what's going on now with *fast and furious,* only this time its liberal hack Eric Holder caught holding the bag lies.

I'm not an authority on this subject—it only crossed my path by association. Those of you who are curious can track down British journalist, Ambrose Evans Pritchard, who writes for the *London Telegraph UK.* I believe he can shed light on the subject.

Perceptively, if you metaphorically align Clinton's legacy with his political inspiration of JFK's legacy, there is a tragedy of ideology. That's if you believe in the Kennedy conspiracy theory. By JFK not sending US reinforcements into the failed secret CIA coup in Cuba, he put his silhouette in the crosshairs of the CIA. And brother RFK, with his relentless effort to bust organized crime, gave the CIA and the Mob a common enemy. So in theory, Clinton's associations with CIA-Mob represents everything the Kennedy brothers fought against and died for. Politics supersedes justice.

You say hogwash, what mob connections does Clinton have? Let me just throw out a few names, starting in Arkansas. Dan Lasater was Clintons money man. Lasater was convicted of cocaine distribution, in 1990 Clinton pardoned him. Paul Begala, part of Clinton's secret police, is a friend and associate of mob lawyer Richard Ben-Veniste. He helped defend Clinton in Whitewater. Veniste is also good friends with mobster Alvin Malnik. Oops, a piece of the Inca treasure slipped out. Yes, that's right. Malnik has ties with George Bush, Sr. I could go on and on but what's the point. As I've done throughout this book, this is just a side bar of intersection of thought.

"So, Mark, in the meantime, what can you give me pro bono about the Clintons?"

"A while back, I heard in the news you guys were trying to get Kathy Ferguson's statement."

"Yeah, that's right. She was once married to Danny Ferguson. She was going to testify about Clinton being all over her in the kitchen at a Christmas party held at the Governor's Mansion. She was also going to tell us about all the stories Danny told her about other women that Clinton had made out with. That's all shot to hell, because I understand she's dead.

"Well, Steve, would you like to see the autopsy report?"

"Yeah, why not. Fax it to me?"

He did and I said, "Okay, Mark, tell me what I'm looking at."

"Let me give you a little background first. The day Kathy Ferguson supposedly committed suicide, she had her nails and hair done."

"So what, maybe she wanted to look good on her way out."

"No Steve, her daughter was going to graduate from high school that very night."

"Really? You're right, man, that doesn't make sense to me either, with her daughter graduating and all, but people do strange things under stress."

"It gets stranger than that. Listen up. See the diagram of the bullet trajectory?"

"Yeah, looks like she got shot in the noggin."

"That's right, but let me walk you through it. When a bullet goes in, it makes a little hole. When it goes out it makes a big hole. Basically, the bullet mushrooms after impact. You with me so far?"

"Like a fly on flypaper, go ahead."

"Okay now, Kathy Ferguson was right handed, so typically a person committing suicide with a hand gun would put the gun to the right side of the temple or in the mouth, right?"

"I guess so, if that's the way you wanted to kill yourself."

"Look at the autopsy diagram, Steve. See the entrance wound on the back lower left-hand side of the head…"

"Yeah."

"Then see where the bullet exits out above the left eye socket."

I studied the diagram a minute and said, "I'm confused, it says here that the entrance wound was in the front of the head and went out just about where the neck and the scull meet, just below the left ear."

"That's right, that's what it says, but look at the entry wound."

"Yeah, I'm looking."

"Now look at the exit wound, see the difference?"

"Yeah—yeah, the entrance wound is the size of a half dollar and the exit wound is really small. Hey, how can the front of the head be the entrance wound if it's that big?"

"Give the man a cigar."

"No…wait a minute. Maybe they screwed up and got it backwards on the diagram, Mark."

"I think not. It gets better. Make your right hand into an imaginary gun and try to put it to the left lower back part of your scull like in the autopsy. Make sure you align your finger as if it were the barrel, for the correct trajectory."

"It's impossible, I can't do it."

"And neither could Kathy Ferguson."

"So maybe she was nervous and used her left hand."

"Give me a break, whose side are you own? Even left-handed it would have been difficult, Steve."

"I'm just playing devil's advocate to see if I can convince myself otherwise. Mark, what hand was the gun found in?"

"Her right hand."

"Where was the bullet found?"

219

"That's even stranger. It was in the ashtray, next to the chair she was found in."

"You're shitting me."

"No, I'm serious. The bullet went through her scull, ricocheted off two walls and somehow landed in the ashtray."

"That's strange, no—that's unbelievable."

"Nope, some bastard tampered with the evidence and dug it out of the wall then put it there as some sick joke mocking the investigation."

Why would they do that knowing that it would...oh, I get it. An inside job."

"I'm not finished, Steve. Kathy's fiancé a Sherwood police officer, was found dead with a bullet hole in his head, lying over her grave with a note that his family swears is not his handwriting."

"Damn, this all sounds too wild to me. Maybe it's some *love-hate* suicide thing, but why would they change the autopsy report. Who would do something like that?"

"Somebody who can, what do you think?"

"Well, I think whatever happened hasn't got anything to do with us. What do you believe, Mark?"

"I believe Kathy Ferguson had a lot of information that someone didn't want out and she was about to come forward because of Paula. I got a statement from the doctors and nurses she worked with. They said that Kathy would have never committed suicide. She was so excited about her daughter graduating with honors.

The nurses on her shift said that when Paula's story broke in the news that Kathy believed Paula, because it happened to her. They said that Kathy was about to come forward to back up Paula's story and spill the beans on that, plus a hell of a lot more. You really want to know what I think? Kathy Ferguson was murdered in the classic execution style—certainly not suicide."

"Scary stuff, but unfortunately, not much we can use, Mark. Maybe the nurses statements could help, but that's second-hand information. I don't think we can use those in Paula's case. What else you got?"

"When the Clintons came back from Hawaii not too long ago, Bill made a pit stop in Little Rock and Hillary went back to Washington. While he was here, he had a *ménage a trios'* with three women at a real estate office in Sherwood."

"Do you know the names of these women?"

"Yep, sure do. One owns a boutique off of Cantrell in west Little Rock. I think we need to meet. Let me talk to Joe and I'll get back to you."

"Hey, Steve, I got a lot of information on Hillary, too. You know she swings both ways, don't you."

"You got any names?"

"Yep, sure do."

"Yeah, I seem to remember reading something about that, where was it? Oh yeah, Gennifer Flowers quite bluntly mentioned something about that in her book. I don't remember the exact words, but she said that Bill told her that Hillary chows down with women more than he does and it's not Chinese food he's talking about."

"All I can say is that I can prove that it's true, Steve."

"Well I'm not so sure I want to go in that direction just yet. I'll be in touch."

I gave the information to Joe, but he didn't seem too interested. Joe was quick to say, "We're not in a position to do any major investigative work, Stephen, but keep me posted on anything else you can find out."

"Oh, you can bet I'll find out more, but Joe, if we can get names maybe we can put a little pressure on Clinton to step up and do the right thing."

We'll see, I'll talk it over with Gil and find out what he thinks."

In the same conversation, Joe told me he had been approached by the producers of *60 Minutes*.

"They want to do an interview with Paula," Joe said.

"Come on, Joe, you gotta be kidding me. They're the ones that helped get Clinton elected. Don't you remember that *stand by your man* remark Hillary gave in that interview?"

"Yeah, I remember, but they've got this angle on Danny Ferguson. Ferguson did that interview with *LA Times* reporter, Bill Rempel. He's got him on tape admitting that Paula didn't do anything in the room because Clinton told him so afterwards."

"Rempel, huh? Sounds like some sort of fairytale to me, Joe."

"No really, *60 minute's* is hurting in their ratings and they need this interview."

"My heart bleeds." I let out with an overload of sarcasm.

"No listen, Stephen, they want to interview Ferguson and entrap him with Rempel's audiotape."

"So it's a Paula and Danny interview, huh, Joe?"

"Yeah, they really want this, Stephen, and they're willing to give Paula the questions ahead of time. It's the real deal."

"I don't know, Joe, I don't trust them. I'll think about it, but for now, my instincts want to say—no."

"Well, discuss it with Paula and see what she thinks. I'll have the producer call you and then we can go from there."

"All right, Joe, we'll listen to his sales pitch."

"Hey Stephen, it's not a he, it's a she, and that was funny, you putting the fairytale of Rumpelstiltskin and Bill Rempel together. You didn't think I caught that did you?"

"You're right, Joe. That was pretty slick of you to hold back acknowledging it until the end of our conversation."

"Yeah, I know you throw things out there for effect and I didn't have time for your antics."

"That's what I like about you, Joe, your bluntness. Talk to you soon."

The producer from *60 minutes* called to give us the low-down. Paula would be handled with kid gloves. All the questions to be asked would be discussed prior to the interview.

Stephen M. Jones, Jr.

Ed Bradley would do the posh piece. Danny Ferguson was to be interviewed about his actions on the day he escorted Paula to Clinton's hotel room at the Excelsior, in accordance to his statement filed with the court.

60 minutes would interview Rempel and play his audiotape. Then, go back to surprise Ferguson with Rempel's interview on a monitor and challenge him on lying about not knowing anything that happened in the room.

So I told the producer, "Well it sounds all good, but you guys and the Clintons are like two peas in a pod. Why would we be willing to help you guys out during May sweeps just because your ratings are in the crapper? *"Frankly my dear, I don't give a damn."* Ha! You have no idea how long I've waited to use that line. I mean, maybe you should re-interview the Clintons. They might be able to *"feel your pain."* Hell, I'm on a roll."

"Look, Mr. Jones, I know how you must feel. You and Paula have had a rough time with the media but I promise you, this time it will be different."

"Yeah, that's what they all say. We're tired of bending over without getting kissed first, savvy?"

"Mr. Jones, a lot of people including myself, believe Paula. Especially the women. They're all on Paula's side."

"Oh really? You might want to ask Patricia Ireland, because the women's organization hasn't said boo about anything."

"No, Stephen. I'm talking about here at *CBS*. And to be honest with you, *60 Minutes* has gone through a reorganization. I think you'll find that we're sympathetic to what happened to Paula. This will help Paula clear her name and the world will know that she didn't do anything to be ashamed of in that hotel room."

Impressed with her pitch I said, "Well, that's one good reason but if we do decide on an interview, I want total control on what's asked of Paula and I want the authority to be able to stop the interview at any time."

"I think I can arrange that, let me make a few phone calls and see what I can do."

Paula was gung-ho and so was Joe. It all sounded too good to be true but if it was true it would go a long way to help clear her good name if there was any good name left after the *Penthouse Hall of Shame*.

Gil called and gave his blessing. Even I started to believe that *60 Minutes* was true-blue. Maybe things have changed for real and if they are hurting for ratings, we can, for once, get our side of the story out without any cheap shots.

The producer called back to say that she was told to give us carte blanche. We told her it was a go! Joe flew down for the interview. We picked him up at LAX and took him to the Long Beach Hilton where the interview was to take place. There we met the producer, coordinator and, of course, Mr. Ed Bradley himself.

Joe found out that Ed was a cigar aficionado. So Joe pulled out a Cuban he had stashed in his jacket and gave it to Ed. He ran the Cuban under his nose and said, "Nice, I'll smoke it later. Thank you."

I whispered, "Say Joe, he's got an earring on. Which ear does it mean that...?"

"Stop it—don't go there, Stephen."

"Hell, I'm just curious, that's all. Chill...Little Joe."

I started casually talking to Mr. Bradley. I don't know what Joe was most worried about...me talking to Ed or Paula's upcoming interview, who, by the way, was having her make-up touched up. Thank God.

So I asked Mr. Bradley, who the most interesting person he's interviewed was?

Ed said, "Jimmy Carter, a very intelligent man, but I don't think he likes me."

"Oh really, why's that, Ed? I mean Mr. Bradley."

"No, by all means call me Ed. President Carter wasn't too pleased about the way he was portrayed in our interview about the Iran hostage debacle. The day after it aired, President Carter surprised me by a personal phone call and said we took his words out of context."

Ed said that Carter threatened never to appear on *60 Minutes* again, plus Carter said a few choice words that he wouldn't want repeated.

Paula's interview went off without a hitch. I think we stopped the interview once for clarification and once to redo Paula's make-up as she began crying when she recounted her story. I remember there wasn't a dry eye in the room. Even the burly, boom man blew his nose afterwards.

The producer came up very excited, and said, "The interview was everything we had hoped it would be. It was so emotional!"

I wanted to respond by saying, "*Yeah...chopping onions has nothing on Paula,*" but who was I to doubt her emotional sincerity. Maybe I've seen it so much lately I've become inoculated.

I guess the producer sensed my lack of emotional response. She deferred my serious nature as still worried about being screwed over.

"Let me reassure you, Mr. Jones, everything's going to turn out fine. Have you met *LA Times* reporter, Bill Rempel, who is to be interviewed after Paula."

"Why no, I haven't. Funny how you've read my mind. Could you introduce me?"

I talked to Bill for a few minutes. I wanted to ask him about his interview with Ferguson. I wanted to see if it jived with what the producer lady was telling me. Rempel ended up telling me the same song and dance, so that made me feel a little better about the pony ride. Afterwards, he gave me his business card and I shook his hand.

They interviewed Joe with some follow up questions like: Where is the case legally now? *I wanted to answer that one, "It's like dragging a jackass through a briar patch by Bob Bennett."*

Next, Paula was asked to go outside with a cameraman and do those indignantly stupid sidewalk cameos. You know, where the guy films her walking so they can edit it into the commentary part of the interview. I've always hated those shots. To me it's in-genuine, but since everything went so well, I didn't dare bark about it.

After the interview Joe introduced us to Lisa Lou. She worked for Peter Brenner who produced the *Judge Judy* show.

I commented, "Wow, Joe! Who's gonna pop out from behind door number three? Andy Warhol?"

"Calm down, Stephen, we're just going to talk over dinner to see what she has to say. We've been playing phone tag and I never got a chance to talk. I left her a message saying when I'd be in LA. She called back and said, "While you're in LA, let's all do lunch. Well, since its past lunch, we'll do dinner." Let's see what she has to put on the table?

"All right Joe, I've never passed up a free steak and Paula was born to be *on the go*."

So away we went.

After dinner, Lisa invited us over to a private Hollywood party that she said was being hosted by a friend of hers. The party was set up like a luau with torches lined around a pool.

I asked Lisa, "So whose party is this anyway?"

"Oh, I'm sorry. I forgot to tell you guys. How silly of me, it's Kato Kaelin's birthday party."

I looked at Joe, as if to say, *"What the hell?"*

Joe responded, "Hey, don't look at me. I didn't know either."

"Oh you guys" Lisa said, "It'll be fun."

She grabbed Paula's hand. "Come on, Paula, let me introduce you to Kato."

Joe and I tagged along like two toy poodles.

In the kitchen, we met the infamous Kato. I don't know who was more surprised to see each other, Paula or Kato. Personally, I wasn't much for the Hollywood scene, but Paula loved it. After the stress of the interview, I guess she deserved a little *R and R*.

60 minute's aired the following Sunday and lo and behold, I had something in common with former President Jimmy Carter. We both got taken to the cleaners by *CBS*.

60 minute's ran Paula's interview, then Danny Ferguson's, making it a *he says—she says* show. They cut the part where the reporter showed Ferguson a TV monitor that contradicted his earlier interview with Bill Rempel. In fact,

Stephen M. Jones, Jr.

Rempel wasn't even mentioned. That was the only reason we agreed to do the interview in the first place.

There are three types of Suns. "Sunshine, Sunflowers, and Sons-a-bitches!" You can guess what category I put *CBS* in. The next morning I was on the horn to the producer, "If you weren't a woman, I'd—"

"Stephen, I'm so sorry. I didn't know either…I was as surprised as you were."

"No, lady, you got that wrong. I'm not surprised at all. I should have known better than to trust you people. What's that old adage, if it looks and walks like a duck…"

She says, "I know, it's a duck."

"Worse, I got quacked up the dirt road by *60 minute's*."

"Look, Mr. Jones, I had nothing to do with it. At the last minute, the executives came in and changed it, literally hours before it was to be aired. That's never happened before. We're just as sick about it as you are. How's Paula taking it?"

"Oh she's just ducky."

"I'm truly sorry, really I am."

"Since you sound so compassionately guilty for your bosses' dirty deeds, do me a favor before this headache I've got breaks my head in two and you get the ugly half?"

"Yes, of course, if I can."

"Send me the *uncut version*."

"It's in the mail, I promise you Mr. Jones. (We never received a copy, frig'em-frag'em figures.)

"Anything else, Mr. Jones?"

"Yeah, tell Ed Bradley that whatever Jimmy Carter said to him after his interview that he wouldn't repeat, tell him that it goes double for me, too."

"What?"

"Just tell him, he'll understand."

Obviously, another lesson learned. As luck would have it, there was a silver lining. I called Joe to see if there was any recourse. Joe's demeanor was ecstatic.

"Damn Joe, I guess you can take it better than me, because I just want to let you know pal, we just got a big ol' soapy enema compliments of *60 Minutes!*"

"Yeah, yeah, so says you. Listen up. After *60 Minutes* aired, I got a call from a woman who wouldn't tell me her name. She told me she had to call me after seeing Paula on *60 Minute's*. She told me she knows exactly how Paula feels, because the same thing happened to her inside the oval office."

"Hot damn—no shit! Oh, wait a minute… What the hell am I getting all excited about? She didn't give you her name. What good is that going to do us, Joe?"

"I'll tell you why, if you'll let me finish."

"Feisty. That's good, Joe."

"Would you please?"

"Yeah, Joe I'm sorry, Paula tells me the same thing. Go ahead."

"Well anyway, she said that her and her husband worked as fund raisers for the Clinton campaign. She continued to say that because of some bad choices, they were financially desperate. Instead of volunteer work she had done in the past, she needed a real job. Now get this, she said the very same day she went to see Clinton, her husband committed suicide."

"You're kidding, what's up with all these suicides, Joe? Looks like people are dying to be around the Clintons. It's like death is attracted to them. Maybe they're involved in some type of insurance scam. Oops, hey, I caught myself this time. Go ahead Joe, finish your story."

Joe took a deep breath of irritated restraint and continued, "She said Clinton came up to her like he did to Paula. He kissed her and put his hand up her dress. Then grabbed her hand and put it on his aroused head of state."

"Oh my God, Joe, this is exactly what this case needs—proof. If we can find her and get her to testify, we can finally get Paula's name cleared and put this ugly baby to bed. You think we can find her?"

"Well, it shouldn't be to hard to track down a woman whose husband was a fundraiser for Clinton and committed suicide.

"So Joe, who do we have that can work on this?"

"Gil and I are working day and night on this appeal of immunity blanket that Clinton is trying to hide under. Looks like we're headed to the Supreme Court. We don't have time to chase down any new leads. I already talked with Cindy Hayes and we don't have the funds for an investigator right now.

"Where did the twenty-five g's go that was from the jeans promo Paula did?"

"I don't know, Stephen, you'll have to ask Cindy that question. I do know that Gil and I haven't been paid *zip* lately."

"What about Izzie, Joe?"

"Who?"

"You know, Michael Isikoff, why don't we toss that bone to Izzie on the understanding that whatever he finds he shares with us."

"All right, Stephen, I'll call him."

Isikoff found her in two days, but told us that he promised her he wouldn't divulge her name. This time a little back scratching turned into back stabbing. *Damned Indian giver.*

However, Izzie did say that she was the one who had called Joe after seeing Paula on *60 Minutes*. Isikoff told Joe that if he could find her in two days, you guys could find her in four.

We did and her name was Kathleen Willey.

Not to take anything away from Izzie's claim to journalistic fame that he's the one that uncovered the lovesick Monica, but he forgot to mention who tossed him the bone in the first place.

Izzie, after getting the boot from the *Washington Post* to the co-owned *Newsweek* could now thumb his nose at his politically correct hacks at the *Post*. His persistent gumshoe investigation eventually led him to unlock the truth that many women who have drifted in and out of Clinton's social club already knew, including his business associate/wife Hillary—that Clinton used his position to acquire sex. *Hello! Big news there.*

I mean...think about it. Kathleen Willey led Izzie to her friend Linda Tripp, who played the secret tapes that spilled the beans on her friend Monica's many rendezvous at the Oral, I mean---Oval Office.

Friends kiss 'n tell. Friends? Where would we all be today if not for our friends?

Funny thing about the Clintons, they knew that we knew about Monica long before her name became public. Yet, they still wouldn't settle with a simple apology.

Win at all cost, but at what price will the American people have to pay? Only historians can dig deep into their souls and answer that question. Where would we all be today if we hadn't elected Clinton for a second term? Better question, where are we all now and are we better off for it?

Chapter Fourteen

I personally didn't give a damn about Clinton's personal life. All I wanted for Paula was to clear her good name or what was left of it.

It was Hillary who fanned the flame by continuous character assassination. You can get pushed around so much until you push back. To me, we had to prove in court that this guy not only sexually harassed Paula, but others as well. No one should use his, or her, power and position to coerce sexual favors from anyone in the work place, no matter who they are. That being, Paula can play the *damsel in distress* better than anyone I know. So where does the truth lie?

I believe Clinton sexually harassed her. I believe everyone matures differently while going through life's transitions. I believe we all, and that includes the Pope, have had particulars with our hormones as a youth.

You sew your wild oats, grow up, settle down and raise a family. Life goes on. Paula was no virgin when I married her. So what? Nor was I. Very few are these days. Unfortunately, there are people like Clinton who never mature in the sexual sense. In public they act and look just like everybody else. They see damsels in distress as an advantage of opportunity.

To be fair, both Paula and Kathleen used their femininity as an advantage, too. Clinton used his power and position to do the same. Who's at fault and where do you draw the line? Who said a little flirting doesn't hurt anybody? Most people are adult and know when to stop when particulars get out of hand. The problem with Clinton is that he is a sexual predator and to him, the word *no* means yes.

Paula went to see Clinton, thinking she could flirt her way to a better job. Kathleen Willey went to the Oval Office maybe to do the same. She was seen by Linda Tripp as having smeared lipstick as she exited. Paula was seen by her two friends and later by both sisters. They all said that Paula was visually shaken. You do the math, looks like a pattern of behavior on Clinton's part to me.

As the case kept grinding to a crawl, I compartmentalized the new information with the old. I found myself thinking more and more about why Paula went to the hotel room in the first place. Is there something in the psyche of an insecure woman that causes excitement when someone of power and authority shows interest that shuts off rationality to the brain, allowing an overflow of hormonal inaptitude?

Obvious symptoms are a flush of blood flow around the face and lips giving a rosy, glowing appearance. That, coinciding with a tingly sensation to the scalp, causing her to continuously toss and run her fingers through her hair with an intentional glance to the person of interest. Then just as suddenly, she turns it off. This tactic causes the unassuming to be intrigued. In the South we call this being hog-tied.

This cause and effect is what Clinton expressed to bodyguard Ferguson as a *come hither look* that he noted in his affidavit. I'll give you a redneck's example; if we were primates, without control, we'd be running around trying to slip three minutes of *wham-bam* into anything short of abstinence. A cute little monkey bent over, busy as a bee merely grooming the fleas off the hairy backs of her girl clans. She's cognitive of the big ape that runs the clan watching her, so she flashes her fuzzy wassy to gain a better position in the clan. She doesn't know it, but he's gonna beat his chest expressing his power and position. The big ape swings over to the cute little monkey. A cry of helplessness shrouds the tree tops for two minutes. (He's a big old ape, can't do the standard three.) Add another notch to his vine—a jungle statistic; like blowing on the end of a coke bottle, she'll never be able to swing from the trees without whistling in a breeze. A bit ridiculous, but we're not hairy primates. When we allow ourselves to receive the call of the wild, we damn well better be sure it's not mixed signals. How do I know this? Because Paula used the same tactic on me. This would be an amusing analogy if it didn't spark some truth of what happened in the hotel room that day. However, believe me when I say, Paula has all the tools to give mixed signals.

I just threw some thoughts out there to give you an idea how my mind has run the gamut. I know what you're thinking; *I've got issues, no doubt.*

Whatever way you want to slice the pie and rationalize it, for me it was all about—*no means no*—not about someone who twists the truth by saying it depends on what is—is. Clinton should've had the mental fortitude, in less time than it takes a monkey to get a hard on, not to confuse flirtation with having his boxers hanging down around his ankles.

Now, if I look at all this as purely strategic leverage and dissociate the human factor, where would we be? It seemed to me, at the time, if we could prove a pattern of behavior on Clinton's part by using Kathleen Willey to testify, it certainly would rattle Clinton's cage. Maybe he'd step up to the plate, do the right thing and apologize. Everyone would be better off for it. Damn that sounds like a line from G.W.

Cindy Hayes, Paula's spokesperson, was flying into LA to meet with us. I certainly had some real issues to discuss with her. Paula and I brought a newfound friend of ours along to see if she could help raise money in LA as well. Her name was Susan Carpenter-McMillan.

We had met Susie through, Jane Chastain, at a press conference. Jane had a weekly talk radio show and was supportive of Paula.

I liked Susan right off the bat. She was head of the Women's Coalition. That perked my interest, because Paula needed support, especially from women's groups. I later learned that Susie and her secretary were the sole proprietary members of her group.

Susie's enthusiasm for controversial issues was unmatched. She pushed legislature for chemical castration for sex offenders. Actually, my approach would've been a little more subtle. Just lay them on a chopping block and let the abused victim do the honors—their choice of axe or ball-ping hammer. The first in line would be that assistant football coach from *Penn State*. Talk about a sick bastard, he has no soul to rape the innocence from a child. My granddaddy said he would take an old tomcat that was causing havoc around the farm and tie a rubber band around his balls to let them rot off. Either way, it's all good.

Susie had spunk with attitude and a platinum hair-do to match. We both were born on the same day, whatever that means.

I saw in Susie a way to voice my opinion against a cult of Clinton extremists. I coined these blind-faith followers as Clintonologists. Their actions reminded me of a well-established Hollywood cult that would lash out when put on the defense. Whenever the faith is questioned by a non-believer—attack the perpetrator like a trailer from a bad B movie. "Come see in Panorama vision how Bubba Buddha fell victim to Bimbo voodoo girl controlled by evil political right-wing vendetta."

Seriously. Yes, there were most defiantly conservative grass root organizations I tapped to support Paula's cause, but not like these over- zealous cult members portrayed.

When they got nasty, I could send Susie Q into the trenches. She could go toe-to-toe and tongue lash any monk the Clintonologists brought against Paula.

The Clintonologists would primarily stick to political talk shows morning, noon and night spouting blatant lies or twisted truths. When asked a derogatory question about Bill's indiscretions, they would go on the attack without answering the question.

It was amazing to watch. If it's professed long and loud enough, then it must be true. It was like these Clintonologist were indoctrinating the masses on every television and talk show radio station by chanting the same script over and over. They would profess what a good job the Clinton Administration was doing, and—oh yeah, they'd say his approval rate has never been better. "All this is nothing more than a right-wing attack. He's doing a good job. His private life doesn't matter."

Tell all and take it home to the masses.

"The American people don't care about these baseless accusations from trailer park trash that's supported by the right-wing agenda. The polls reflect what the American people want."

Now square up to the camera and talk over everyone else for the final pitch.

"Are you better off than you were five years ago?" Actually that's a President Reagan line, but why not borrow something that works from the *Gipper*.

Hot damn, they kicked butt! A well-tuned spinning machine—as long as the economy kept bringing home the bacon to the American people. However, history would've dealt Clinton his worst nightmare if the nation had been in a recession at that time.

What really smoked my ham were the continuous accusations that this was all about money and that Paula's just a gold-digging bimbo. Hot damn, sons-a-bitches!

If they want a fight by God, I'll give 'em a war! Instead, I gave them Susan McMillan. I needed to find someone to front my emotions for me, someone who could play the same game of *low down and dirty*. I found that quality in Susan; a real mud slinging trench fighter. The only thing with Susie was that she brought politics into the arena. It's not that it wasn't always there—like some shadowy intruder hidden in a murky causeway, but with Susie, there wasn't anything hidden. It was in your face blatant. She had a bad habit of being a loose canon as Paula's attorneys found out.

Susie wanted Paula on tabloid shows that she felt would give Paula exposure, "Frankly Susie, I think Paula has already been exposed enough lately." I said.

"No, no, Stevie pooh, I'm not talking about clothes off exposure, I'm talking about letting people see Paula like I do; a sweet, shy and insecure little girl."

"Two things Susie; don't play that Stevie pooh crap with me, it may work great with Paula, but it pisses me off. Second, Paula can be sweet and she can be a spoiled hellcat on wheels when she doesn't get her way. Shy—I think not.

Paula could have a satisfying conversation with a deaf mute. Insecure is what got her in this mess to begin with. Oh, and to answer your question about tabloid shows… the answer is not just no, but hell no!"

Susie wanted Paula to go on the *"Sally show."*

"Oh, Stephen it'll be fine. I've personally talked to Sally, and she said it would be a pro Paula audience. Paula will get first class treatment."

"Yeah, I've heard that before and the answer is still no."

"Well, do you mind, if I go on the show?"

"Knock yourself out, Susie, but don't say I told you so."

Susie did and the surprise guest was Paula's sister, Charlotte, who had been touting that Paula was in it for the money. Then Sally gave the mike over to the booing Paula audience that Sally said would be pro- Paula. The first person asked Susie about five guys having sex with Paula in the back of a van. Susie squinted her eyes and said, "I know you—you're Mark Brown, Charlotte's husband."

Sally acted so… surprised and said, "I had no idea." *Yeah and pigs fly.*

Anyhow, Susie did what Susie does best, "Here's the real trailer park trash. They do live in a trailer."

No matter how Susie struck back trying to moderate damage control, it was a lose—lose situation for Paula. The Clintonologists conspired confrontation between the two sisters as a tactic to delay and take focus off the lawsuit.

In between commercial breaks Susie called, "I'm eating crow, you told me so, Stephen."

I made sure it was the last time Susie appeared on that type of tabloid trash. It certainly fed into Bennett's quote, "This lawsuit is tabloid trash with a caption."

By now, if you're not able to see the web of deception being spun by these Clintonologists, then you're living in a tar-pit of denial, but read on, maybe you can be healed.

Soon Susie was on every legitimate talk show slamming her adversaries by saying, "You liberals can't control your boy's zipper."

Stephen M. Jones, Jr.

I think she's the one who coined the phrase *Zipper Gate*.

Joe and Gil went ballistic. However, it was too late; Susie was now family to Paula. She was Paula's big sister. She spent time and most of all, money on Paula.

Susie also helped me keep Paula focused on the lawsuit. When I had problems with Paula wanting out and wanting to give up, I called Susie to the rescue. Paula was feeling the heat and Susie came with the water hose.

Paula's continuing feeling was that I was too controlling and not cooperating with the attorneys gave me an idea. I used Susie as a balance between the tug-of-war being waged everyday between Paula wanting to give the attorney's carte blanche and me wanting Paula's good name restored without giving away the bank.

There was a price to pay for Susie, but not in monetary value. The downside would be allowing her to sometimes cross the line from being Paula's spokesperson to interjecting political mud slinging. *We all have our vices.* I told Susie that she was pissing off the attorneys by bringing politics into the case, "They feel you're a loose cannon. They say Bennett called up wailing about you."

"What do you think, Stephen?"

"I think they're right—stop the political bashing, but the gloves stay off on everything else. I don't give a damn what Bennett thinks. Let the Clintons taste a little of what they've been dishing out."

Susie cooled her heels for a while, but soon she had to have her fix and was back in the saddle politicking. *I wonder if they have a room at the Betty Ford institute for that type of dependency.* She was a thorn in the side, but she was someone I could trust and right now, I needed her for Paula.

In the meeting, Cindy Hayes advocated through teary eyes how ungrateful I was at the hard work they'd done on the *Paula Jones Fund*.

"Save the tears, sweetheart. I get cried on by the best and it's going nowhere with me."

I leaned over to Susie and whispered, "What do you think?"

"Get rid of them. I can help you set up a fund and you don't have to pay me a dime."

That's all I wanted to hear. Cindy was out and Susie was in.

Susie's husband, Bill McMillan, was a medical malpractice attorney. To me, a sharp pencil in a stack of broken leaded number two's. Of the entire attorneys I have ever met, Bill McMillan is as honorable as they come in a profession where cash flow and ego dominates ethical standards.

If one man in this book deserves recognition on the settlement of this case, that one man is Bill McMillan. To watch him during negotiations is like watching a master craftsman pulling together all the components, then cutting off the dead ends void of any emotional interest.

Toward the end of Paula's lawsuit, Bill and Susie were going through a tough marriage separation, coupled with a multi-million dollar business investment that went belly-up.

My point is, that in between the personal chaos, Bill McMillan helped settle the highest profile case of the century and never asked for one red cent. Two words describe Bill McMillan—class act.

After the settlement, I learned that he was about to lose his mansion of a house. I called Margaret, the secretary of the Paula Jones Fund and told her to pay off all outstanding bills and give me a call back with the balance. She did. I gave her a bonus check and thanked her for all her hard work. I then had her cut a check for the remaining twenty-five thousand to Bill and then closed the account. I picked up the check in Burbank and drove to Bill's office in Pasadena. He wasn't there, so I gave it to his secretary. *I left a note inside, apologizing because it was not more. Who was I kidding? The check probably didn't cover a month's worth of lawn care on his estate, but it was something, at the very least—a token of gratitude.*

Since Paula and I were headed toward splits-ville anyway, the only thing left that I had control of was the Paula Jones Fund. And I'd be damned if the one guy responsible for settling this albatross of a case, would get nothing.

Although Bill was having a rough time, I wasn't fairing any better myself. I was still unemployed from being fired for nothing by Al Checci, owner of the company I worked for and personal friend of the Clintons. I'll get into that a little later, but right now, I do think for historical value, it needs to be noted, before forgotten by time or journalistic hedging of truth, how many people owe a debt of insurmountable gratitude to an honorable man as Bill McMillan.

Another honorable mention is Bernie Warner. Getting an apology was like a quest for the Holy Grail and Bernie was a knight of statistical value. A year or two of waging war against the Clintons was causing a cost and effect deficit that I couldn't afford. After the *Penthouse* scandal, the *Landmark Legal Foundation* that was funding the lawsuit was now distancing themselves. Checks to Joe and Gil were few and far between. Soon, I feared that Paula's lawyers were going to advertise a bargain basement sale to Bennett for something far less than an apology. The white-washed picket fence was coming up fast, just ahead on the left. So it was paramount that I surround myself with people I could trust. Bernie was one of those true blues. Anytime I needed the numbers ran, I turned to Bernie. *Thanks for all the help, a bit late in coming from my end I'd say, but your friendship and contribution for holding the moral high ground was greatly appreciated.*

Right about this time unrest was raising its ugly head. Paula and I were starting to see the lawsuit in different ways. The more worms that Hillary's investigators made to come out of the woodwork about Paula's past, the more I was hell-bent on keeping her good name and reputation.

Paula, however, saw it as a way out of being stuck away from home, sort of a cash cow to buy her a new house in Arkansas. A free get-out-of-jail pass from me, who she felt had locked her away from her family and friends. I guess being held up in a one bedroom condo, with media camped outside watching your every move, could drive anyone a little bonkers. But besides all that, the slightest impression that Paula's sister, Charlotte, could be right about her smelling money wasn't going to happen under my watch, by God—I was bull-headed enough not to allow myself to be wrong about whom I married. I'd be damned to hell before I let Paula break her promise and cash out like all the other bimbos had done. Having what the Clintonologists were spewing come true would be the ultimate disgrace.

However, Paula was starting to worry me with comments like, "I don't give a flip about my good name. I don't care anymore what people think about me. They've already made up their minds who they think I am, so what good is it to keep on fighting, Steve Jones."

"You don't mean that, Paula?"

"Oh, yes I do—what we're doing ain't gonna' change nobody's mind. With all this mess I been through, I feel like I deserve money to buy me a house in Arkansas and have a little extra left over just for spending."

"Paula, who've you been talking to, Debbie?"

"I kin think for myself, thank you very much. Anyhow, it don't matter if I've been talking to someone or not. This is how I feel—you never pay attention to how I feel. You always do what *Steve Jones* wants to do. This ain't about you, it's about me! Can't you get that through your thick skull? I don't care about your good name that I have. If people really knew you like I do Mr. High and Mighty, your name wouldn't mean squat to anybody anyways. You got that! I'm tired of this whole mess and I jus' want out."

At that time I didn't know whether she had said those things just to push my buttons or if she really meant it. Whatever her justification, I couldn't drop the ball now. Anyone who ever wanted to fight back against sexual harassment in the work place would be eaten alive by power and position. *I honestly felt that if we caved, no one would ever want to come forward, speak out and seek judiciary penance.*

I can tell you that Paula's attitude about my/her good name had put a wedge between us. The longer I kept Paula involved in the case, the more she resented me. My solution was Susie and Bernie. Susie would constantly take Paula on a girl's day out to some posh spa or shopping spree, trying to keep her happy. Bernie would call Paula when I couldn't convince her that settling now would cost us more than we could ever pay off in three lifetimes.

Stephen M. Jones, Jr.

Bernie had the patience and edification of a father figure. Susie would baby-talk Paula to hang in there for the greater good of all women who have been sexually abused on the job.

Paula played into it beautifully when she had support from others. She was a poster child for sexual harassment. When she saw newspaper cartoonists drawing her nose shaped like a penis surrounded by her big hair pulled up in a polka-dotted bow she wanted to bow out. One day she was a crusader for women's rights, the next, she wanted her house in Arkansas *right now*. Paula's opinion could change with the wind. Keeping her focused was a battle in itself.

Her strength was in others that supported her. When negotiations did occur, it was paramount that a clear apology existed and enough money to pay for all outstanding fees that had generated from the lawsuit. That's Bernie's forte. As I said before, he was my numbers guy. Any time money was brought to the table, I had Bernie go over it like a *fly on flypaper*. Between Susie and Bernie, they kept Paula on the same page without Paula thinking I was trying to persuade her to change her mind. I know it sounds a little skullduggery, but that was the only way to hold Paula to her promise. She promised me just before we filed that she would not give up, as I would never stop supporting her right to clear her good name.

I want to thank both of them for their true friendship to Paula, and unyielding support. Even in the end, when some people distanced themselves when Paula chose a different course, Susie and Bernie were always there for her.

The Clintons used Bennett to intentionally leak out a story that Paula satisfied a bunch of guys in a van when she was 19. Paula denied the story, but said that she did know one of the guys. Her reaction was, "It's all lies. I was never with more than one guy at a time—ever. I always had a boyfriend."

I have no idea if it really happened; however, the *Penthouse* saga tainted my overview. Unfortunately, Bennett had forgotten to mention that these same guys they'd dug up were all convicted felons.

Without Apology

I think Paula could tell that all this was taking its toll on our relationship. As I said earlier, a couple living in a small condo, it was impossible to seek solitude from one another's resentments. A halo of friction and tension was a constant reminder of how different we were. I guess it's true what they say about how *opposites attract*, but in this arena of circumstances, it was becoming intolerable. How could it get any worse? Shazam!

Needing to get out of the condo, if for only a few minutes, I went to get the mail. "Look, honey what the mailman brought. I got a letter from the IRS. Must have gotten above our means. Nope, that can't be…"

Wrong again. I got hit with an IRS audit, compliments of the Clinton's appointed director and good friend, Charles Rossotti. *Now how could that be on an airline employee's income? Better start soaking some pinto beans.* I would be audited for the next four years.

So let's put the Clinton's squeeze play strategy into perspective. Smear Paula's name publicly by using *Penthouse* and the blow-job boys in the van so everyone will know she has no reputation to protect. Have Stephen fired with the help of Clinton's buddy, Al Checci. That way, they won't have income. Audit me so I will owe money that I don't have to begin with. *Pretty damn daunting perspective for two people to live harmoniously under one roof, don't you think?*

So, if you were me, what would you do? Well, if you were part of the growing society where you don't know who your daddy is then maybe having a good name doesn't mean much anyway. But if you feel that your good name means something honorable, then you stay and fight. The only problem about that perspective is that I was internally losing faith in Paula and becoming more judgmental. I was no longer fighting for her good name, but mine. Like Paula said, maybe it was that way all along and I could never admit it to myself. Ahh, the refection pool—you can't help looking down into the dark pool of self-analysis. The subtle ripples soak into the mind's eye, shaping mirror images that reflects your future or so one imagines in deep despair. Confucius say, "Bird cannot build nest in bare tree."

I mean, we got to where we hardly ever touched each other. When we did come together there was no emotion at all.

Paula said all too often, "Can you please hurry up? It's starting to hurt. Aren't you finished yet?"

I leaned over her back to kiss her shoulder, trying to show some affection while still embraced. I noticed her body seemed to be moving in rhythm, I thought, *maybe a reflex of mutual satisfaction*, but when I looked over her shoulder, I was shocked to see that she was filing her nails! Oh no she's not! Damn that's raw! I stopped, grabbed my pillow and headed for the couch.

As I was leaving, Paula hollered out, "And take that farty-ass dog of yours with you."

I turned around and called out to Mitzie, who began to make her way out from under the bed by sinking her toe nails into the carpet. *Man's best friend.*

"You know, Paula?" I said, "I could have had more interaction with a blow-up doll wearing one of your hair bows."

"Maybe you should go out and buy yourself one then. You want to talk about interaction mister. You hardly ever kiss me anymore, you jus' want to jump on and jump off."

Male egotistically pissed, I responded, "Oh really—okay Paula, you want me to tell you why? It's that damn hair removal cream you use. You walk around looking like Colonel Sanders and after a few days when it's grown back it feels like I'm kissing a man and it grosses me out. I don't know why you feel you have to use that crap. All women have fine hair on their lip. But for some odd reason you're so self-conscious about it, probably because your mama has a real mustache and it shows."

My voice echoed from the hollow depths of a sinking ship. She clinched her teeth and narrowed her eyes and repeated after me emphasizing each word.

"My-mama-has-one!"

Oh no, I've gone an' done it now. I brought her relatives into the mix. Whatever you do in a relationship, never ever bring mama into an argument, especially derogatorily. Hell has no fury than a woman whose mama you've just badmouthed.

Without Apology

It was too late to stop now, though. Maybe I'll try and sugar-coat the bitterness by injecting a sweet word, which is the usual mistake we all make. I've been told it has the same emotional impact as handing her a dozen roses then hitting her over the head with a sledgehammer.

"Now, now honey, you've been putting that damn cream on for so long until it feels rough when it grows back, that's all."

Paula burst into tears, "I hate you for saying that, Steve Jones!"

"I guess this means I'll be a night-time couch potato from now on."

"You betcha, Mister!"

Walking to the couch, I looked down at Mitzie. "So which side of the dog house do you want?"

Mother Nature is a lot like human nature, just like after a bad storm, a rainbow appears signaling new life and regeneration.

At a time in our lives where turmoil was who I went to bed with, then woke up on the couch with, it was a miraculous conception when Paula became pregnant with our second son. Paula's labor was a walk in the park or rather canoeing. I mean, we were literally talking about river rafting while Paula was in labor.

I couldn't help noticing all the accents in the delivery room. Paula's Doctor was from South Africa. He had a, *Cheerio, deeply embedded,* English accent. "I say old boy, do you mind very much if I play the real doctor and you stand over there like a good chap."

It left me wondering if he really meant it.

"Look, will you bloody well move out of the way!" He then sternly blurted.

Yep, he meant it.

The nurse had a sultry French accent. "Monsieur, if you like, you can stand next to me."

Paula, in her Ellie May accent, "Don't even think about it, Buster."

And in my Tennessee accent, "No problem sugar-bugger, I'll just get on the other side."

Stephen M. Jones, Jr.

"So tell me, old boy, what's there to do if I'm... how do you put it? Oh yes, now I remember the phrase, if I'm in your neck of the woods, so to speak?"

Still feeling the sting from the doctor's remark, I said,

"Well Doc, I can tell you what we don't do, is put gasoline soaked tires on people and strike a match. I hear that sort of thing happens in your neck of the woods."

"Oh quite right, we've had our share of atrocities not un-similar to those in the south, where I've heard they wear pillowcases over their heads."

"That was a generation or two ago, Doc, and it wasn't thousands of people in less than a week. How do you people say it, oh yes, now I remember, it's called ethnic cleansing. Just the other day on the news, I saw that hundreds of mutilated people in your country had been chopped up and were floating down some Congo River like logs."

"Really, old man. I don't' believe this is the time or place for such a discussion."

Paula gave me the usual *stink eye* and chimed in, "What is it with you? You gonna start with this doctor, too?"

Knowing exactly what she meant, I started over again on a clean slate.

"Hey Doc, you ever been white water rafting? No? Oh man you should go. What an adrenalin rush. Paula goes with me and she can hardly swim a lick.

Paula interjected, "I kin too! Well...jus' a little. Anyways, enough to keep my head above water—thank you very much."

Looking down and smiling, I said, "Yeah, I guess all those swim lessons I had to make you take kinda' came in handy, huh baby?"

Without even so much as an ouch, Preston Corbin Jones was born August 14th 1996. Both Paula and I were surprised; miracles do come in pounds and ounces.

CHAPTER FIFTEEN

In 1996, not a lot was going on with the lawsuit, but the Presidential elections were red hot. Bennett made sure that every venue of attack was ground down to a snails crawl. He was obviously trying to stall the lawsuit until after the '96 elections and with the help of Judge Wright, he was doing a pretty damn good job at it. The only highlight that sparked interest back into the case was an article in the *American Lawyer* magazine by Stuart Taylor. He directly contradicted the Clintonologists spin machine by saying that the Jones' lawsuit was not some frivolous suit as alleged. Taylor continued by saying that the Jones' suit had merit and should be taken seriously. That Paula did what most victims do right after an assault—they immediately inform close friends and family. All Paula's witnesses corroborated what she had told them within the first few hours of the encounter. Stuart Taylor said, "That's the crucial part of believability… when it's a *he says—she says* lawsuit."

With that, Izzie called and wanted to put Paula on the front cover of *Newsweek* along with a fair article.

There were plenty enough times that both Paula and I were offered a platform to speak out against the Clinton duo re-election campaign, but I turned them all down. I wanted to send a clear message that this was not about politics, but about sexual harassment. We put out a press release, at the disgust of some conservative supporters, stating that all Paula wanted was *her*

Stephen M. Jones, Jr.

day in court and we were not going to take part in any partisan politics during the elections. I was content to allow Clinton to live, or die, on the vine without any assistance from us.

When Clinton was re-elected, Bennett couldn't stall the appeals any longer. His indicative accomplishment of delay afforded the Clintons four more years.

I believe one guy's response summed it up perfectly, when asked why he voted for Clinton, "Hey man, I voted for him just to see the rest of the show!"

Um, um, um. Pitiful. I mean, it makes you wonder how we traversed intellectually to where we are now.

Some years back, while working at the ticket counter, I checked in a woman going to Papeete. I looked at her passport for proper documentation and noticed she was born in 1889. Then it struck me—she was well into her 100s. I couldn't believe my eyes. She walked normal and by all accounts, I would have guessed she was in her sixties. So I asked her what the secrets of a long life were. She remarked, without missing a beat in a quaint Polynesian voice, "You Americans, you over-indulge in everything. You over-eat, you over-work, and with her pointy little finger directly in my face, you over-do everything! You are so wrapped up in keeping up with everyone else's business, you lose you're sense of balance."

I thought about what she had said and she was right. We do over-do everything, missing our balance in life. We Americans love to see a good scandal. What better way to watch it or read it while super-sizing it. Go ahead, curl up your lip and say, "Hey baby, put some chili on my cheesy fries, thank you...thank you very much." *I think there's a message in there somewhere. Go jump on a scale, you'll figure it out.*

As the gears of appeals crept in our direction, Clinton took the approach that you cannot sue a sitting president. He backed his brief to the court with the case of Fitzgerald vs Nixon. To make a long story short, Nixon fired this guy, Fitzgerald, who then sued President Nixon. The case went all the way to the Supreme Court where it was narrowly ruled in Nixon's favor. The Justices cited that a sitting President couldn't be sued for his official duties. *Bingo.*

This didn't have anything to do with his official duties. In fact, our case was before he became President.

Reed Irvine told me a story about JFK. When he was still a Senator and running for the Presidency, he loaned his limo and driver out to some delegate. The car was in an accident and soon after Kennedy was elected President, the delegate sued him. JFK took the same approach and said that he couldn't be sued while in office. The Judge ruled that the case could go forward, because he was not the President when the accident took place.

Too bad Judge Susan Webber Wright didn't have the judicial fortitude to do the same.

Kennedy settled out of court. Except for the claims, the dynamics between the Jones case and the JFK case were the same. Clinton claimed he was immune from being sued just like JFK and Nixon did. When Clinton couldn't put that in his pipe and smoke it in public, he changed his strategy and said that the case should wait until he leaves office. *Well, hell yeah, I guess so! He gets re-elected you're talking four more years. Who knows where we'd all be in four more years. If something happened to Paula, the case is thrown out.*

Clinton based his claim on the *Soldiers and Sailors Civil Relief Act* (SSCRA). The act serves to suspend enforcement of civil liabilities in order to enable such persons to devote their entire energy to the defense of our nation.

Now think about what he's trying to do here. Given Clinton history, you think the best legal minds working for him would have had a little foresight. The dumb son-of-a-biscuit eater who suggested that Clinton use this act should have been tossed outside the White House gates, given an accordion, tin cup, and pet monkey. So with this theory tucked under his belt, Clinton reasoned that since he was ultimately the Commander in Chief, that he would be covered by the SSCRA.

Wrong!

What it did do, however, was cause an uproar in the military community. One Vietnam veteran commented by saying, "How could Clinton wake up and look at himself in the mirror? For him to say that he falls under the

Stephen M. Jones, Jr.

SSCRA, when he dodged the draft and I had buddies come back in body bags, is a disgrace to all veterans."

What's more amazing is that Judge Wright must have agreed because she ruled that Clinton could wait. It's beyond comprehension that a Judge, sworn to apply the law evenly, can be used in the political arena. It's one thing for an un-elected citizen to gather support on the belief of injustice, but an appointed Judge, using the flimsiest of excuses, to justify her ruling for purely political means is monstrous. It undermines the legal system when a Judge politicizes a citizen's right for due process.

Thank God we didn't file in California where the 9th Circuit Court of Appeal could have ruled. If our laws were based on the interpretations of the 9th Circuit, we'd all be sitting around smoking what Clinton said he didn't inhale, and wearing girlie dresses, uh... Arnold. Speaking of Arnold, he couldn't work with the political hacks in Sacramento and now California is billions in debt. And who do we elect to pull us out of economic wows but Jerry Brown. One resident from Oakland, Ca. where he was mayor said, "If there was a dog hurt on one side of the road and Jerry Brown on the other, I'd help the dog and leave Jerry." Man that's cold, but seriously, when Jerry left town he left the Oakland tax payers with a huge I.O.U. His 10k project costing 61 million stalled in the recession. Building plans reviewer Kenny H. Lau hated to see Jerry go. His salary went from 76 thousand a year to 271, 694 dollars with overtime. In fact, hundreds of city officials' had their salary doubled. It's good to work for Jerry when it's off the backs of the tax payer. While governor in the late seventies and early eighties he took a 6 billion surplus and turned it into a 1 billion deficit spurring a state spending increase of 120%. Oh, and what do we do? We elect him when we're already billions in the hole... Brilliant!

I've got to get back on track before I throw-up a blood clot. Where was I? Oh yeah Clinton's weak link of staying the lawsuit.

We, of course appealed, so tack on another delay tactic. The appeal process slowly worked its way up to the Supreme Courts.

Without Apology

Let me now say a few more accolades about Judge Wright. She did not want to try this case—period. She bent over backwards for Clinton to the point of being chastised by her peers. More than once, her rulings were overturned. Judge Wright imposed gag orders while her professor husband had a case of loose lips and gave interviews to the press.

In my opinion, she pretty much threw her gavel out the back window. With that being said, it could have been a hell of a lot worse. From the random pool of Judges, Judge Wright was the only one who was not a Clinton appointee or a flaming F.O.B.

However, the way I was told, she had some personal history with Clinton. She had been a law student under Professor Clinton at the University of Arkansas Law School. I understand that Clinton actually lost her final exam. He offered her a B+ but Wright refused and requested to take the test over for a better grade. I guess she wanted grades with honorable mention at a time when honor meant something.

Obviously, Judge Wright had no hard feelings toward her old alma mater seeing how lenient she was *threw out* the case. *No, I meant to spell throughout that way.*

If I seem a little harshly derogatory toward Judge Wright and others I have mentioned in this book, I do so without impunity of soul. I base this on Newton's third law:

"For every action there is an equal and opposite reaction."

To help Joe and Gil prepare for the upcoming battle royal in the Supreme Court slated for argument on January 13th 1997 were a few people behind the scene, they called themselves Elves: Jerome Marcus, George Conway and Ann Coulter are the ones that I knew of. I mostly talked with Ann Coulter. We seemed to be on the same page, although she surprised me in casual conversation that she, at the time, was dating Guccione's son, Junior.

"You're not talking about that *Penthouse* bastard's son are you, Ann?"

She said, "He's nothing like his daddy."

"Um…The hell you say. Well, only time will tell how far the toupee falls from the scalp."

Stephen M. Jones, Jr.

The funny thing about her was, because of her association with Jr., I wouldn't open up until I was reinforced on her ideology. Come to find out, she is to conservatism what Al Franken is liberalism.

My association with the Elves was mostly informative. Ann kept me abreast on the appeals process and that says a lot for Ann Coulter. The question begged to be asked, and by now you know I had to get it off my chest. I'm not one for formalities, so I asked Ann *flatly*, "If you guys call yourselves Elves, then who the hell is Santa Clause?"

She never answered my question, but I assumed it was someone at the *Landmark Legal Foundation*. I don't think Joe and Gil at that time were aware how informed I was being kept. I also knew that Joe and Gil had very little to do with drafting the arguments going before the Supreme Court. That's one reason why I felt that they didn't deserve any settlement money after they dropped the case.

Unbelievably, the ACLU attached a brief in support of our position that a President can be sued while in office. *Go figure.*

This is how the Supreme Court showdown was played out.

Gil, the more elder statesman, would go before the Supreme Court Justices. Joe would appear on all the top news shows leading up to, and after, the hearing. To help Gil prepare, Judge Robert Bork and Theodore Olson, a justice official in the Reagan years, set up mock arguments of sorts to prepare Gil as best they could.

I didn't want Paula, along with myself, to go to the festivities. That would have just generated the usual circus animal atmosphere and I wasn't about to give the other side free tickets to a *Paula bashing concert.*

I asked my dad to fly to Washington to be my eyes and ears at the hearing, which ultimately turned out to be a bad calculated move on my part. Later, Joe and Gil used the relationship they had gained with my father as leverage to try and get me to accept an unacceptable settlement.

On the defense, Walter Dellinger would parlay Clinton's position. From what I could understand, he was a law professor on loan from Duke University. I wondered if he and Carville were mutatedly related. Dellinger was the interim Solicitor General for the Justice Department. Bennett seemed to be sidelined and didn't offer anything to the Justices that my dad felt was worth commenting about.

On the day of reckoning, inside the Supreme Court, my dad said that either side could barely get a word in edgewise. The Justices came in with guns a'blazing. When Dellinger said something in the nature of, "The public interest should take precedence over private litigants and a President's schedule is too busy."

Dellinger was caught coming out of the movie theater—shot full of holes by Justice Scalia, "We see Presidents riding horseback, chopping firewood, fishing for stick fish, playing golf. *Really?* The notion that he doesn't have a minute to spare is just not credible."

Afterward, I remember that we were all on pins and needles watching press releases and trying to read tea leaves at the same time. All the news stations verified what my dad had said earlier, that the Justices had drilled both sides with equal enthusiasm.

The Clintonologists were quick to say that if Paula wins the appeal, then it will make any sitting President vulnerable to an avalanche of lawsuits. As usual—bullshit. Presidents are surrounded by secret service, security cameras and appointed associates around the clock. The possibility of such an occurrence is so remote that it wouldn't even register on a percentage scale. Rarely would a private citizen have an opportunity to get close enough to subject a President to any civil litigation, especially sexual harassment. Gurus like Bob Beckel professed that type of ideology. *I swear these guys could sell fresh scat to the public and make it look like a banana split. He's now getting paid on Fox News to provide the liberals opinion. The devils advocate.*

On May 27th, 1997 the Supreme Court ruled *nine to zip* that a sitting President had no special immunity to delay the case.

Justice Stevens echoed those same sentiments. He wrote that in his opinion, Clinton's presidency had nothing to do with his unofficial conduct.

Stephen M. Jones, Jr.

How about them apples Judge Susan Webber Wright? Looks like you're going back out to the courtyard to pick up that gavel you threw out the window. "You're court is in session…"

After the big ruling, we tried to live out from under the microscope of the media and get back to the basics of raising a family. However, throughout June and July I kept hearing distant drums from Ann Coulter and others that settlement negotiations were being discussed.

"Well hell's-bells Ann, that's news to me. As far as I know, nothing's going on, but I'll call Joe."

I called Joe immediately, "Hey Joe, are you guys talking to Bennett about any settlement negotiation, because hey, you'd think these guys would be ready to play ball after losing in the ninth inning of the Supreme Court, right?"

"Nope," Joe said. "Gil and I haven't heard a word since our last offer, Stephen. All's quiet on the western front."

"Um… all right then Joe, but let me know if you hear if the other shoe drops."

"Yeah, sure thing—you and Paula will be the first to know."

One week went by and I was starting to see smoke signals with the thrum—thrum rhythm of the drums getting closer.

I called Gil. "Hey, I talked to Joe just last week and he says there's no negotiations going on. How 'bout it? What say you? Cause listen, I'm getting calls from everybody telling me otherwise. I mean, even my dead aunt Esther called from the grave and I don't have an aunt Esther."

"No, Stephen, nothing's going on. It's just the media's usual crap. It's a slow news week and they've got nothing better to do than spread rumors. They gotta fill up those pages with something."

The very next Saturday morning, we received a FedEx package containing a settlement proposal from Joe and Gil. Needless to say that I was angry, doesn't even scratch the surface.

I think deeper, a core eruption—Pompeii-ish maybe. "Don't piss down my back and tell me it's raining." To be lied to all along, and kept in the dark without any participation in the negotiation from Paula's own lawyers was one good reason to place the proposal inside my Weber BQ for a weenie roast.

I struggled with the inner me. Get over it, Steve. It's the substance on the proposal that counts, not how it was contrived. Exactly! Be open minded, I told myself. I tried real hard, honest I did.

Joe and Gil emphasized that this was a complete victory for Paula. That she got everything she wanted and would have money in her pocket to boot.

The proposal was basically a white-wash. There was no admission on Clinton's part for inappropriate behavior. Any money that Paula received would be paid back to the attorneys by way of selling the sealed affidavit describing Clinton's anatomy. It wasn't spelled out exactly that way, but they mentioned that it would be just a matter of time before the sealed affidavit became public and we'd lose any monetary value.

To me it was about restitution of Paula's good name. How could selling some cheesy affidavit for profit to pay back legal fees be a complete victory? That played right into the trailer park trash theory and I didn't walk over hot coals dragging Paula every inch of the way to eat crow now.

To complete the deal, they wanted Paula to sign over all book rights as part of their reimbursement. To push their point to accept or else, they said, "Chasing after a lesser victory is folly in light of the fees and expenses you personally will have to pay pursuant to your legal services contract with us. Especially since legal fund receipts have not met expectations."

Well, hell yeah, why not just string me up by my nuts. Since it was you guys who wrote that scrotum stretch into the contract in the first place, that if a legal fund was opened, the contract reverts from a contingency to an hourly rate. *So, let's see how this all transcends.*

Gil has his personal friend, Cindy Hayes, open a legal fund that never meets expectations, but stinks enough to draw flies from Hillary's investigators who sics the IRS to come a' knocking. *Wow, it's a beautiful thing to owe you guys a balance from your failed expectations if we don't accept this proposal. Now...I'm fighting from all sides, it's a coup d'etat!*

I sent the proposal to Bernie for a Vatican verification; you know, grab *your ankles and pray the priest will be quick scenario.* He confirmed that it was!

I also called Susan to ask her to come over, because I couldn't talk on an unsecured line, thinking Paula's attorneys might hear from their newfound buddies.

Joe and Gil were very specific. No one was to know about the proposal and they needed an answer by noon Monday. I had to talk to Susan in a hurry to ask her how hard it would be obtaining new attorneys.

Joe and Gil stressed that because this proposal was a complete victory for Paula, that continuing the case would only incur more expenses that they could no longer afford. If Paula turned down the agreement, they would withdraw from the case without prejudice. *Got to love the ultimate pressure tactic.* The most powerful word in the human language is *no*, and for some, it's hard to say. I didn't like to be put in a corner and forced into an ultimatum. Joe and Gil made it easy? Hell no!

Susan asked her husband, Bill McMillan, to help search for new attorneys. In the interim, Bill arbitrated the proposal with Joe and Gil. He opened dialogue with Bennett that wove a relationship, which proved invaluable in a final settlement two years later.

A court appearance was fast approaching in front of Judge Wright. Joe and Gil would continue to represent Paula, dropping the dead line until after the court appearance.

On August 22nd we appeared in a Little Rock court room. Judge Wright ruled that the case could go forward against both Clinton and Ferguson, but threw out the claim that Clinton had defamed Paula. Then she got down to the business of scheduling the trial. Bennett acted as if he wanted the trial date to be set as soon as possible.

Yeah, right—stall for four years but now you're all gung-ho to get it on. What a political hack job.

Visually, Bennett was short with plenty of double chin crammed inside a dark blue, two-piece suit accented with a two-tone shirt that went out of style with fat ties and polyester. Although, I've noticed people who think their pooh doesn't stink seem to have that white collar—blue shirt thing going on, sorta' like wearing penny loafers without socks. You know, one of those weird, high society cult statements. Funny how personal attacks bring out the worst in rhetorical feelings when it comes to reputation and good name.

I then looked over and saw Paula talking to Susan, not a revengeful bone in her body, carefree—just chirping away like a lark, oblivious of my internal sentiments. Glancing back at Bennett, I began wondering how different he was from his brother William, who wrote *The Book of Virtues*. One brother writes about it, the other is paid to allow others to exploit it. Someone told me that they came from a broken marriage, same as Clinton. They were pretty much raised without a father figure. Hum, *the good, the bad and the ugly*, void the cool background whistle.

After the court hearing, Paula and I were in Joe and Gil's hotel room. I sat on the corner of the bed alongside Paula. Joe pulled up a chair and said, "Look, it's even worse now than we expected."

"How can that be, Joe?" I said.

"Weren't you paying attention? Judge Wright threw out the claim that Clinton had defamed Paula."

"Yeah, I heard it, so what? The case still stands and we're in a better position to re-negotiate for better terms. Clinton isn't going to want to go to trial if he knows that we really mean business."

"No, you're not getting it, Stephen." I sensed the frustration in his Joe's voice as he continued. "The claim Judge Wright dismissed allows Clinton's (sexual harassment) insurance policy he had with Chubb and State Farm off the hook from paying out any settlement. As it stands, the counts that are left probably won't add up to a hundred-thousand. We're already at seven times that figure now."

"Joe, correct me if I'm wrong, but it was never about money to begin with, you knew that before you took on the case. But if Clinton's not going to apologize in that agreement you guys worked out behind our backs, I might add, then Clinton has to show it by paying through the nose."

"He's never going to apologize, Stephen—it's not going to happen. You get that?"

"I got it."

"Good! This proposal is the best Paula is going to get. Gil and I have put our hearts and soul into this case, but we can't continue to do it for free. I don't know if the settlement offer is still open after today, but if it's still on the table, you and Paula need to let us know what your answer is." Joe paused for a long time, then said, "So what is your answer?"

"Well guys, we'll have to think on it. We're not going to be pressed into a knee-jerk action. I've been there—done that, but if you want an answer right now—it's no."

Paula and I were back in Long Beach when Joe and Gil sent us a final letter strongly encouraging us to accept the proposal. In nine underlined reasons, they outlined why we should accept.

First: The language was all about Paula and nothing to do with Clinton and Trooper Ferguson. "Paula you brought this case to clear your name, not to prove they were bad people."

Second: "In our opinion, that after litigation and Clinton sustained damage from pre-trial discovery, there would be virtually no hope for such a favorable settlement."

Third: "Chasing after a lesser victory is folly in light of the fees, and expenses you personally will have to pay pursuant to your legal services contract with us. Your reputation will suffer greatly in pre-trial discovery. In that regard we have learned that a former boyfriend, whom you know well, and several others, will testify about a supposed event. These matters will be brought out to show that you allegedly did not enjoy a good reputation."

Reality check—now are some of you deniers starting to come to the same conclusion about collusion with the other side?

Fourth: "The court dismissed your claims for defamation. However, our opponents (Really!) are still willing to hold open the offer."

Yep, it's the same claim that you guys helped script, now it's not worth the paper it's written on.

Without Apology

Fifth: Payment to you of $700,000. is more than you could possibly obtain from Clinton. We estimated a maximum verdict of $50,000. and it will be much less, if the jury gives you any judgment at all."

Possibly true.

Sixth: "Another benefit is that you will not be subjected to Ferguson's efforts to show that you could not be defamed, because of an alleged scandalous sexual past. Instead, Ferguson appears to be willing to agree to settlement language, which strongly implies that he lied to the *American Spectator*.

Seventh: "Your reputation for truthfulness is no longer at issue in the case against Clinton, because the claim has been dismissed in which you were called a liar. The court dismissed your claim for liberty interest in reputation. A trial therefore cannot redeem your good name and reputation for truthfulness."

Eighth: "The court, in its memorandum and order of December 28, 1994, noted this lawsuit came about in an effort to clear your name of allegations of sexual activity involving *then* Governor Clinton. As we have told you, the proposed settlement clears your good name."

Hmm...I must have missed that part.

Ninth: "This settlement will put money into your pocket as we explained in our August letter. In our opinion, you will never again be able to obtain money for yourself and your family directly from the lawsuit itself. You will also lose all possible money from the sale of the affidavit. *There it is!* We regret the necessity of seeking withdrawal. We will prepare and file a motion to withdraw with the court on Wednesday, September 3, 1997."

Well, kick me in the teeth and call me snaggles. So, tell me Joe and Gil, how will selling the affidavit restore Paula's good name and reputation?

To be fair, they did continue to say in their summary that this was Paula's decision alone and that she should not feel pressured to accept a settlement with which she is not completely satisfied.

Wow, I don't know, what would you call it when Paula's attorneys wheel and deal without your knowledge and then say take it or you lose your legal representation? I say bull-crap with a caption. No question it was a combined effort to put pressure on Paula. Need further proof you say? Read on...

I think the second week of September, or maybe later, we got a call from a court clerk in Arkansas. There was to be a conference call between all parties involved. We were warned that this conference must be kept secret and held in accordance to the court's gag order. Judge Wright went further to say that if any word of this conference leaked out to the press, then the person responsible would be held in contempt of court. She emphasized that if asked—this conference never happened.

On the day of the call, I rushed home from work, but was stuck in LA traffic as usual. I used my cell phone to connect to the conference call just in time to hear Judge Wright's admonition that I described above. As I was about a block from home, I lost my signal. *Damn Nextel!*

I blew in the door to see Paula and to my surprise, Susie. I grabbed the extension from Susie and gave her a *What the Hell* look. She, in turn, put her finger up to my lips as if to say...shush.

Judge Wright did roll call, all of Clinton's lawyers were present including Bill Bristow, Ferguson's dirt bag attorney.

Joe and Gil were given accolades by Judge Wright feeling that they were due fair compensation for all their hard work. Judge Wright then chastised Paula for not accepting what she felt was a good and equitable settlement between both parties.

Obviously the Judge didn't have the full story.

I then said, "Judge Wright, this is Stephen, Paula's husband. Let me explain why Paula couldn't accept the settlement."

"Excuse me, Judge Wright, this is Bob Bennett speaking. I don't believe Mr. Jones is part of this complaint and to my knowledge he is not part of Mrs. Jones' counsel."

"Oh, I'm sorry Mr. Bennett. I didn't know that anyone would object to Mr. Jones being involved."

"Judge Wright?"

"Yes, Mr. Bennett."

"I have no objection to Mr. Jones listening."

"Mr. Jones, you will reframe from any further communication; however, Mr. Bennett has been gracious to allow you to listen. Mr. Jones, do you understand?"

"Oh yeah, Judge Wright. You bet I do."

I put my hand over the phone, and said, "Paula you're going to have to try and explain why."

So Paula tried to explain, "Well Judge Wright, I couldn't accept a settlement without an apology."

"Mrs. Jones, without accepting this settlement you have put your personal needs above what I feel is a reasonable solution for all."

"Yes Ma'am, but I just feel that their needs to be some admittance of wrong doing from Mr. Clinton."

"Mrs. Jones… your attorneys have worked long and hard on your behalf to come to a fair settlement for you. Don't you think you're being a little selfish by not accepting a settlement that's good for you and the country?"

"Yes, Ma'am."

With tears in her eyes, Paula looked at me for help. I whispered into her ear, "You tell her that you didn't do anything wrong!"

At that point, I felt so badly for Paula. I had carried her to this place and sworn that I'd be there for her and all I could do now was listen. *Damn you to hell Bob Bennett!*

Paula couldn't defend herself and was resolved to sobbing, Yes Ma'ams. Joe jumped into the mix in an attempt to help Paula, but was quickly cut off by Bennett. He never attempted again.

Bennett came in for the kill, "Judge Wright, I have motions that need to be answered."

"Mrs. Jones, I'm awarding your counsel's request for withdraw. Understand Mrs. Jones you will be responsible to respond to all motions in a timely fashion or your case will be thrown out. Do you understand, Mrs. Jones?"

"Yes Ma'am."

Stephen M. Jones, Jr.

That had to be one of the worst felt emotional lows of injustice of the case. Being paraded in a three-ring circus and smacked into submission of unequal liberties by Bennett's bullwhip of due process.

Well, go ahead eat that cotton candy and enjoy the show. "The fat lady may be humming, but she's not singing yet."

With the help of Bill McMillan, we countered within our own ranks. I remember what the greatest coach of all time, Vince Lombardi, said, "It's not how many times you get knocked down; it's how many times you get up!"

We began negotiating within the settlement proposal negotiations. Joe and Gil gave us nine reasons to accept, we proposed eight stipulations. They agreed to all but one, the eighth one, which I called, *The Eight Ball*. It was the deal breaker. Instead of a paper façade with no teeth that put us in the hole financially, this really put "Money in Paula's pocket."

From what I remember, here's how it worked. We upped the ante, from $700,000. to $850,000. If there was to be no apology, then Clinton should say it in the monetary form. Paula would receive $450,000. We keep the affidavit. Later, if all things went well and Clinton stayed out of the spin zone, we would give the sealed affidavit to Clinton—no strings attached.

Paula would have no further legal liabilities to Joe and Gil. Paula would pay all outstanding liabilities incurred outside the realm of legal fees. A sweet deal, just like a hot day with two scoops of vanilla icecream on a sugar cone. Ya' don't know which side to lick first. Oh yeah, I almost forgot...and no signing over book rights.

The *Eight Ball* was if Clinton wouldn't accept the $850,000 counter proposal, then Joe and Gil would walk away from any monetary interest in the case.

Looking back, it was a great counter proposal, monetarily speaking. However, I still have that pee in my chili feeling of how the whole dim lit back room manifesto was contrived in the first place. I can't prove it, but it has all the hallmarks of Hillary's sticky fingers all over it. On top of that, it wasn't about the money, but an apology for an indiscretion. Without some forum of responsibility on Clinton's part, the case, if it had stopped right then, would've gone down in history as a complete mystery of circumstances. With that in mind, and knowing me from what you've read so far, who do you think put the *Eight Ball* into play? Exactly! It was to fail by design, knowing that Joe and Gil would never accept the eighth stipulation.

Also, truth be known, the last-minute negotiating bought us time for Bill McMillan to help us search for new representation.

In the search for new and improved lawyers, Bill McMillan put the word out that we were having open house interviews. By the same token, Bill was instrumental in answering documentation requests that Bennett shot out from his circus cannon.

My problem was I wanted a team of attorneys to be able to put together a superior force of trial lawyers, not so much versed in settlement negotiations which put us in a disadvantage with the Clintons.

To do battle on an even plain with the Clintons who, by virtue, defines whatever is, is. I had to change the dynamics. I wanted meat eaters! I had already learned the first time around that if we stayed on the same course, we'd get the skinny end of the lamb.

I studied their tactics. Bob Bennett was a hard-nosed negotiator, *Mr. Intimidator* of sorts, but he hadn't tried a case in years. What's that old saying? "If you don't use it, you'll lose it." Well, that saying kept tolling in my ear. This time by damn, I'll have the sun at my back!

So here it is in a nutshell. There were more than a few qualified candidates posed to hop aboard the bullet express. However, bringing their egos in line was like smashing protons with a wiffle bat. All wanted to be big chief—not one was willing to come together to form a team of equals.

While out to dinner in Pasadena with the McMillan's, Bill said he had received information about a group of attorneys from Dallas. No one present that night gave them a second thought except me. Their firm was not associated with, nor recognized as, having a prestigious pedigree. This was right down my *back alley mentality* of taking the gloves off a southpaw and releasing the arm that's been tied behind our backs. I wanted a bare knuckle fight! I didn't give a damn about semantics and pedigrees. What mattered to me was how much trial experience they had, and they had plenty! I asked Billy to send me a dossier from the Dallas boys. I liked what I read, so I put in a call to their lead attorney, Donovan Campbell, of the law firm Rader, Campbell, Fisher & Pike.

Chapter Sixteen

I requested a meeting with the Dallas boys and they flew in to meet us at Billy and Susie's house in Pasadena. After the preliminary invocations, we get down to the sermons. I told Donovan that Joe and Gil's approach was mentally hamstrung by settlement negotiations and taking Clinton to trial was never realistically on the table. That's not to say that settlement wasn't an option, it was just no longer a focal point.

I made it clear to Don that this was an uphill battle. I emphasized that Paula's case was not a cash cow. The total torts in the lawsuit amounted to around $80,000.

I continued by saying, "You'll be infested with media, constantly looking over your shoulder, trying to second guess your next move. The upside—if there ever is one, is that your firm will become newsworthy overnight."

Don wanted their firm, if they took Paula's case, to be the only source of disseminating information. Everyone else needed to have a *no comment mentality*.

"Really?" I said. "Well…add another spout to your tea kettle, brother, because Susie will be Paula's spokesperson. So if you take this case you'll have to coordinate closely with her. I don't believe *"no comment"* exists in Susie's vocabulary!

As I continued, I intentionally looked at Susie. "I'd like to adhere to the theme, "loose lips sink ships."

Susie responded quickly. You have to admit, Stephen, I've gotten better!"

"Exactly my point, Susie. You have gotten much better…at it!"

After that, Don and Jim left to powwow with their partners. A few hours later, Bill and Susie's doorbell rang. Both attorneys walked into the foyer of the big house with seriousness in demeanor. At first, I took it that they were going to decline the case. Jim Fisher spoke directly to Paula. He spoke with a smile slowly emerging across his face, "The firm of Rader, Campbell, Fisher & Pike would be honored to represent you in a case to restore you're reputation, ma'am."

Wow, a Texas-style introduction—I liked it, a style of southern formalities that cannot be mimicked outside the *Lone Star State*. One word—genuine—a rare commodity. For one moment I almost forgot about *Penthouse*.

The *Posse*, as I sometimes called them, didn't come without a hitch in their *giddy up*. Both Paula and I signed the contract in Don's hotel room. I learned that John Whitehead of the *Rutherford Institute* came along with the package deal. The Institute would financially back the case. I'd been there—done that with *Landmark Foundation*. The difference was that Rutherford was up-front about it. I voiced reservations about it, but not loud enough to back out.

John Whitehead and I butted heads on two fronts. First it was dealing with his ego. I thought that I had nipped that in the butt with hiring the *Posse*, but no. John was on every talk show circus, east and west of the Pecos.

I had some influence on Susie, but not with John. He was on *The Geraldo Show* so much, I thought John might sit in while Rivera was out collecting forensic dust possibly left behind from one of Al Capone's old shoes.

Secondly, John wanted me to shut down the PJ fund which conflicted with their fund-raising program. I told him that I'd shut it down and donate the entire amount to the *Rutherford Institute* if he could guarantee me I wouldn't owe a dime after the case was over. You guessed it—death and taxes. He balked and the PJ fund stayed open.

265

The *Posse* didn't waste time rounding up the Jane Does. Judge Wright set the parameters for defining a Jane Doe. Basically, it was anyone who'd had a sexual encounter with Bill Clinton and was promoted in position or given a job. Their real names kept in secrecy due to public exposure.

We knew that once we turned over the witness list to the other side, Hillary would have them scatter like a light switch flipped on in a New York diner. So began the absurdity of cat and mouse. Clinton's women of indiscretions past and present mysteriously disappeared or were conveniently out of the country. Sweeping the countryside, Kathleen Willey was first, but she didn't come out of the *hole in the wall gang* easily. Working in conjunction with Clinton's attorney, Bob Bennett, she stalled with surgery issues and denied everything—right up until we put her son on the stand. After Kathleen flipped, she got a little taste of what we'd been going through with threats and intimidation.

Next, out of the badlands, was Judge Jane Doe, aka Beth Coulson, who Clinton had appointed. We calculated that she had an on-going relationship around the same time Billy the Kidd was plucking Gennifer's flowers. Ethically speaking, she never admitted guilt, even when presented with documentation witnessed by the State Trooper who accompanied the Kidd.

What's that Line? "Well…that's my story and I'm stickin' to it—#**!"

Judge Doe was asked specifically, on one of the nights in question when her husband was out of town, what she was doing at a local park half past midnight in the back seat of Clinton's dark blue Lincoln. Judge Doe answered by saying that she and Clinton were Bible studying. Okay…but from the trooper's testimony, the rocking of the suspension from the hot rod Lincoln, combined with the moans of pleasure, must have somehow been misconstrued as praising the Lord. I understand some of the words climactically spoken that night could have "Oh God" biblical connotations.

Another raid on the Clinton saloon house produced Jane Doe # 4, aka Shelia Lawrence. You might remember her better by her husband, Larry Lawrence. Still doesn't ring a bell? Well, let me give ya' a little background. Larry was a wealthy Jewish real estate mogul who donated millions to the

DNC, plus a quarter of that went to the Clinton's campaign fund. Larry's notoriety comes from being dug up from Arlington Cemetery because he never served in the military as purported. After the Army, *who presides over who* is entombed in our most sacred ground, found no military record, so they questioned his admittance. The Clinton administration forced the issue, using the excuse that Larry was appointed by Clinton as ambassador to Switzerland and that should be good enough. Come to find out, he had dodged the draft just like Bill, which was a disgrace that he was buried there in the first place.

Not only was Bill a good friend of Larry and gave a eulogy at Arlington, but Bill was a bigger friend of Larry's wife, Shelia. They were known to do a little puttin' around on the golf course. I understand she could really drive the balls down the fairways.

Trivia: The word golf stands for <u>G</u>entlemen <u>O</u>nly, <u>L</u>adies <u>F</u>orbidden. Thought you might like to know, or not. So anyway, the *Posse* had her on their *most wanted list* and Shelia went on the lamb. We got a tip as to where she was hiding out. You know where we found her? After three weeks staking out Bruce Lindsey's home, (*Chief White House Deputy Council for the President*), Shelia finally came out to accept the subpoena. I guess she got sick of being hold up without Bill's number two iron to putt-putt-putt around with her. Poor Larry, I guess they had that old guy young wife thing going on. Or maybe he did the Eskimo. You know, in days of old where it was tradition to give your wife to a cold shivering friend in need, or in Bills case…liberal. I'm just saying…it's good to be king of the DNC.

Like newborns, we headed out to Dallas to assess the witness list. The deadline that Judge Wright had set for the final list was fast approaching. I argued to have Hillary and Bill's little brother, Roger, on the list. Mr. Pike, one of the attorneys, felt that it could be judged by, *you know who*, as being mean spirited; therefore, losing a tactical position of holding the moral high ground. So I said, "What's the name of that country and western dance song that fits your direction of thought, Mr. Pike?"

Without Apology

He looked at me perplexed at my inference, so I said, "Oh, now I remember—Bullshit! So why the hell am I on their list?" Silence…I got their names on the list, but that's as far as the gambit ran in that direction, dammit.

Discussion falls on Linda Tripp's signed affidavit and her willingness to allow us access to the tapes between her and Monica. Since I had still worked for an airline at that time, I volunteered to fly down to pick them up.

Un-damn-fortunately, a few days later, Ken Starr, crashed our party and crossed over from Whitewater and seized all the tapes. Barn burner!

The *Posse* makes several attempts to depose Monica, but her attorney in the beginning was working in conjunction with Bennett, stalling and using the same dog and pony act of medical excuses that Kathleen Willey had used. I understood that Monica had a dependency on fudge brownies. I heard that some people over at *Jenny Craig* had given her thousands to lose weight and kick the habit. I'm sure that it was a shrewd move on some exec's part over at *Jenny Craig*. Again, give that person a monkey, a tin cup and an accordion.

Within a few months, Paula and I were in Arkansas for her deposition. Bennett, with the help of Hillary's detectives, tried to attack Paula's reputation in public and got chastised for going after the victim, so she used Bill Bristow, Danny Ferguson's attorney to do their dirty work. Bristow fit the bill. You know the type—skuzzy looking with dirt under his nails. Hillary's cronies dug up every Tom, Dick, and Harry who'd ever had a sexual encounter with Paula in order to discredit her reputation.

I have to say what became known was best suited for the Heimlich position and not for my ears. No matter how much you're prepared, it still bleeds you.

After two days of mental disgrace, I flew to Dallas for my deposition, still wondering why me, and not Hillary? What's interesting is that they wanted a copy of my screen actor's card; to be able to work in the movie industry you have to be in the Guild. "What the hell does my SAG card have to do with this case?"

I was told that I needed to surrender it for purposes of photo copying. Well, a couple weeks went by and I couldn't get an audition for an *Oscar*

Mayer wiener commercial. Not that I was burning down the house as an actor...I'd get a call back—here and there, but now it had dried up and blown away like the Oklahoma dust bowl. My agent wanted me to use the notoriety of the case to solicit work. To me, that would undermine the principle of what the case was about. I like to make money just like the next man, but not off the back of an intertwined, high-profile case. I may be a lot of things to a lot of people, but I couldn't find it in myself to do that.

Hell, anyway the Clintons were worshiped in Hollywood, still are. Maybe not as passionately as before, but you can bet they still carry a black *American Express* line of credit in Tinsel Town when it comes to donations for re-elections. Speaking of which, I hear a rumbling to have Biden say he's to old for another term as Vice-President and motion Hillary as his stand in. I can only say if that happens Obama has a good chance to be re-elected. Hillary is perceived as very popular along with clout under her belt. And don't forget, you get Bill as the kewpie doll. A package deal. Barak would be best advised to tell Bill to stay the hell away from Michelle. I'm just saying, the guys got history.

After my deposition, I flew back to Arkansas and the next day I got a call from the vet where Mitzie has been kenneled. He advised me that she was dying. I flew back to LA and drove directly to the veterinarian's clinic. I rushed back toward the back area and found her lying flat with an IV taped to her paw. When Mitzie recognized me, her tail slowly slapped at a puddle of glucose that ran from her vein and trickled out her other end like a leaky facet. Her kidneys were shot. I lay down next to her and cried like a baby.

After I was able to pull myself together, I drove home and found a shut-off notice taped to the door. Huh, I guess Paula forgot to pay the bill. I opened the door and walked into the darkness, no flashlight, no candle—no nothing.

An arid smell lured me into the kitchen. Having already kicked my shoes off my aching feet, I stood in front of a defrosted refrigerator with my socks soaking up whatever had permeated inside and leaked onto the floor. Reluctantly, I opened the fridge door to allow the stench to enter my nostrils as if committing toxic inhalation suicide. I turned quickly and put my head under the sink to splash cold water in my face to keep from throwing up. You guessed it—Paula didn't pay the water bill either.

Early the next morning, I got a call saying that Mitzie had died during the night. I should have stayed when they told me to go on home.

Later, newspapers ran a story that was leaked out by Hillary's investigative squad about how the Paula Jones Fund was abusing money by paying for Mitzie being kenneled. I always felt that the stress of Mitzie being kenneled for so long during our depositions contributed to her fate, but to say I abused funds was ludicrous. Wow, I'm deposed for hell knows why and the pro-Clinton media hacks think the expenses should come out of my pockets. Two words—dirty bastards.

I argued with the *Posse* and arranged to set the settlement price tag to two million dollars for two reasons: One, I wanted the Clintons to understand that we were under new management that meant business. Two, it was either pay through the nose or apologize. Our legal liabilities were well beyond the amount the golden egg had laid earlier of seven-hundred thousand.

After putting the settlement price tag on the Mount Gibraltar pedestal, we picked up the pieces from continuously being land-mined every step of the way by finally scheduling Clinton's deposition to be held at the White House. The venue was changed to Bennett's law office in downtown DC. I was told by our attorneys who had talked to their attorneys who said that Hillary was worried that Bill's deposition at the White House might be scrutinized by the public as being legitimate. Duh!

We depose Clinton on January 17, 1998. Strategically, Bennett arranged the law office building to be blocked off on one side with large trash containers and a coupla' cross-country buses. I can't pin that tail on Hillary's shenanigans. See, I can be fair. I know I keep bringing her up a lot, but it was like Bill was sidelined to his official capacity as President, while Hillary was imbedded with the Jones case. Most people never knew how deeply involved she was. Now you do. I wouldn't say that she had total control of the case, but she was never sidelined either—she played the entire game.

Stephen M. Jones, Jr.

My sources told me that Bennett's office leased the cans and buses. Anyhow, this forced us to enter from the front plaza causing a vacuum.

As we got out of the taxi, hundreds of media surged toward us from everywhere—it was a *madhouse* of pushing and shoving. A camera guy fell backwards onto a twelve-foot ladder with another camera man standing on top. Like the domino effect, as the ladder fell, so did everyone else in its path. I seized the moment and literally stepped on fallen people with Paula in tow. I thought of Bennett looking down at the spectacle, from high above the chaos, enjoying the tripe he helped arrange. Our lead attorney, Donovan Campbell, used to refer to Bennett as, *dough boy*, but right about then, I was thinking more like... *asshole*. That thought didn't fair well with the guy's face that I had just stepped on—sorry dude.

Safely inside the green zone, I noticed that Wesley Holmes, one of our attorneys had his jacket and shirt almost ripped off. While he was huffing and puffing and tucking his shirt back in, I said, "Hey Wes, are you a lawyer or rock star?"

He found no humor in my remark. His contorted expression, if plastered, could have sold as a Halloween mask, it was that scary.

There was a staffer from Bennett's office, along with the Secret Service, checking our identification thus allowing only Paula and her select attorneys up the elevators. As for me, unfortunately I was chaperoned into the lobby by the Secret Service guy with squeaky shoes. No kidding, every time the guy walked, it sounded like an old door hinge, or better yet, the box springs in the Lincoln bedroom. *Like how the hell do I know?* All I do know is that every time I started pondering how things were going up there, the guy would stretch his legs throwing my thought process completely out of sink, buggy. *I stood all I can stand, and I couldn't stand no more,* so I told him, "You can't be too secretive in the Secret Service with shoes like that. Hey Bub.., could ya' take your shoes off next time you decide to do a walk-about?"

"Sure!" He said, only he didn't, and now he moved around constantly just to piss me off. Thinking about it now, it seems ridiculous; *I mean—to think the guy was going to walk around in his stocking feet just to pacify me.* I know

271

what you're thinking and if it's about me, you're probably right. Maybe you could recommend one who's not too expensive, but that was then, and this is now. Actually, writing this book is therapeutic.

In the conference room where Clinton's deposition took place, Jim Fisher was our point guy. He passed over a list of what constitutes sexual relations. Pretty much everything physically arousing between two people except kissing. While this was being mentally digested, *Brucey Baby*, aka Bruce Lindsey, was playing waitress extraordinaire by serving iced tea every few minutes to Clinton who sucked them down like happy hour at Bubba's Sweet Tea Tavern.

After looking over the list, Bennett loudly objected and Judge Wright, who made special arrangements to be there in person, weighed in.

The Judges conclusion, with the help of Bennett, deemed the definitions too sensitive for public scrutiny and would be scandalous to say otherwise. Hee, hee, hah, hah…that would be funny if Judge Wright wasn't trying to protect the sanctity of the presidency by sacrificing the plaintiff's rights. So there you go—without a clear, concise understanding between both parties of what constitutes oral sex. Then all that's left is vagueness which muddies up the water of clarity.

Shrewd move. Instead of pinning the tail on the donkey we got our doorbell rung. Left on the front steps, with a brown paper bag lit on fire for us to stomp out and scrape off. *Hold on—the fat lady's humming, but she's not singing, not just yet.*

Unbeknownst to the Clinton camp, Wes had flown into DC a day early to interview Linda Tripp, the day after the Feds wired her to milk Monica. Wes took the cream right off the top. We had very detailed information on times, places, gifts, and the knowledge of a personal video tape that Monica had made for Clinton.

When Clinton was asked direct questions, under oath, he perjured himself, or for you nonbelievers out there still living in a gopher hole of denial, he gave grossly misleading answers. Oh, and as a footnote, he admitted having a sexual affair with Gennifer Flowers. I couldn't have cared less, other than the fact that it could weigh in as to how truthful he would be in our case, since he had continually lied about it publicly for years.

So, after the deposition, while we were out celebrating at the *Old Ebbitt* restaurant, the candle was burning at both ends at the White House trying to track down Betty Currie, Clinton's personal secretary. The Clintons were desperate to tell Betty to tell Monica to return the gifts that Bill had given her. Yes, that's right, Hillary knew of Monica at that point.

Betty Currie kept the returned gifts in a box under her bed. Such devotion to deception. I think every sexual predator needs a secretary like Betty.

Unbelievable—As if taking the tapes were not enough, Ken Starr informed Judge Wright that we are interfering in a possible Federal indictment by deposing Monica. So, get this, she disallowed Lewinski's deposition. If you opened a dictionary to see Judge Wright's definition as to what she constitutes as a Jane Doe, you'd see a picture of Monica revealing her polka dot thongies underneath that blue cocktail dress.

A) She worked for Clinton.

B) She had sexual relations with Clinton.

C) She was given a job or given a promotion. Well, attempted by good friend Vernon Jordon until leaked to the press. The pawn is sacrificed to preserve the greater cause. Starr's Whitewater goldmine turned out to be fool's gold, so Starr crossed over to our plight for justice, claiming imminent domain. *Damn claim jumper!*

"So Hillary, where's the collusion theory of a right wing conspiracy that the Jones' camp was imbedded with the Feds?" Okay—okay, so maybe Starr used us like last year's catalog in an Arkansas outhouse, but I wouldn't go so far as to say it was collusion.

On April 1, 1998, Judge Wright, on the flimsiest of reasons, tossed out the lawsuit. Oh, and if you think it's just coincidence that she did it on April Fool's day, then you need to stand under the apple tree, Sir Isaac Newton. Judge Wright's underlying statement, along with her ruling, was loud and clear to Paula, and all women who stand up against sexual harassment. "You're a fool!"

Without Apology

Late that night, I stared into the one eye cable monster in disbelief, agonizingly watching Clinton celebrating in South Africa beatin' on bongo drums and smoking a cigar, probably an infamous Monica dipped cigar, as I understand he has done on other joyous occasions. The robust flavor, I imagine, falls just short of a soiled Baby diaper. After purging my mind of Mr. puff n stuff, I thought that if Paula stops now, no one would ever come forward after seeing how a Judge could be in the pockets of the executive branch.

On April 6, I was fired from my job of eighteen years for no reason. As I mentioned earlier, Al Checci, owner of the company I worked for, is good friends with the Clintons. The company is Union, so the firing had to have been arbitrated before a labor lawyer could interfere. The arbitration was conveniently postponed for almost two years before I won my job back.

Bob Bennett called Paula's attorneys the day after I was fired and said, "I don't see any reason to appeal Judge Wright's decision to throw out this frivolous suit. I understand that Steve and Paula are financially strapped now, so why don't they go ahead and write a book."

Now are you starting to see the screws being wrenched tighter? I didn't mention being fired for nothing; let me fill in the blanks. I'm not going to dwell too long in this area because the people who caused my firing either no longer own, or work, in my station. What's that old saying? *We're under new management now.*

The day in question; I clocked in, worked my shift, and clocked out. However, there was a station freeze because a flight was returning to the gates. At the end of my shift, I was not told by any supervisor that there was a freeze and to stay, which is the normal protocol. Actually the procedure is to ask for volunteers and then hold over junior agents in reverse seniority if a flight is delayed or canceled.

Now, just five minutes before my shift was to end, I walked in the office door to clock out at exactly the same time as a manager was going out and we bumped into each other, and I commented, "Would you like this next dance?" She smiled, but mentioned nothing about a freeze. I then noticed that someone from the Airline's Executive Club had put a magazine in my employee box about the Jones' suit. I grabbed it and went to the restroom. Ten minutes later I clocked out and walked out.

They, the company, said that they had a witness that said I removed a freeze notice taped to the time clock then clocked out and re-taped it. When I told the manager that wasn't true and requested that she bring in the witness, she said she'd get back to me. A day later, she said their witness said he hadn't seen anything. *I guess that was nothing more than a big fabrication of circumstances, huh?*

So continuing the Q & A session, she asked if I'd seen the posted freeze notice taped to the time clock. I told her that employees tape all kinds of messages there—most were requesting trades for days off, and I don't pay any attention to them. If there was a notice taped up there, I don't recall seeing it. In fact, of all my eighteen years with the company, I've never seen a freeze notice. I've always been told verbally before my shift ends. I reminded the manager how, on the day in question, I ran into her when we both went through the door at the same time and she never mentioned anything about a freeze. She confirmed to me that she remembered, because I recorded the entirety of the Q & A session.

A few days later, close to the end of my shift, I was summoned to the manager's office. I was handed a termination letter and told to turn in my badge and keys. The letter said that I was being terminated for lying about not seeing the freeze notice taped on the time clock. *I'm confused, where's the lie?* Oh, and to make matters worse, I found out that the manager didn't even post the freeze notice until five minutes after my shift was over. The only reason I was still there was because I had gone to the restroom before clocking out. Technically, I was off the clock. The company doesn't pay you after your shift, unless an overtime slip is signed by a supervisor.

An insider at the White House informed me that I should request transcripts from the two phone conversations that Clinton had with Checci prior to me being fired. I tried to subpoena the transcripts, but Janet Reno's office refused on the grounds of national security. *Why would a CEO and Clinton have anything to do with national security?* Answer: if it had to do with anything about me being conveniently fired, Clinton would have a bigger suit on his hands, as well as the company. I tried a second time, requesting they black out anything to do with national security, but it went nowhere. Little guy—short end of the stick.

Almost two years later, and after the Jones' suit was over, my firing came up for arbitration by a company-paid arbitrator.

Three key factors:

First: For one thing the witness for the company gave conflicting testimony about the position of the freeze notice. By the way, this was the same witness the manager brought in to lie about seeing me remove the freeze notice. He, the witness for the company, said it was not covering the slide, whereas the management said it covered the slide where you could swipe your badge to clock in/out. He later tried to change his testimony to say that it was covering the slide. Who's the liar?

Second: Time reports showed that employees who were not affected by the freeze (ramp guys) clocked out just before I had and could have removed the notice.

Third: Testimony was given, including mine that no one had ever seen a freeze notice posted before.

The arbitrator asked me if I had an obligation to read the notice that I don't even remember seeing. I told him no, because I didn't know that materials taped on a time clock were official and mandatory to read. Aftermath, I got my job back, but since the arbitrator felt that I should have read something that I don't remember seeing in the first place, he denied me any back pay.

So there you have it, you be the Judge and Jury. Bottom line—pretty much financially screwed at a critical point in the case. Interesting to note, is that for two years prior, I constantly had my credit history checked by the Clintons to see if we were receiving money for personal gain from right-wing organizations. I constantly got TRW and Equifax letters each month that I never applied for or requested a credit history. They knew that I was the sole

Stephen M. Jones, Jr.

supporter of our family and that losing my job would squeeze us big time, calculatedly evil.

Chapter Seventeen

Funny thing, it never crossed my mind not to appeal after Judge Wright's decision to throw the case out. I must be a glutton for punishment, as if to say, "Thank you sir, may I have another?"

Paula just wanted out. I wanted to appeal and the *Posse* called to say they had just poured the coffee grounds over the camp fire and was riding into the sunset. I got on the horn again looking for an attorney just to get the appeal filed.

Ironically, I get a call from my friend, Paul Rodriguez, then editing manager for *Insight Magazine*. He wanted to invite us to the White House correspondence party. "Hmm, hold on while I check my schedule Paul—no job, no case, no problem.

Actually it was my way of sending the Clintons a personal message. I knew it would be front page if we went. I also knew that Paula would be bombarded by the press. What better message could I send them than by crashing their party; reminding them we're still here, still a burr under the saddle you might say, like an uninvited relative that sits at the diner table belching and farting immune of conscience. A continuous reminder that's whispered and jeered just short of ear shot. It worked beautifully too. I could see Bill and Hillary looking down on us every time the flash bulbs flickered in continuous succession. The table lit up like the 4th of July. A little sweet revenge knowing that they knew I was mocking them in their own backyard. *God, if only I could have thought to bring my own bongo drums.*

Don Imus was the entertainment for the night. He heckled the Clinton's by exaggerating that a Mercedes was parked outside with Arkansas tags, knowing full well he was talking about us. Our car had more camera time than the Rose Bowl Parade.

Paula wore an aqua blue cocktail dress, accented with rhinestones that I had picked out special since the color blue was in rogue for White House events. Paula loved the dress and bought some costume jewelry to match. She had her hair prepared at some salon down the street from the hotel.

Paul, accompanied by his wife, picked us up by limo from our hotel. We were greeted by some cheers and a host of organized jeers that somehow knew exactly when we'd arrive at the Hilton. For Paula and me, by now we were preconditioned for it, but it really upset Paul's wife. I thought she might have a nervous breakdown on the spot.

Every prominent newspaper and magazine represented that night had a private party room inside the hotel. I remember holding onto Paula tightly while being hustled from *Newsweek*, to *Vogue*, to *Vanity Fair* in standing room only rooms. As we walked into the *Vanity Fair* private party, I noticed Walter Cronkite being interviewed, and as soon as the crowd noticed us, a hush of silence hovered across the room, along with an intense goggle, as if a tomato was about to be thrown.

The interview with Walter stopped and the interviewer rushed over to us. The only time Cronkite was ever up-staged and shouldn't have been. The Hollywood elitists snubbed us by immediately leaving upon our arrival. Personally, I didn't give a rat's ass, except for the fact that they couldn't help walking by to take a closer gawk. Michael Douglas strode by, making a dramatic exit looking all the more condescending. Well, Michael, be careful—after all you married a Jones, and I have to say she's definitely helped your reputation. Then there was Ellen DeGeneres and her mate, Anne Heche. Anne stood next to me and our eyes met, we gazed at each other until

Without Apology

Ellen gave her a pull. All I can say is that it wasn't a look from a woman who just likes women. I guess history proved me right on that.

The party spilled out onto an outside veranda. I needed some fresh air with room to breathe, so I left Paula to hobnob on her own.

Robin Leach, with his English accent, came up to me like we'd been friends for years. We talked for a few minutes, then I spotted Mary Bono standing alone. I admired her for her strength to continue Sonny's work in Congress, especially with two young children. So I asked Robin to introduce me. I found her to be warm-hearted, but feeling a bit like me at the moment—out of place.

A reporter for *Vanity Fair* came to apologize on behalf of the magazine because Paula was to be on their front cover wearing Vivian Leigh's green gown in the movie epic, *Gone with the Wind*. She had already had the pictures taken and interviewed. He said, off the record, that the Clintons were to do a follow-up interview but Hillary told them that if you print Paula's story you won't get the President's, so they canned it.

I told him to stay far away from Paula because he might get a drink splashed in his face. I asked him if he would send me the pictures of Paula in the dress and he did. Finally, someone in print that kept his/her word. It's like falling asleep on fresh linen and goose down for the first time after being curled-up on the floor.

After all the hob-knobbing, we finally sat down for dinner. There were a few other guests at our table. Paula sat next to Victoria Toensing, a DC lawyer who supported Paula's case. I sat between G. Gordon Liddy, and a retired FBI agent, Gary Aldrich, who wrote the book *Unlimited Access*. Talk about sitting between a lot of exploitive history there! Gary gave agitated remarks throughout Clinton's speech. With Liddy, I asked questions about wiretaps. *I needed to know more about the subject and who better to ask, right?*

I noticed Paula drinking, but not eating. She was talking louder than usual, then I saw that nasty furry-boom mike hanging over her head picking up Paula's inebriated conversation. Again, I pushed it aside and told Paula to eat something to soak up all the wine she was having.

Stephen M. Jones, Jr.

She told me in a loud, slurred voice, "Stephen Jones, why don't you mind your own business! With all the crap that I've been through, I deserve to have a good time."

The friction between us was noticed by everyone at the table. Paul pulled me to the side and asked me not to cause a scene. I questioned Paul's veracity, *Excuse me—I'm causing a scene?*

I decided to let it go and to let Paula be Paula.

Paula and Victoria went to the restroom, no big deal right? Wrong again. Because of the threats from the crowd of hecklers, we, that is, us men and hotel security, lined up across the restroom door to keep away any unwanted intrusion. I told Paula to make it quick because I'm sure others needed to go, too. Well five minutes turned into twenty and I felt so bad for some of the ladies that obviously had to go, but were rejected. So I sent in a lady who had to go so badly, she had tears in her eyes, with a message to Paula. "What the hell's taking so long?" A few minutes later, the lady came out and said that Paula and Victoria were talking and smoking. Boy was I pissed. All those people held back while Paula was in there taking her own sweet time. Well, after that, I went back out again on the veranda and clipped the back of a stogie and shared it with Donna Rice Hughes who, if you remember, got caught up with Gary Hart's 1988 Presidential affair.

We talked about her program called *Enough Is Enough*, a website that protects kids from internet predators.

A few hours later and back at our hotel room, Paula was heave-hoing in the porcelain goddess of regret. It was a night to remember for those who should've known better.

Meanwhile, back at the ranch, Judge Wright was highly criticized for throwing out the case by fellow justices in numerous press releases. They said that if we appealed, the chances were good that her decision would be overturned.

The Dallas boys called to say that they want another cattle drive and will stay on throughout the appeals process. We flew to Dallas to do a little renegotiating on our contract. Next day, we held a press conference announcing our intentions to file an appeal with the 8th Circuit Court of Appeals.

Hear ye, hear ye, read all about it—Clinton gets impeached by the House of Representatives due primarily for lying in the Jones case. Now it's up to the Senate to rule on Clinton's fate. Rumor has it that the 8th Circuit will rule in our favor. *Damn, that's bad news for Clinton.* If the Jones lawsuit resurfaces, right in the midst of senate impeachment hearings, it could sway a few votes in favor of impeachment.

Smells like an opportunity to me, except one minor problem. Lead attorney, Don Campbell, has a passion of dislike toward Bob Bennett that rivals my own. Don sent me a fax stating that any negotiations for settlement are at an impasse. He reminded me that the firm was already 1.3 million into the lawsuit. *Well, Goddamn! It's not like I've been rolling in a field of clover myself lately.* I faxed Don back a letter reminding him what we'd talked about in the very beginning. I reiterated that this was never a cash cow and it sounds to me like you're putting a dollar figure ahead of his client's best interest.

I think the word *pissed* doesn't adequately describe Don's reaction to my fax. He relayed a message from his secretary suggesting that if I had anything further to say, to say it through Paula. Neither he, nor anyone at the firm, would continue to accept my calls. Not thirty minutes after the *go to hell from Don*, I got an anonymous UPS package containing a video tape. As I played the black and white security quality video it appeared to be Clinton and Gennifer Flowers doing the wild thing on a big brass bed. I immediately called Don to tell him that if the tape could be authenticated, we had Clinton by the balls, but I couldn't get a word in edgewise.

"Stephen, I don't give a damn what you have to say." And he hung up!

Clinton, you damn lucky son of a biscuit-eater. I mean, what are the chances that I get a tie-breaking advantage the same time I have a blowout with Don? *Hot damn—shit fire!*

So I pulled the plug on Don and handed the negotiating reins over to Bill McMillan. Bill had a good history with Bennett when we were internally negotiating with Joe and Gil. Plus, everyone wanted out except maybe me and the media who had mutated into genetically oversized Paraná. *Who was I fooling?* Internally, I knew it was a lost cause, I couldn't hold it together any longer bound with baling wire dipped in piss and vinegar.

The best I could do was try to break even.

Entertainment Tonight was beating down the door for an exclusive interview with Paula. I'd pretty much stayed away from paid interviews, but now it was time to pay the plumber. I knew that what we'd squeeze out of the Clinton's wouldn't come close to what we owed. I worked out a deal with *ET* for Paula to fly to New York for the interview. *ET* started at fifty-thousand and I stroked it up to double that.

The plan was to settle with Clinton somewhere between eight-hundred thousand to a million. I knew the threshold was not over a million. I was told that Clinton had a poll taken. *He must take a poll if his tub water is too tepid.* A great resource don't you think? Clinton having the American taxpayer paying for the national endowments of meaningless polls. Anyway, the poll showed that if he paid out a million, the public would surmise that to be a *wow* figure and make him look guilty. *Well, yeah, that was the intention, Einstein!* Thus the Clintonologists would have a hard time spinning the settlement as a frivolous case that hindered his duty to the American people.

Now, after settling with Clinton, I had no intention of giving a dime to Joe and Gil who had filed an $800,000. dollar lien against any settlement.

Like they deserve a damn thing—after removing themselves from the case as a pressure tactic to force an unacceptable settlement.

My personal feeling resonated into Arkansas law which states that attorneys who elect to dismiss themselves from representing a client must forfeit any monies in association with that case.

I asked Bill McMillan if he could find any loopholes in the handwritten contract Paula signed at the last minute prior to filing the case in Little Rock. (Later Joe and Gil sent a revised one and I asked Paula not to sign it. Luckily, one of the few things she did that I asked.)

Bingo! Bill called me back and said that the contract was a contingency, but would revert to an hourly rate if a fund was set up. In a contract between client and attorney it has to be one or the other. Basically, you can't have your cake and eat it, too. So it could be argued that the contract was ambiguous, thus rendering it null and void.

Next, I called upon women's groups around the country for speaking engagements for Paula, so she could give back to so many who had supported her against sexual harassment in the work place. Paula received thousands of letters of support. Some were from women's organizations wanting her to be a spokesperson. I thought this would be a perfect opportunity for Paula and some of these groups offered to pay. It wasn't some huge amount, but for me it wasn't about that anyway.

Everyone on Paula's side fought hard for years against the Clintonologists who spun her as *trailer park trash*. Paula was starting to be perceived by some as a heroine for women's rights.

I remember one letter in particular. It was from a very old lady who said that she had marched in the streets in 1919 with her mother for the right to vote. She said that she wanted to give five dollars to the *Paula Jones Fund* and wished she could give more, but she was on a fixed income. Her letter touched me so much that I kept the five dollars and replaced it with my own. Every time we cut checks from the fund, I'd pull out her five dollar bill to remind me to make sure the money went where it was intended. Just in case you're wondering, after Paula took a different direction than what I had hoped, I took the five dollars and had it laminated into a certificate honoring the lady who had sent it as a true heroine. I mailed it back to her, along with a letter thanking her for letting us borrow it for a little while.

Best laid plans: Paula flew to New York to do *ET*. The day after the interview, news broke that the Jones case had been settled. Jeff with *ET* called and blasted that they had just paid a hundred grand for yesterday's story and wants an exclusive follow up. I told him it would cost him another twenty-five thousand. He countered by threatening to stop payment on the checks. I told him that Paula, in good faith, did the interview and if you stop payment I'll sue you for breach of contract. I told him that I'd just gotten off the phone with *Extra* and they wanted an interview and were willing to pay big, but since you guys are in a bind, I'll give you the follow up for an additional twenty-five thousand. After Jeff's voice returned from soprano to alto, he said he'd call me back in ten minutes. When he called back, he told me that we had a deal. "Our camera crew is already in the hotel lobby. Have Paula ready for a five-minute follow up in twenty minutes. Oh, and by the way, I'd bet you a steak dinner there was never a deal with *Extra*, but what do I care, it's not my money. It's the King brothers."

Jeff I said, "I feel much better knowing that!"

Guess I owe him a steak dinner, huh?

Excitedly, I call Paula thinking, *Damn I'm good*. All you have to do is...don't have a pot to piss in, along with a take it or leave it attitude. I guess the lawsuit has taught me a few things after all.

Paula sounded groggy when she answered the phone and said that she and Susie had stayed out late last night.

"That's nice, honey. I'm in the middle of changing Preston's poopy diapers. Oh, by the way, your suit is settled—it's all over the news. H-E-L-L-O—you getting all this? Anyway, I struck another deal with *ET* for a five-minute follow up for—get this Paula, an extra 25g's...sweet huh?" To my surprise, I heard nothing on the other end of the line. Paula didn't say one word. "Paula did you fall back to sleep on me?" Again, I heard nothing but silence. PAULA!

"Yeah," she mumbled.

"Good, now stay awake and listen up. They want you ready in twenty minutes, so get your birthday suit on."

"That's nice, Stephen...sounds like we'll have plenty of money now. But I don't care 'bout no five-minute follow up. Call me later."

"Paula, I don't think you're grasping the situation. We're in debt up to our eyeballs—get it! We owe a hell of a lot of money to a hell of a lot of people, so get your chicken feathers out of bed, now!"

"Don't bother me, Steve Jones, I got a hangover and right now, I don't care." With that, she hung up the phone.

Smoke was literally coming out of my ears. I called Susie in the next room for help. She got Paula up and downstairs with no problem.

I then called Bill McMillan to tell him to make sure that Paula's name was the only name on the settlement check. Too late—the check had already been made out to Paula, Billy, Joe, Gil, the Dallas boys, and if Bennett had thought about it, maybe Aunt Bee. Bennett wasn't going to forget about the good ol' boys who had helped him out behind our backs.

Now...damn unfortunately, the check has to be floated around for everyone to endorse, leaving the door cracked for Joe and Gil to try to needle in.

After Paula got back from New York, she headed out to Little Rock with the boys by train. Paula has this phobia about flying. In two weeks she'd meet with Judge Wright as to divvy-up the check. I stood there in the train station waving and looking up at the window hoping to get a glimpse. The cars lurched forward as I walked alongside, waving until my arm ached, even though the end car had passed me some time ago. I felt a surge of emotion run through me. My throat strained and my jaw clinched as if to hold back the tears welling in my eyes.

Paula didn't put the boys in the window as planned, so they could wave back. Why? At that moment I knew that she had done that purposely. A few days earlier, we'd had a huge argument, in the heat of the moment I told her I loved her for being the mother of our sons but I was not in love with her. *Yep, that would about do it, but there was a hell of a lot more to it than that.*

For the past few years of the case, our marriage had disintegrated for many reasons. If you asked Paula she would say that I was too controlling, not letting her out of the suit when she so many times wanted out. She said she hated me for keeping her away from her family and friends by living in California. The final excuse was infidelities. Throughout our relationship, just like her mother and sister did to their husbands, her insecurities would cause her to have bouts of jealousy. So, when an unsubstantiated rumor floated around that I had been unfaithful, Paula jumped on the band wagon. I believe it gave her the excuse that she was looking for. *I wonder how that rumor got started...Freud?*

Stephen M. Jones, Jr.

A friend at *USA Today* called and said that an anonymous fax came over the AP and said that I was messing around on Paula. Nah, could I possibly think that Hillary, in particular, who has enough inside clout, would spread unsubstantiated rumors to all the news agencies? Yeah, I do—her forte is dirty pool. The Clinton finale of sorts, a twisted crushing blow of reverse accusation aimed right at Paula's insecurities.

For the record, I'd like to weigh in my two bits. Yes, it would have been easy to eat the greener grass when the bedroom door had been closed for almost a year. We were living more like roommates than husband and wife. So to answer the question as to the rumor mills, I'll quote a famous actor and say, "I'd like to say it's all true, what they say about me and anything else they continued to make up along the way."

All I know is there wasn't one clear cut answer as to why, just a combination of all of the above.

Within two days after arriving by train in Little Rock, Paula called me and said that she'd found a house and wants to put down half. When I blew up and said that we should wait until everybody's been paid off to see where we stand financially, she hung up on me. Within the next hour, the bank called and said that Paula was withdrawing large amounts from our account. Luckily, I had moved twenty-grand to a trust account for taxes and that's what I lived on until I got my job back. Since both our names were on the account, the manager asked me what I wanted to do.

"It's her money, let her take it," I said. That was a big mistake because emotion plays a big part in stupidity.

Paula hired a local attorney in Arkansas to help arbitrate the eight-hundred and fifty thousand dollar check. She paid him forty grand to tell her that she doesn't have to pay Joe or Gil, the same thing I had told her for free. It seemed that whatever I said, she did the opposite. Paula was on a roll, in her own words, "I kin make up my own mind, thank you very much!"

She gave Joe and Gil two-hundred thousand; she got two-hundred thousand plus 1 dollar. Paula proudly told me that it was her idea to get at least a dollar more than Joe and Gil. The Dallas boys got the rest.

Without Apology

As I mentioned earlier, not a thin red dime went to Bill McMillan except the money I pulled out of the fund. The one guy who helped broker a resolve heard around the world fell silent to historical value. There's probably a moral of immorality to the story somewhere, but damn if I know.

Paula purchased the house in Arkansas, then signed with some fleabag agent who used to be married to La Toya Jackson. Later, I heard that she had struck a deal with a psychic network that paid her to have her face on ads with 800 numbers so the *intellectually challenged* can foresee the future—Impressive!

Then the big slam. She posed for *Penthouse*, the same magazine we had sued and then dropped to preserve the Clinton case. Not exactly what I had in mind when fighting for her good name and reputation for the past five years. I'm sure our sons will carry that embarrassing baggage around for life.

A few weeks later, I get a call from Paula's attorney saying that I could see my sons if I signed papers in an Arkansas Court House. Well hell if that's so! I filed in LA and served her first. Our divorce was final in 2002, close to two years later. I don't know which was more draining on my soul, the lawsuit or our divorce.

Someone once asked me if I had to do it all over again, would I? The answer to the question is a resounding, "Hell no." What's that old saying, "If I only knew then what I know now!" Boy, how the world would've turned differently. That said, I truly believe the crusade for good name and reputation for which I fought so hard to preserve, whether now ignominiously justified will one day be weighed and measured—then promptly digested into the bowels of forgotten history. That being, if history is as one sees it as so.

In Summary

Looking back, there was a tremendous good that came from the Jones vs Clinton case. It cannot be underscored the impact the case had on redefining sexual harassment policy in corporate America.

Integrity is defined in *Webster's* as *"firm adherence to the code of especially moral values, incorruptibility."* People with integrity know the difference between right and wrong—between truth and fabrication. So written by Dr. Thomas J. Stanley, he also quotes a business entrepreneur as saying, "Never lie. Never tell one lie. If you tell one lie, you will eventually tell fifteen more to cover up the first lie."

I don't think this principle exists in today's politics, but it should. Hillary presented an award to Anita Hill for standing up against sexual harassment on one side of her face, then hides her other side by secretly implementing a scorched earth policy against every woman that accused her husband (I use the term husband loosely), all in an effort to preserve her self serving interest to become the first woman President. Oh, and maybe you feel the reason is because she's still in love with the man. If so, you've got your account in the wrong bank. Well, 2008 is history, but 2012 could still bear the name Hillary Clinton on the ballot box if Joe Biden retires. It's hard to say, but I do know it would tremendously help a lost Obama campaign. I do know that Hillary has a double standard when it comes to sexual harassment. No matter who the accused is, no one is above the law of accountability. I believe Bill, with the help of Hillary, just got his hand slapped by Judge Wright for lying in a deposition when many people today are serving time in prison for doing the exact same thing. So in reality, the bar of morality is lowered for all when it is perceived as a mockery of justice.

But for me, the Jones lawsuit lives and breathes today in the voices of every woman and man faced with insurmountable odds and stands up to shout, "I'm mad as hell and I'm not going to take it any more!"

AUTHOR'S APOCALYPSE

Now wait a minute, isn't about half of Obama's administration made up from Clinton's appointees including Hillary herself. What happened to his campaign theme---Change? But there is change, the deficit is at 16 trillion and climbing. I know, it's Bush's fault. Only the statistics don't lie. After 8 years in office, G.W. contributed 4 trillion to the deficit. After three years in office Obama gave us 6 trillion in change. Go ahead you ignorant souls that voted for him and give him another 4 years and see what comes after trillions. It's imminent infinity, that's long enough for your ancestors to evolve back into one cell organisms. We are in a radical movement of changing into a socialist country and most of you don't even know it. By now you know it's what I do, so once again let me line up the ducks for you. We're still in a recession with unemployment at 9%. But realistically speaking, it's more like 22%, because the government doesn't count those who gave up looking for a job and simply stopped filing for unemployment.

Small companies are regulated out of business. Ever go into a *Wal-Mart, Target, ToysRus, GE appliance,* or *Apple* store and try to find anything made in the USA? Damn near impossible! China erroneously deflates their money (*Renminbi*, Chinese currency) so these fat cat mega corporations can buy and manufacture products in "Red" land at 10 cents on the dollar. Mom and Pop companies can't compete. Thank you Mr. President for allowing unfair trade agreements while your cronies keep spending on *Capital Hill* and we keep owing China 2 trillion and up. I wouldn't doubt Mao Tse-tung is tattooed on one ass cheek and Rev. Jeremiah's epithet, "God damn America" on the other. I remember not to long ago when most everything you bought was made in the USA. Can't you see it? Can't you see their tearing America down to equate us with every other European nation. Look at Obama care. It's government institutionalized which forces every American to buy insurance. Even religion is no longer separate. The church may be forced against their beliefs to pay for contraceptives. Where do some of these congress-women and feminist groups come off saying it's their right to get free morning after pills and contraceptives? So now we the taxpayer and religious organizations have to pay for sexual pleasure. And these liberal women championing the cause; I mean have you seen some of these women on the news? Let me tell you, they don't need to concern themselves personally, because no male "seaman" will ever launch a boat in their canal. Seriously, why do liberal feminist look like former White House press corps reporter, Helen Thomas?

When a government enforces its citizens to buy a commodity, that's socialism. Come on! Get your finger out of your crevasse and listen.

Now let's talk about the bailouts of Fannie Mae, Freddie Mac, Countrywide, and Wall Street. Barney Frank, who was the chairman of the house financial committee, oversaw and said that Fannie and Freddie were "fundamentally sound" all the while enjoying a little man love with a Fannie Mae executive. I swear, I'm not making this stuff up. Yes I'm blunt and up front. But nevertheless, it's a conflict of interest don't you think? He co-authored the Frank-Dodd financial reform legislation that single-handedly helped cause the housing bubble to burst by forcing banks to give loans to people who couldn't afford to live in a shoebox much less pay a mortgage. The guy should be retired behind bars. Tack on another 145 million. Ok, just to be fair, G.W. can split the difference of irresponsibility. We have mechanisms for companies that find themselves in the red. It's called Chapter 11, hello...

Oh, and there's the *GM* auto industry bailout to the tune of 27 billion, that's roughly 25% of capital we the people still own. Oh, and just a side note, *GM* just recently hired a overseas British advertising firm for a mere 3 billion.

Stephen M. Jones, Jr.

Hell, Obama bails them out with our tax money and GM out sources. Bravo! Due to the tsunami in Japan that gutted their automotive export, GM made a profit, so they gave 7 grand apiece to their union employees, but not one thin dime went back to the American taxpayer. Come on… you occupy Wall street comrades burning the American flag and draping yourselves in China's red flag of fascism and vote for him again and see where you are in four more years. You Jersey Shore intellects want equality without sacrifice. You wreak of entitlement and believe the rich should pay for your needs. Take all the money from the rich and it would run the country for about six months. No you say, just tax them at 60% instead of 45%. Do that and the corporate rich will sit on their money more so than now. They will not hire anyone in the private sector and the 45% that don't pay taxes will soon be over 50%. Our economy can't sustain all those freeloaders and you'll see that what's happening in the streets of Greece will be all across middle America. If Obama gets another term, our forefathers that fought and shed blood to preserve a Constitution of freedom for all will be dismantled and vanish before your eyes like a bad magician and the "days of days" will be the end of days. Damn it, I got off point again due to ignorant ideologies taught by fascist professors to our young people. One more point and I'll stop. You young bucket heads that feel entitled, take a look at your young Chinese counterpart who starts at age 12-working, and lives in the factory for less than you spend on cappuccino's in a year. They work 14 hour shifts and if they screw up the quality engineer takes it from their pay. The worker sends most of the money they earn to their parents who send only one child to school. Think about that next time you want to burn the American flag and poop on a cop car, dumbass! Let's move on before I bust a blood vessel. The *Cash for clunkers* cost us a mere 3 billion. That's 24k a car Mr. President, but what really ripped me a good one was instead of re-selling them to a third world country and minimize the snatch of the taxpayers Band-Aid they scrapped them. I'm sure Fidel could have replaced all those 57 Chevy's with some newer gas guzzlers thus causing Hugo Chavez to export more oil to Cuba, but no, Obama junked them all. I know a bit ridiculous, but you get my point.

Without Apology

The *Shovel-Ready* jobs bailout to get America off the unemployment lines cost us about 800 billion and netted very few private sector jobs with no growth to the GDP. As Obama said laughingly; "I guess shovel ready wasn't as shovel ready as we thought." Then there's the Obama government void of any checks and balances taking hard-earned tax payers money and funding failed so-called green projects like *Solyndra* with 535 million flushed down the toilet. The *Chevy Volt* at 250k a car, and *Fisker Automotive* at 93 million. After which, *Solyndra* gave themselves bonuses off the sweat of the taxpayers brow. And you bozos on the left still think he's re-electable? Maybe so, if you're a conformist to the socialist party. You still don't get it? What we're going through now is by design. America is on the verge of becoming just like every other country. No stronger, no better, just the same as the rest of them. That's the big plan, wake up and smell the totalitarian roses. I hear a world currency is just waiting for the right time to be introduced. Where you gonna go if you don't like something, it'll all be the same. I can't imagine a one-dimensional society, all living in a one world order. You think it's coincidence that all the dictators are being knocked off one at a time? Saddam Hussein, Iraq; Hosni Mubarak, Egypt; Muammar Gaddafi, Libya; and soon to be Bashar al Assad, Syria. Bad people to be sure, but it's not about that. It's about world order. So some of you say that's why I'm voting for Newt. Well brother, I like his fire and brimstone, too. But that won't change a leopards spots. He's a progressive and sees the future in the same rose-colored glasses as our liberal friends except for conservative ideologies. Newt is close friends with the Clintons and Pelosi. They will cut each other's throats politically, but go to the same toga parties behind closed doors. Something to keep in mind, Newt, when they spill the beans on what you did in the eyes of the ethics committee. Newt has a tall hill to climb when Romney can outspend him 10 to 1. The same goes for Rick Santorum. I think Rick would win hands down 20 years ago, and hopefully in 2012. But Americans are becoming less and less a Christian nation and more a anti-Christ movement. When you can have Liberals in SFO eat-out at a family restaurant openly in the nude void of morality and impunity from any indecency laws, we are surely becoming absorbed in a nation of European ideological behavior. Nevertheless, Obama will out spend whoever wins the nomination 100 to 1. What burns my pickle is that a President can fly around campaigning on Air Force One at the taxpayers expense. Let the DNC or the RNC pay expenses not related to Presidential duties. Every time he hops on Air Force One there goes a million on jet fuel and security logistics, poof! That's a helluva lot of damn tacos, amigos. Obama said he would cut the deficit by 4 trillion in his 1st term and said that he shouldn't be re-elected if he can't. So what's the big woo? Take him for his word. He keeps writing checks the taxpayer's ass can't afford to cash. Obama hasn't balanced the budget in a 1000 days and his budget he just proposed won't even have democratic support to pass through congress because it adds another 1.3 trillion to the deficit, duh! I understand he's going to change his campaign slogan, "*Change*," to something inspiring and less-challenging to entice the 25% *Jersey Shore* intellectuals to vote. Maybe they can have *Black Panthers* hand out free pot at polling stations with an immunity declaration by Eric Holder.

Osama's "*Change*" is counterintuitive, where we criminalize the good guys and give compassion to those who want to vaporize Israel from the face of the earth. There are real threats from fascist regimes looking for the weakest link in the chain of command. Now think about it, there'll always be scapegoats like Sandy Burger to shred the evidence. So what is one to do when democracy hangs in the balance? I say vote the sons of bitches out of office when re-election rolls around. Be careful, don't allow your "love and let live" *Woodstock* theology to corrupt and cloud your brain. Remember, Rome wasn't built in a day, but it burned to the ground in the middle of the night. Sometimes change is not so good.

ABOUT THE AUTHOR

Stephen M. Jones Jr. has experience with every aspect of this book because he lived it. Someone once said, "It's not so much what you do in life, but how you live it."

Born in 1960, he attended Christian Brothers College and the University of Memphis. A member of the Screen Actor's Guild (SAG), Stephen has worked in many theaters of life, more importantly, his family. He lives in Southern California with his wife, stepson, and during the summer his two sons.

His interests are broad and he maintains close relationships with friends and colleagues in the media on both sides of the political pulpit. In his leisure time, he can be found sailing the California coastline.